SAINSBURY'S

Book of

PARTIES

SAINSBURY'S

Book of

PARTIES

GLYNN CHRISTIAN

FRANCES BISSELL

JOSCELINE DIMBLEBY

CLARE FERGUSON

SOPHIE GRIGSON

GERALDENE HOLT

PATRICIA LOUSADA

NIGEL SLATER

WINE NOTES

OZ CLARKE

INTRODUCTION

ROZ DENNY

Published in the UK exclusively for J Sainsbury plc,
Stamford House, Stamford Street, London SE1 9LL
by Webster's Wine Price Guide Ltd, Axe & Bottle Court,
70 Newcomen Street, London SE1 1YT

First published 1990

ISBN 1 870604 06 7

Typeset by August Filmsetting, UK
Colour separations by Reprocolor Llovet s.a., Spain
Printed and bound in West Germany by
Mohndruck Graphische Betriebe Gmbh, Gütersloh, Düsseldorf

Conceived, edited and designed by
Websters International Publishers

NOTES ON RECIPES

Menus with a green menu 'box' are suitable for vegetarians.
Menus with a pink menu 'box' are relatively low-budget.

All spoon measures are level.
1 tablespoon = 15ml
1 teaspoon = 5ml

Eggs are size 3 unless otherwise stated.
Pepper is freshly ground black pepper unless otherwise stated.
Milk is full-fat unless otherwise stated.

Ovens should be preheated to the specified temperature.
Page references on recipes refer to photographs.
For all recipes, quantities are given in both metric and imperial measures. Follow either metric or imperial measures but not a mixture of both.

THE AUTHORS

FRANCES BISSELL is a leading food and cookery writer with a weekly column in *The Times*. As well as television and radio broadcasts here and abroad, she is much in demand as a guest cook at some of the world's leading hotels. She is also the author of *Sainsbury's Book of Food*. Her recipes have been described as 'exactly what one dreams of being fed in other people's homes.'

GLYNN CHRISTIAN is best known as the entertaining and innovative television chef and food reporter on *Breakfast Time*, *The Garden Party* and *This Morning*. He is also a regular radio broadcaster and the author of 17 cookery books, including *British Cooking at Its Best* and *Pies, Pâtés and Terrines*.

OZ CLARKE, wine correspondent of *The Daily Telegraph* and a regular on BBC Television's *Food and Drink Programme*, is known for his entertaining and unpretentious approach to wine writing. He is author of the annual *Webster's Wine Guide* and the best-selling *Sainsbury's Book of Wine*.

JOSCELINE DIMBLEBY, food correspondent of *The Sunday Telegraph* and author of many best-selling cookery books, including *A Traveller's Tastes* and *Marvellous Meals with Mince*, is a frequent guest on radio and television shows. Her personal and creative approach to cooking and her appreciation of a wide range of foods stems from a childhood spent abroad.

CLARE FERGUSON, author of several cookery books, including *Chicken Dishes*, and previous food editor of *ELLE* and *She*, contributes to major newspapers and magazines. She has worked extensively as a food stylist for television, notably for the BBC series *Madhur Jaffrey's Far Eastern Cookery* and has presented a series of television programmes on South Pacific food.

SOPHIE GRIGSON is the cookery correspondent of the *London Evening Standard* and writes regularly for the *Sunday Express Magazine*. She has contributed pieces to *Taste*, the *Observer*, and *The Sunday Telegraph* among others and has made a number of television and radio appearances.

GERALDENE HOLT is an outstanding authority on French cuisine. Her *French Country Kitchen* and *Recipes from a French Herb Garden* have been highly acclaimed, and in1988 her *Cook's Garden* in *Taste* magazine won a prize as the most outstanding series of the year. She is the Food Correspondent of *Homes and Gardens* and writes regularly for *BBC's Good Food*.

PATRICIA LOUSADA is the author of many cookery books including *The Book of Chocolate*, *Game Cookery*, *Pasta Italian Style* and *American Bake-In*. She grew up with a love of cookery gained from her Italian mother, a singer and inspired cook with a wide knowledge of French and Italian cuisine.

JEREMY ROUND Before his death in 1989, Jeremy Round was awarded the Glenfiddich prize for restaurant writer of the year, as well as being overall winner of the competition 'for his special and significant contribution to raising the standard and knowledge of what we eat in this country.' As food correspondent for *The Independent* he was particularly admired for his wit, enthusiasm and judgement.

NIGEL SLATER is Food Editor of *Marie Claire*. The simple style of his monthly food pages won him a Glenfiddich Award in 1989. He writes regularly for the *Sunday Correspondent* and works as a food stylist in London and Paris and for New York photographer Christopher Baker.

CONTENTS

ROZ DENNY

INTRODUCTION

For a large party, there should nowadays be a vegetarian alternative, though if the salads are substantial and interesting, they can do the job more than adequately – especially if there are also some interesting cheeses on offer. Otherwise pasta dishes or vegetable pâtés or terrines can solve the problem of feeding large numbers of vegetarians and keeping the carnivores happy at the same time. Some of the menus in the book such as Jeremy Round's Brunch (above) are entirely *vegetarian (distinguished by a green 'menu' box).*

Home entertaining and party-giving are rapidly increasing in popularity, and the excuses for such pleasurable pastimes are similarly multiplying. In addition to all the major milestones in our lives such as weddings, christenings, anniversaries and birthdays, more and more of us are dreaming up all sorts of reasons and excuses to throw parties and show how we cherish our families and friends and have fun into the bargain. No doubt many of us nurture the hope that the compliment will soon be returned.

The main purpose of a party is sheer enjoyment but there are also other benefits 'by the way'. The host has taken time to give the party and the guest to attend. In the mutual atmosphere of conviviality new friendships can be started and old ones reaffirmed and built on. A party, if you like, recharges one's social batteries. Away from the bustle and stresses of everyday life people can relax and temporarily take time off from problems and anxieties.

Entertaining can take many guises and you'll find a host of wonderfully creative ideas for parties in this book from intimate dinners for two to rumbustious carefree brunch parties, wholesome homely teas and lavish celebratory feasts. If entertaining for the first time, many of us feel more confident in small groups, and for new party-givers this is the best way to start – with a small group of one's closest friends so hiccups or mis-timings are forgiven or tolerated. As your success rate grows so will your confidence.

What makes for a really good party? Why can parties work so well on some occasions and not on others? Is there a magic formula for entertaining success? The answers regrettably are not straightforward. There are no precise rules to guarantee a memorable event. One thing is certain – money is not one of the main ingredients. It helps, but a party with coffee and sandwiches can linger as long in the memory as, say, a Champagne and caviar celebration.

There are some things, though, that inevitably help make a party go well: a welcoming smile, food and drink prepared with care and attention, good company and conversation that sparkles with genuine enthusiasm; all these help promote feelings of wellbeing and warmth. But, above all, the one essential element is a calm, relaxed and happy host. And the secret of being a calm, relaxed and happy host is to be organized, plan ahead and give yourself plenty of time to get everything done without panic.

PLANNING THE PARTY

In this book you will find complete menus for all kinds of parties – parties for different occasions, with many themes, and for varying numbers of people. They come from authors with utterly distinctive approaches to food but they all have one thing in common, the food is well planned and balanced in terms of texture, colour, lightness and blend of flavours. Party food should be easy and uncomplicated. That is not to say the dishes should be unadventurous. Some of the best flavour combinations are surprising blends of two or three simple ingredients. If you are nervous about your culinary capabilities its wise to limit the number of dishes. Better to do a few dishes well than a great variety badly and have to spend the party excusing your mistakes.

Choosing the right menu for the occasion is important and these parties should give you plenty of scope. Obviously it helps to know your guests' tastes. Are there religious constraints? Do they eat only white meat? Are they vegetarian? Some of the menus in this book are entirely vegetarian (distinguished by a green menu 'box'). Others are relatively economical (distinguished by a pink menu 'box'). Detailed recipes are given for at least four dishes in each menu, but nobody expects that you're going to cook all the food for your party. These days it's possible to buy in all kinds of wonderful foods to complement your cooking, that may need simply to be assembled or arranged, and the menus include suggestions for 'extras' of this kind appropriate to each meal. In fact all essential components you might need to serve are mentioned right down to the bread and butter, condiments and coffee. Some bought-in ingredients can take the place of whole courses, cold cuts of meat, bags of washed mixed salad leaves, cheese and fruit, for example.

Crudités, raw vegetables, and dips are an excellent trouble-free buffet dish or starter to a lunch or dinner party.

Hors d'oeuvres should keep hunger pangs at bay and also get tums in the mood for digestion. You might have a small bowl of exotic olives, some salted almonds, a few carrot and cucumber sticks, maybe even some of the newer up-market crisps. Instead of dotting these about the room where they could be overlooked or consumed by a passing family dog, group them together attractively on a tray. First courses, too, can be bought in. A selection of delicious salami, or some slices of Parma ham with fresh figs or melon, would make a wonderful starter to a dinner party, or, on a larger scale, excellent buffet food.

Cheese is a life-saver for busy party-givers. There are now so many wonderful cheeses available that there is no need to apologize for offering cheese and fruit instead of a dessert, for example. And at a buffet party, a well-endowed cheese board is ideal for the party grazer – a nibble or two, then away for some animated party conversation then back to the board for more slivers or chunks. You don't need to serve lots of cheeses – on the contrary three or four cheeses well chosen and carefully presented is much better than lots of bits and pieces – and one very special whole cheese, a perfectly ripe Brie, for example, or a Baby Stilton – can look just spectacular.

For an attractive presentation buy more than you need in generous wedges and full rounds – the leftovers will keep. As a rough guide allow 250g/8oz each of at least three cheeses for every eight people, decreasing the proportions as numbers of guests increase. Make sure there is a good mix of familiar favourites such as Cheddar or Jarlsberg, a Brie-type cheese, a sharp but creamy blue cheese and, possibly, a goats' milk or ewes' milk cheese. Around this core build up some surprise flavours or your favourite new discoveries – apart from anything else they will be a good talking point. Take cheeses out of the refrigerator some time before serving, about an hour for hard cheeses, 30 minutes for soft cheeses. Don't cut soft cheeses until about to serve as they may run. Cover the cheeses loosely with foil or cling wrap, uncovering just before the guests arrive.

With the cheeses offer a mixture of cheese biscuits, oatcakes, Bath Olivers, bread sticks and some freshly sliced French bread.

DIPS

Dips for crisps or *crudités* are very quick to make using a base of fromage frais or curd cheese or purées of pulses or other vegetables. Greek yogurt makes an excellent base for dips, such as this spiced mango cream: fry a chopped onion in oil until softened with a teaspoon of mild curry powder, then blend with a carton of Greek yogurt and a tablespoon of mango chutney. Or serve a Chinese dipping sauce: mix two tablespoons each of light soy sauce and dry sherry, a little fresh grated root ginger and a few drops of sesame oil.

Desserts If you are not an experienced cook or have precious little time to prepare puddings, there's no reason why you should not buy in some ready-cooked special desserts. There are now so many high-quality ready-made puddings available, such as tortes, sorbets, mousses and gateaux, or make a magnificent display of fruit. It doesn't have to be expensive. One of the nicest Christmas buffet centrepieces, for example, is a pyramid of satsumas with holly or ivy leaves tucked in between the layers plus small bows of silver or gold ribbon or coloured sugar almonds.

A large arrangement of grapes only, mixed black and white, looks wonderful, especially if snipped into smaller hand-size bunches which guests can help themselves to easily. And some perfect just ripe pears or peaches could make an ideal finale to a dinner party.

Fruit is such a useful standby for parties and you can be as simple or elaborate as you like in presenting it. This stylish arrangement of prepared fruit is for Sophie Grigson's Japanese Barbecue (page 148), but a more traditional fruit bowl is also attractive as well as appetizing.

Have, for example, a base of crisp well-flavoured apples and pears, decorated with a scattering of kumquats or lychees, grapes or fresh dates. Or build a Victorian-style fruit bowl, using a tall pineapple core (fix it to a fruit stand with some children's play clay). Pile up the fruit around it, using small bunches of grapes or miniature bananas to cascade over the rim. A few artistically positioned ribbon bows or leaves add to the effect.

SERVING THE FOOD

Some party-givers like to serve the food ready-plated, but this is only really practical for smaller numbers: you will need a large amount of tabletop space to lay plates out and some guests may have to wait for their food, so this method suits cold food better.

The stand-up table buffet is perhaps the most popular these days, but it too needs planning. Is there enough space in the room for queueing? Can people get in and out of the room through the same door? Some hosts find it useful to work out a flow of guests before they start planning. For larger buffets repeat the same dishes at either end of the table so you can have two queues.

For more formal buffets you may want to divide the menu into courses, but remember that increases the number of trips to the buffet table. Sit-down meals could have a cold starter ready-plated and on the tables, with a serve-youself main course, while the pudding or dessert is plated-up during the meal for serving.

Crockery and cutlery So many people worry that holding a big party means they have to hire a great collection of china, cutlery and the like. It's really not necessary unless it is a very special celebration. Borrow from good friends, making a list first of what you need and who can lend what. In fact, if you are having a sit-down party with individual tables it's quite a fun idea to lay up complete services and sets per table. If the lenders come as guests, they'll feel quite at home.

Stand-up buffets really need only forks, spoons, knives for buttering bread maybe and lots of serving spoons. Wrap the forks in napkins or lay them out on a small tray. Sit-down parties need a full set of cutlery – again borrow if need be and when you come to lay up, try and keep the sets together.

PLANNING AHEAD

Some impromptu parties are great and memorable successes, but invariably they happen when good friends get together and all muck-in. A special party does need a certain amount of planning if only to make things easier for you. There's no substitute for lists. First, having worked out exactly what form of party you want, a sit-down or stand-up, and the menu, read through the recipes carefully at least a good week in advance. Some recipes involve marinating a couple of days' ahead and it's no good discovering that the day before.

Clear your freezer if you want to prepare some dishes ahead or buy meat and fish in advance to freeze. A whole salmon, for instance, can take up quite a bit of space. Work your way through the recipes, mentally cooking as you read, to see if there are stages you can prepare ahead – pie shells, sauces, vinaigrette, stocks and so on. For major parties it might help to draw up a timetable and write in any shopping, pre-cooking and preparation that can be done ahead. It saves those awful last-minute panics. You will find the menus in this book already give guidelines about what can be done in advance.

If you're planning a large party, storage may be a headache. Dried goods though can be packed into boxes and stacked in a spare room. Part of the garden shed could be cleaned, lined with paper and also used. The major problem though, summer or winter, is fridge space. Clear out all non-essential foods like bottles of oil and squash that don't actually need to be chilled. Alternatively, borrow space in your neighbour's fridge or freezer (usually no problem as long as they're invited to the party).

Buy in a good supply of cling film, wrapping foil, food bags and bin liners. They are indispensable when preparing food ahead. A pasta salad, for example, will take up less fridge space in food bags, stacked on top of one another. Similarly, store things in square containers, not round. You could also use cool-bags or insulated picnic boxes on the day to store salads or chilled drinks, but *always* make sure dishes containing meat, fish and dairy produce are kept well-chilled in the fridge.

SHOPPING LISTS

Detailed shopping lists will take much of the headache out of planning any party however small. Check the 'planning ahead' section of each menu for dishes that can be part-prepared in advance and work out when you need to buy what. Then write out lists in sections – meat and fish, groceries, vegetables and so on. Have a spare list pinned in the kitchen for items you remember in the middle of doing something else. You may need to do the shop in two or three trips, buying dried goods first. Certainly the drink can be bought well ahead.

DRINK

Some parties can be held with little or no food, but none worth remembering with little or no drink – and except, of course, for tea and coffee parties, and children's parties, drink usually means alcohol. What you serve will depend on your budget and on the type of party. Wine is the popular choice for most parties and with the huge variety available you can match the wines to almost any type of food and any budget. For large easy-going buffet parties you might pick a couple of cheap and cheerful wines, one red, one white which you can happily afford to buy in quantity. For smaller lunches or intimate dinner parties you'd probably want to go to a bit more trouble and expense. Most of the menus in the book include wine suggestions from Oz Clarke specially chosen for the food and the occasion. But there are no hard and fast rules about wine and food and the main thing is for you to serve something which you and, hopefully, your guests will enjoy.

If the party is fairly casual, some people may prefer beer rather than wine but, unless it is a lunch or dinner party when you may want to serve drinks before or after the meal, I would steer clear of spirits at parties. At large parties as an alternative to wine, beer and spirits serve a punch – fruity and with plenty of ice in summer, hot, spiced and welcoming in winter.

Whatever the party there must also be plenty of non-alcoholic or low alcoholic drinks. Many people do not drink alcohol at all and others are limiting their intake, especially if they're driving. Mineral water is, for many, the preferred alternative. Have a choice of still and sparkling and offer ice, and slices of lemon, lime or cucumber and sprigs of fresh mint to spike it up. Standard mixers such as

Few people have enough plates and dishes to be able to use matching sets at big parties – but a mixture of styles can look just as attractive.

QUANTITIES

How much drink you serve depends on the occasion and the guests – but it is much better to buy too much than too little.

In general allow from a half to a full bottle of wine per head. For beer drinkers allow at least 1 litre/2 pints per head and get in about a quarter as much mineral water as you have wine.

tonic water, dry ginger ale and soda water, are also excellent alternatives to alcohol. Have a choice of fruit juices on hand, too – bought or homemade – and allow people to mix their own non-alcoholic or low-alcoholic cocktails or spritzers. At the end of the party serve hot coffee or tea to those who would like it.

SERVING DRINKS

If you're taking trouble about choosing the drinks you'll want to do the same about serving them. Again it depends what you've got. Most white, rosé and sparkling wines, most non-alcoholic drinks and many beers will need chilling and that can be quite a problem especially for a large party in the summer months – particularly if the fridge is full of food. Drink though can be chilled without a fridge, albeit in a slightly unorthodox fashion. The best and quickest way is with iced water. Use the bath if you have to or a large plastic dustbin or borrow lots of buckets. Buy bags of ice on the day, or ahead and store in the freezer. Alternatively, on the preceding days freeze your own ice in big chunks in strong food bags. A couple of hours or so before the guests arrive, half fill the bath, dustbin or buckets with ice and cold water, then add the bottles. Room temperature is the rule of thumb for red wines – but that also depends on the room – and the wine, so don't overdo it. If you stand the wine in the dining room for a few hours before serving it, that should be enough.

If you're having a stand up buffet – have a special table set aside for the drinks, and not too near the table with the food or there's likely to be a traffic jam. If possible put someone in charge of opening and dispensing the drinks, and have a couple of people going round topping up. Have at least two corkscrews – opening bottles takes time, and besides, one might break.

If there's Champagne make sure it's opened by a responsible person who will point the bottles well away from themselves and anyone else. The trick is to hold on to the cork firmly, and twist the bottle slowly. To be absolutely safe put a cloth over the cork. Have glasses ready, and keep holding the cork when it pops.

Wine certainly tastes better from proper glasses, but if you run short then small tumblers could be used. Make sure you have larger glasses for beer and water, and, when calculating how many you need, add on ten per cent or more as spares. Give all glasses a good polish with a clean dry tea-towel, especially if they've been tucked away in some dusty cupboard. For children's parties use paper cups.

PRESENTATION

Presenting food and arranging tables and rooms requires little more than thinking carefully about shapes, colours and textures.

The Room Think of your guests' initial entrance. The idea is to make them glow with anticipation as they walk through the door. It's often a case simply of setting up suitable lighting, rearranging furniture for the maximum floor space, clearing away clutter and dressing up the room and the table with fresh flowers. Think of the rest of the house too. Is the bathroom sparkling; are there clean fresh towels and dainty guest soaps? Even a small arrangement of flowers on the bathroom window sill shows care and attention. Dust and hoover the day before, it needn't be thorough but it looks so much better and, if it's a large party, tidy a couple of bedrooms to take people's coats. In winter an open fire is wonderfully welcoming, even if it does die down during the party.

Create a pleasant atmosphere at evening parties with side lighting so

Candles on the food table or dotted around the room in cosy corners add a special touch, but do watch them in case they get knocked over or need replacing. They come in many different shapes and sizes, and scented ones also help to perfume the room.

borrow spare lamps if you have to. Evening barbecues also benefit from good lighting. Buy in special torch flares or, if you've overhanging trees and branches, try these simple fairy candle lights. Tie string round the necks of large thick jam jars. Fix a candle on the base of each with melted wax, making sure the wick is below the top. When it gets dark, light the candles and hang the lights up in the garden – the effect is quite magical.

The Food Since food comes in different shapes, sizes and colours, it makes sense to choose dishes to emphasize this. A matching dinner service may look lovely as a display but won't necessarily do all foods justice. If the food looks good on each dish, then you'll find the whole meal will automatically look well co-ordinated. Different textures can blend very well together – white china looks good with earthenware, glass blends both with wooden boards and pretty bone china. You'll find traditional and modern styles can blend quite happily together.

Obviously, hot food must be served in heatproof containers, which could limit the style of dish. A sprinkle of parsley won't make a casserole look any better in a half-full battered old pot, but spoon it into a shallower dish, garnish it with some sprigs of fresh herbs, celery leaves and toasted nuts and it will look much more appetizing. Similarly rice or pasta mounded up on a large flat platter with some shredded cucumber or watercress bunches or sliced tomato will make more of an impact than if it had been allowed to languish in a deep bowl. Coleslaw or potato salad can be served on a flat plate edged with pretty salad leaves; tomatoes and cucumbers can be sliced and arranged in layers.

Garnishes Generally make any garnish appropriate to the dish. If it contains prawns, use pretty prawns in shells; if carrots, onions or courgettes – use a few thin slices as a garnish; lemon, lime, sliced hard-boiled egg and the like all help lift a dish. If you've time and inclination, try your hand at some spring onion brushes, trimming the green tops and slashing the white bulbs a few times, then soaking in cold water until they curl up. Radish roses can be made up cutting them almost to the stalk end in a six-point star and soaking again. However, it is not necessary to resort to these simple garnishing tricks. Some halved cherry tomatoes, a sprinkling of cress, slices of radish and shreds of spring onion will be just as effective. And don't forget the beauty of fresh herbs – roughly chopped parsley, coriander, dill, or thinly shredded basil always look wonderful. You'll find lots of ideas for using these and other garnishes in the following pages.

For desserts if you can't control a piping bag, then spoon softly-whipped cream in mounds round the edge of a dish and top with grated chocolate or nuts or trickle over with runny red jam. Edible flowers, such as rose petals, violets, borage flowers, nasturtiums and pansies can also be a pretty, and unusual decorations for all kinds of cakes and puddings and sometimes even for salads, too.

Finally, as host, *you* are the most important person at the party. Without you there would be no party, so take care of yourself and make sure you too are able to enjoy the event. Get the rest of the family to help with the shopping and preparation, and when drawing up your planning lists, try not to give yourself too much to do during the party – delegate as much as possible. In your timetable or schedules, add in a final hour for a relaxing bath and time to dress up. A happy, calm host enjoying his or her party is quite infectious.

CLOTHS AND TABLE LINEN

These need not be the real thing. Old white sheets can be given a new lease of life as table liners, with prettier small cloths on top. If you've time (or willing help) then iron out creases first. Even bedspreads, curtains and cheap lengths of fabric are good covers. For napkins, white damask really are a treat – you may have an elderly relative who has a good horde, but there are now many lovely large and thick paper napkins (and, indeed, table cloths) that are just as suitable. Again, make sure you have spares.

GLYNN CHRISTIAN

Breakfasts & Brunches

Breakfast is such a perplexity. Should you believe it to be the day's most important meal and stuff yourself? That might be a direct path to being overweight, overdosed on fat and cholesterol. Do Europeans do it better, ruining digestion and shattering equilibrium with strong coffee and a bite of croissant? Don't expect answers from me. Except to say breakfast is important simply because it is first, a preparation for what is to come.

In the less structured pleasure of holidays and weekends I like entertaining breakfasts, late-ish ones, perhaps combined with lunch to become, neologically, brunch. A later morning event means children can come and go, or parents may, while children safely do Saturday things. New babies may comfortably be displayed and it is easier on the old. The drink/drive problem is solved, too. Those who want alcohol can more easily find public transport: those who do not, feel under less pressure. It's not rude to stay a short time, and acceptable to hustle late stayers because you must shop, or garden or something. Maybe they'll help?

Breakfasts and brunches encourage the kindness of strangers. So there is casual exchange over tea-making, unexpected pairings with sugar-sharing. Involuntary revelations when toast-making together have much resonance...

It is easier for the inexperienced host or hostess to breakfast friends well, and to do it on a budget. The sincerely hospitable offering of croissants, jam, tea and coffee makes more friends than a posturing dinner. But you can go further, and I do.

I like to offer something soothing and something startling, something that is clearly naughty and something specially nice. There must not be an imbalance of fat for that clogs the palate and, these days, there is bound to be a vegetarian.

Whatever the formula we will have been properly prepared for the challenges of the day. Could one be more grateful to a meal?

Opposite **AMERICAN BRUNCH** *PAGE 24*

Jeremy Round's Amsterdam Brunch for 16

A feature of eating all over the Netherlands – particularly in Amsterdam – is the influence of former colonies, especially Indonesia with that part of the world's love of flavours which play savouriness, tang, spice and sweetness off against each other. This brunch party centres on three South-East Asian dishes served with two cooling accompaniments.

In the Netherlands pancakes are eaten with a whole range of sweet or savoury fillings according to the occasion and time of day: for lunch perhaps with crisply fried bacon and thick, sweet *siroop*, or at teatime with fruit and cream. This buffet finishes up with the type of small, relatively thick, spongy griddle cake that North Americans call pancakes and eat stacked high for breakfast, again with bacon and maple syrup (an idea which must surely have crossed the Atlantic with Dutch settlers).

The aubergine dish, barbecued vegetables and the hash are all suitable for vegans. They will, however, have to skip the raita and the egg-and-milk-rich griddle cakes and Chantilly cream, although the fruit salad should be good enough to eat by itself.

MENU

*

INDONESIAN AUBERGINE, GREEN BEAN AND BANANA WITH COCONUT

BARBECUED BABY VEGETABLES

SPICY POTATO, MUSHROOM AND CHICK PEA HASH

*

GRIDDLE CAKES

*

German Beer
Mixed Fruit Juice Cocktail
Coffee

SPICY POTATO, MUSHROOM AND CHICK PEA HASH, INDONESIAN AUBERGINE, GREEN BEAN AND BANANA WITH COCONUT, BARBECUED BABY VEGETABLES

INDONESIAN AUBERGINE, GREEN BEANS AND BANANA WITH COCONUT

This unlikely mixture produces an utterly delicious vegetable dish and perfectly reflects the Indonesian love of contrary flavours. Non-vegetarians could try it as an accompaniment to meat or fish.

750g/1½lb aubergines, peeled and cut into 1cm/½in cubes
750g/1½lb dwarf green beans, topped and tailed
12 shallots or 3 medium onions, finely sliced
9 fat cloves garlic, finely chopped
3–6 teaspoons cayenne pepper
1½ tablespoons ground coriander
1½ tablespoons sugar
175ml/6fl oz freshly squeezed lime juice
1–2 teaspoons finely grated lime rind
1½ teapoons salt
1·3 litres/2¼ pints water
375g/12oz desiccated coconut
6 tablespoons vegetable oil
6 tablespoons roughly chopped fresh basil leaves
6 bananas, thickly sliced

Put the aubergine cubes, beans, shallots, garlic, cayenne, coriander, sugar, lime juice, lime rind, salt and water in a large saucepan. Bring it all to the boil. Cover the pan and cook for 5 minutes.

Add the coconut and oil. Stir. Allow the mixture to bubble rapidly until all the liquid has been absorbed by the coconut.

Continue cooking over a medium-hot flame, stirring from time to time and letting the coconut catch on the bottom between stirs. When the mixture is dry, richly flecked with brown and smelling nicely of toasted coconut, stir in the basil leaves and bananas. Take off the heat.

Serve hot, warm or at room temperature.

BARBECUED BABY VEGETABLES

To cook evenly the vegetables should be roughly the same size so if sprue asparagus is not available use thick asparagus cut lengthwise into halves or quarters. Use any trimmings in stock or soups, or chopped up and sautéed to eat with omelettes or scrambled eggs.

48 baby corn cobs
3 red peppers
3 bunches spring onions
2 bunches sprue asparagus (optional)
1½ tablespoons sweet sherry
3 teaspoons sesame oil
1½ tablespoons soy sauce

Wash and dry the corn. Take out and discard the stalk end and seeds from the red peppers. Cut into strips. Wash, dry and trim the spring onions to about the same length as the corn. If using, cut the top part of the asparagus spears to about same length as the corn.

Cook the vegetables in batches until the spring has just gone out of them and they look scorched and blackened in stripes as if they have been cooked on a charcoal grill. This effect can be achieved on a charcoal grill, on a very hot griddle, under a grill pre-heated to high or – most successfully – in a heavy, dry, preferably non-stick frying pan preheated over a medium flame. Keep the batches moving with a spatula.

When nicely coloured, remove each batch to a warm serving platter. Boil the sherry, sesame oil and soy sauce together in a small pan and drizzle over the vegetables.

EXTRAS

With the savoury dishes in this menu serve a herby tomato salad, using the most flavoursome tomatoes you can find. Slice them thickly and sprinkle with a little salt, freshly ground black pepper, chopped chives and fresh thyme. If the skins are tough, peel them by holding the tomatoes one at a time on the end of a long fork in a naked gas flame until they scorch and wrinkle, or by blanching the fruit in boiling water for a few seconds. Chill this salad well before serving.

Also good with the vegetable dishes will be some raita – set yogurt beaten until smooth then mixed with finely chopped fresh mint leaves and well chilled. And don't forget to provide some crusty bread and Dutch butter.

You'll also need toppings for the griddle cakes. Serve a variety of preserves – the likes of clear honey, maple syrup, golden syrup, apricot jam and blackcurrant jelly. Preserves with large bits in them are not suitable. To make jams and jellies runny in the same way as syrups (much more satisfying to trail across pancakes from a spoon), you may like to heat them, strain and keep in a bowl over a basin of very hot water.

Chantilly cream is another possibility. Whip double cream until light and frothy with a few tablespoons of your favourite sweet liqueur (Drambuie, Grand Marnier and Benedictine are particularly good) or a little sugar and a tot of brandy or rum. This can be heaped on the griddle cakes with a sprinkling of mixed toasted nuts.

A fresh fruit salad can be used as a griddle cake topping or served separately with the Chantilly cream. Choose from whatever fruits are in season, wash, dry and chop or slice them if necessary and pile into a large bowl with, perhaps, sugar to taste.

Have plenty of fresh coffee, and make up a tropical fruit juice cocktail from whatever juices are available

PLANNING AHEAD

In advance: Make the pancakes up to two days ahead and store them in the refrigerator wrapped in foil, in layers separated by sheets of greaseproof paper. Alternatively make them well ahead and freeze them.

The day before: Make the Indonesian aubergine, green bean and banana with coconut. Make the spicy potato, mushroom and chick pea hash. Both these dishes are actually better made ahead of time and either reheated or served cold.

If they are frozen, take the griddle cakes out of the freezer and leave overnight in the fridge to defrost. Toast and chop the nuts.

The day of the party: Make the raita and put to chill in the refrigerator. Make the herby tomato salad and put to chill. Prepare the baby vegetables ready for 'barbecuing'. Make the fresh fruit salad and put to chill. Prepare the Chantilly cream. Make up the fruit juice cocktail and chill. Reheat the vegetable dishes if they are being served warm.

As the guests arrive, grill or dry-fry the baby vegetables and put the griddle cakes in the oven to reheat.

PRESENTATION

Have everything fresh and clean-looking with lots of white linen and lace, clear glass bowls or plates and simple white china. Serve chunks of bread in a basket lined with a starched white napkin. Use mugs for the coffee – it's so much easier to wander about the garden or wherever with a mug than with a cup and saucer which needs two hands.

Since this is Amsterdam there must be flowers. Tulips? Why not?

SPICY POTATO, MUSHROOM AND CHICK PEA HASH

New or old potatoes can be used for this recipe but small new potatoes will hold their shape well and give a better-looking result. This dish can be made the night before and reheated or served cold.

2kg/4½lb firm, waxy potatoes
½–1 teaspoon black pepper
½–1 teaspoon ground turmeric
750g/1½lb button mushrooms
175ml/6fl oz vegetable oil
3 teaspoons whole fennel seed
1½ tablespoons finely grated fresh root ginger
5 fat cloves garlic, finely chopped
3 large onions, finely chopped
3 fresh green chillies, very finely chopped
1½ teaspoons ground cumin
3 teaspoons ground coriander
450ml/¾ pint tomato juice
4–5 tablespoons chopped fresh coriander
1½ × 425g/15oz cans chick peas, drained
Salt

Peel or scrape the potatoes. Unless quite small and new, halve, quarter or cut them into smaller pieces so that they are all about the size of a quite small new potato. Put in a saucepan, just cover with cold, slightly salted water and bring to the boil. Reduce the heat to a simmer, cover the pan and cook until the potatoes are just tender (about 10 minutes for most new varieties, up to 15–20 for others). Drain and leave them at room temperature until quite cold (they are even better if left overnight). Sprinkle the potato pieces with a little salt plus the black pepper and turmeric. Toss them to distribute the seasoning evenly.

Wipe the mushrooms and, unless very small, halve or quarter them until they are about the same size as the potato pieces.

Heat the oil in a heavy pan and in it fry the potatoes until lightly browned and crisp on all sides. This may take up to 15 minutes. Remove from the oil and set aside.

Add the whole fennel seed to the oil, sizzle for a few seconds, then add the ginger and garlic. Sizzle briefly, then add the onion and chopped green chillies. Stir. Reduce the heat and cover the pan. Cook, stirring from time to time, until the onion is soft, then stir in the ground cumin, ground coriander and tomato juice. Stir and cook – scraping up all the stuck-on bits from the bottom of the pan as you go – until the sauce is thick.

Add the mushrooms, potatoes and 2 teaspoons of salt or to taste. Stir to mix. Cover the pan tightly and cook over a medium-low flame for 10 minutes, until the mushrooms have shrunk and given off much of their liquid. Stir in the fresh coriander. Now boil, uncovered, stirring frequently, until the sauce is reduced again to a thick consistency. Stir in the chick peas and leave the whole dish to stand for at least 10 minutes.

Stir again before serving hot, warm or cold.

SEE PAGE 16.

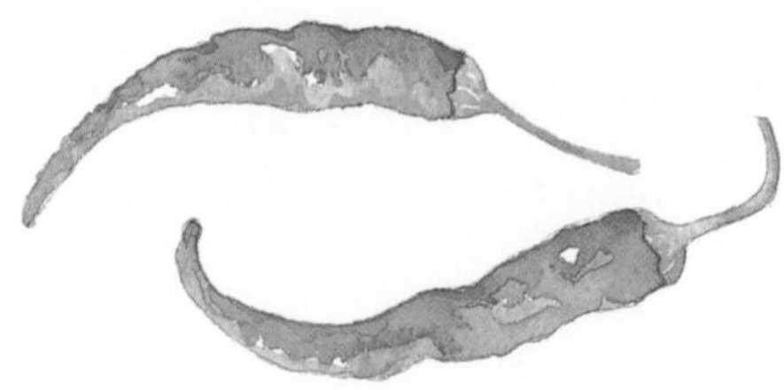

GRIDDLE CAKES

These marvellous light griddle cakes can be served with a host of different toppings – clear honey, syrups, smooth jams and jellies, fresh fruit salad, various creams, natural yogurt and a variety of toasted chopped nuts.

375g/12oz plain flour
2 tablespoons baking powder
½ teaspoon salt
125g/4oz caster sugar
4 eggs
450ml/¾ pint milk
2 tablespoons set yogurt
75ml/3fl oz water

Sift the dry ingredients into a large mixing bowl. Beat the eggs thoroughly together with the milk. Beat the yogurt with the water. Mix in the egg and milk mixture. Tip the liquid ingredients all at once on to the dry ingredients. Very lightly mix with a fork or balloon whisk until the lumps disperse. Do not overmix.

Heat a non-stick griddle, skillet or large frying pan over a medium flame. When hot, but not searing, spoon on several separate tablespoons of the thick pancake batter. These will spread slowly into discs about 7–10cm/3–4in in diameter.

Do not disturb until the upper surfaces of the batter discs are a mass of bubbles then flip them over with a spatula. You should find the bottoms of the discs are a deep, smooth, even brown. Cook for a minute or two on the bubbled surface until that is light brown in patches.

Dish out immediately, or remove the griddle cakes to a platter covered with a clean tea towel which can be folded over them until the rest are ready.

If you are preparing these ahead of time, separate them with greaseproof paper. If you freeze them, defrost the cakes before reheating in single layers in a medium oven.

To serve *Place a platter heaped with griddle cakes on the table and offer a variety of toppings separately for your guests to help themselves.*

Oz Clarke's
WINE NOTES

You might look at this brunch in two ways: there's the wonderfully inviting cool austerity of a Dutch interior for one – all white lace and linen and polished wood – but equally with that riot of tropical flavours you might imagine a verandah, the warm mist rising off the dark green forest, the sun already high in the sky over the tousle-headed palms. Either way, a thirst's coming on – and it's not for wine.

It's for an ice-cold beer, really cold, searing the throat, snapping open the eyes. We could drink Dutch beers but they're pretty bland nowadays, so I'm going to go for German, in particular wheat beer – from north and south Germany – low in alcohol, with a very slight refreshing sourness to it – and sometimes a flavour of cloves. Perfect.

FRESH FRUIT SALAD, GRIDDLE CAKES AND TOPPINGS

Celebration Breakfast for 4

Sometimes a weekend breakfast, served late, is the only time to celebrate with people who are too busy or far flung for dinners – lunch would be a banal compromise.

Celebratory breakfasts are a delicious way to extend the fun and friendship of other celebrations. Rather than making them busy affairs for the hordes, I think they should be intimate, showing special thought for special people. They are flattering ways to welcome out-of-towners before an afternoon wedding or a christening; a special time to talk with those about to leave for a new life or someone newly returned; a less pressured time to enjoy a new godchild.

But what about the day after the wedding, after the engagement party or the school reunion? This is often the time when anti-climax dissolves the fun – but not if you are serving breakfast in style!

Whatever else you decide to do to this menu, serve the soufflé. It will be so unexpected a celebration is guaranteed. That said, nothing has excited quite so much comment at my celebrations as the fruit butters. A simple trilogy of toasts or croissants, fruit butters and the Champagne would be wonderful enough . . . especially if you have invited only one other guest.

MENU

*

ORIGINAL SWISS MUESLI

SMOKED SALMON SOUFFLÉ OVER CREAM SPINACH

SHERRIED KIDNEYS WITH GREEN OLIVES

FRUIT BUTTERS

*

Buck's Fizz
Bloody Mary
Pink Champagne
Coffee or Tea

EXTRAS

Croissants or small brioches make wonderful accompaniments to both the soufflé and the kidneys but you will need a second oven so they can be served hot. Allow two or three each.

An alternative to kidneys, or a third choice, might be special sausages and mash using interesting sausages, slowly baked, with a mash of potato and another root vegetable in roughly equal portions – potato and white turnip or celeriac are the most popular – made very smooth with masses of butter and milk and a small amount of very finely chopped garlic and enough parsley to make a definite green colour.

Even the coffee and tea should be special. I might offer a Formosa Oolong tea, and for the coffee, a lightly roasted Colombian or Kenyan. Serve hot milk for the coffee or a bowl of whipped cream and finely grated, very dark chocolate.

ORIGINAL SWISS MUESLI

Crunchy grains of varied persuasion upon which you tip milk moments before you eat them isn't really muesli at all. When Swiss Dr Bircher created it, the oats were always soaked overnight to sweeten and tenderize them. He used mountain water; many people these days would use skimmed milk. I use orange juice. This is better for you than milk because the vitamin C of the juice unlocks the iron of the oats. Use a volume measure for the grains to save time and effort.

300ml/½ pint loosely packed rolled oats or mixed rolled grains
150ml/¼ pint fresh orange or other fruit juice
1 tablespoon clear honey or demerara sugar (optional)
1 tablespoon lemon juice, or to taste
½ teaspoon ground cinnamon
1 large crisp dessert apple
Sliced dried fruits, such as prunes, apricots and peaches (optional)
Toasted hazelnuts, fresh fruits, fruit-flavoured fromage frais, yogurt, to serve (optional)

Combine the oats, fruit juice, honey if using, lemon juice and cinnamon. Coarsely grate in the apple, including the skin. Mix, cover and refrigerate for up to four days.

Sliced dried fruits can also be incorporated in the mixture, in which case increase the amount of juice to allow for absorption.

If you find the muesli is too damp, stir in more oats before you serve; if it is too dry mix in more juice.

To serve *Serve with a scattering of toasted chopped hazelnuts, seasonal berries or exotic fruit, plus a dollop of yogurt or flavoured fromage frais.*

SMOKED SALMON SOUFFLÉ OVER CREAM SPINACH

A voluptuous cushioned balloon of soufflé soothes the most beastly breast on a celebratory morning. Much can be prepared in advance, and the soufflé can be popped in to cook while you enjoy a drink and the first course. Miniature croissants make a good accompaniment.

ORIGINAL SWISS MUESLI, SMOKED SALMON SOUFFLÉ OVER CREAM SPINACH

300ml/½ pint milk
Bay leaf, peppercorns, parsley stalks, a little onion, cucumber skin, for flavouring
50g/2oz butter
40g/1½oz plain flour
250g/8oz frozen spinach
250g/8oz smoked salmon
150ml/¼ pint double cream
4 egg yolks
¼ teaspoon freshly grated nutmeg
25g/1oz grated fresh Parmesan
5 egg whites
Soured cream, to serve (optional)

The night before, bring the milk slowly to the boil with the flavouring ingredients then remove from the heat. Make a roux with the butter and flour and cook for 2 minutes without browning. Remove from the heat, strain on the hot milk and whisk until thick. Cool, cover very closely with clingfilm and refrigerate overnight.

Defrost the spinach thoroughly then squeeze it in every possible way to drain it. Cover and store overnight. Chop the smoked salmon, cover tightly and refrigerate overnight.

Next morning, butter and lightly flour a 1·5 litre/3 pint soufflé dish (or eight small ramekins). Lightly salt and pepper the spinach and spread it in little clumps over the base. Pour on the double cream and scatter a quarter of the chopped smoked salmon over everything.

Preheat the oven to 190°C, 375°F, Gas Mark 5. Warm the prepared sauce until it stirs easily, then whisk in the egg yolks, followed by the nutmeg, Parmesan and remaining smoked salmon. Whisk the egg whites until peaked but not dry and boldly stir a third of this into the salmon mixture. Tip the mixture into a large clean bowl and carefully fold in the remaining egg whites. Ladle (most important) rather than tip the soufflé mixture into the prepared dish, put it into the oven and close the door as quickly as you can. Bake for 30 minutes (or 8 minutes for the ramekins) until well-risen and nicely browned on top.

To serve *Lift off the top crust and divide that evenly among four warm but not hot plates; divide the soufflé quickly by serving with a big spoon. A large dollop of chilled soured cream would make this into something rather like heaven on a plate.*

SHERRIED KIDNEYS WITH GREEN OLIVES

PLANNING AHEAD

In advance: You can prepare the fruit butters up to a week in advance and store them covered in the refrigerator or freeze them for up to four weeks.

Up to four days ahead put the muesli to soak, refrigerated. Toast any nuts you are serving and store in an airtight jar.

The day before: If you have frozen the fruit butters, thaw and inspect them to see if they need a gentle warming and whisking to reamalgamate any escaping fruit juice.

Prepare the roux-based sauce, spinach and smoked salmon for the soufflé, cover carefully and refrigerate.

Blanch the olives for the kidney dish and store in cold water. Prepare the kidneys, cover and refrigerate overnight.

Prepare the trimmings for the muesli. Set the table if you have time and do the flowers.

The day of the party: Take the fruit butters out of the refrigerator and put the Champagne in to chill. Do whatever else is needed to the table.

Take the ingredients for the smoked salmon soufflé from the refrigerator so they return to room temperature. Put the sausages into a low oven and roast as slowly as you can, allowing a generous hour – at least.

Discreetly assemble the soufflé and put it into the oven. Pop some croissants or brioches into the oven too if you have the space.

Fifteen minutes before the soufflé is due, sit your guests to eat the muesli, then if necessary ask one to help you cook the kidney dish so that it and the soufflé coincide. Stir the parsley and other final flavourings into the mash and serve as suggested. Open the Champagne. Make the toast while the tea and coffee are prepared.

FRUIT BUTTERS, SHERRIED KIDNEYS WITH GREEN OLIVES

Although this is the sort of combination you might expect to find in a Spanish *tapas* bar, kidneys with sherry and olives have always seemed better at breakfast time. They are also very good as an accompaniment to the smoked salmon soufflé rather than as a further course, in which case you might want to serve only half the amount. Speed is of the essence and thus you need to have two pans and everything prepared before you cook, or a willing helper.

75g/3oz stoned green olives
12 lambs' kidneys
75g/3oz butter
2 tablespoons olive oil
175g/6oz button mushrooms, sliced
250ml/8fl oz Amontillado sherry
8 tablespoons brandy
8 tablespoons double cream
Coarsely chopped fresh parsley, to garnish
1 lemon, cut into wedges, to serve

Blanch the green olives in boiling water for 2 minutes, drain then store in cold water until needed. Skin and core the kidneys then cut them into thin slices, lengthwise if your knife is sharp enough. Heat about a third of the butter and all the oil together then fry the kidneys over high heat until just cooked through. Remove from the pan and keep warm.

Heat the remaining butter in the second pan and cook the mushrooms only until they are heated through, then add the olives and reduce the temperature to its lowest setting.

Deglaze the kidney pan with the sherry, adding the brandy and cream, then reduce rapidly until half its original volume. Tip the kidneys, mushrooms and olives into the sauce, turn gently until heated through and simmer for only 1 minute.

To serve *Sprinkle the kidneys with coarsely chopped parsley and serve with lemon.*

FRUIT BUTTERS

These are not the old-fashioned fruit butters, which were purées of fruit cooked and cooked until most of their moisture had gone. My fruit butters are a combination of lightly cooked fruits and rich Normandy butter, naturally sweet without added sugar. Fruit butters are equally good at tea time, when you might further lighten them by folding in whipped double cream. Only two things are essential. As the butter and fruit mixtures are cooling you must whisk them gently which ensures that as the fruits lose juice this is incorporated into the butter; the whisking lightens the butter and as the butter sets ensures even distribution and a good rugged texture. And you must not heat the butter more than is necessary to melt it or you will change its sweet flavour.

Grape and walnut butter:
250g/8oz red grapes, halved and seeded
175g/6oz unsalted butter
2 tablespoons chopped, toasted walnuts

Plum and prune butter:
175g/6oz stoned red- or yellow-skinned plums, sliced
50g/2oz prunes, sliced
150ml/¼ pint apple juice
175g/6oz unsalted butter

Apple and orange butter:
2 Golden Delicious or similar dessert apples
2 oranges, preferably navel oranges
150ml/¼ pint freshly squeezed orange juice
Finely grated rind of ½ orange
8oz/250g unsalted butter

Spiced dried fruit butter:
125g/4oz dried fruits (apricots, peaches, pears, apples, prunes), sliced
300ml/½ pint apple juice
½ teaspoon freshly ground cinnamon
175g/6oz unsalted butter
2 tablespoons toasted flaked almonds

To make the grape and walnut butter, cook the grapes over gentle heat for 3 or 4 minutes, until the grapes are plumped and quite a bit of juice has been expressed. Allow to cool a little, stirring from time to time to tempt more skin colour to flow out. Melt the butter, and mix into the grapes. Keep stirring to deepen the colour until almost set, then mix in the chopped toasted walnuts.

If the butter appears to separate, stir everything like mad and it will all incorporate again and stay that way if then quickly chilled. If you don't like skins you may remove them, but then you will have no colour in the butter.

To make the plum and prune butter, put the plums in a saucepan and add the prunes and apple juice. Poach the fruits in the juice, stirring from time to time, until tender. Add the butter and keep stirring as it melts into the mixture to break up the fruit a little and to encourage a deepening of the flavour. Pour the mixture into a pot and chill quickly.

To make the apple and orange butter, peel and core the apples and cut into 1cm/½in chunks. Cut the peel and pith from the oranges with a long sharp knife then remove the segments between the membranes. Put the apple and orange into a saucepan with the orange juice and poach over low heat for 3–5 minutes until the apple is soft but still holding its shape. Stir in orange rind, then the butter. Stir until setting to ensure a coarse texture and even flavouring.

To make the spiced dried fruit butter, put the dried fruits in a saucepan with the apple juice and poach until really tender. While still hot stir in the cinnamon and butter. Allow to cool slowly, stirring from time to time. When the butter is almost set, stir in the toasted flaked almonds.

Oz Clarke's *WINE NOTES*

What time in the morning are you going to have your celebration breakfast? There's a big difference between a sort of dawn chorus of revellers continuing the night before's high jinks and a sedately celebratory late Saturday morning affair after a busy week at the office. It makes a considerable difference to what drinks are going to work, because about the only time I actively don't want a glass of Champagne is at a traditional 8–8.30am kind of breakfast time. Four in the morning – sure, anything goes; 10am is just about right for a bright and breezy glass of fizz. Mostly in between these times I'd rather have freshly brewed coffee and orange juice.

That's where the Bloody Mary comes in (two parts tomato juice, one part vodka, a squeeze of lemon juice and plenty of ice). Especially if you spice it up with a good splash of Worcester sauce – and a dash of Tabasco – it can do no end of good in waking you up with a bang. And I must say, if I'm going to make a Buck's Fizz (one part orange juice, three parts Champagne) I'm going to use blood oranges for the extra delicious perfume of their juice. Add to that a measure of Cointreau or Mandarine Napoléon, and suddenly, I'm wide awake and raring to go.

PRESENTATION

This should be all stops out, as long as you do not run the risk of outshining any preceding or following celebration, which would be churlish. Starched linen napkins rather than paper, please, and the silver and crystal you save for celebrations. If you have a large table and plain white linen it is sensationally good to scatter flowers directly on to the table – white and purple crocuses, roses or rose petals, blossoming boughs, holly and ivy, according to the season.

AMERICAN BRUNCH
for 20

Believe me, the United States does breakfast better – all the delights of the famed British start to the day but so very much more too.

Now, I'm not talking the diet-victim nibbling of California, you know, a 10-mile back pack and double aerobics before water-melon pickle and raw fish. No, I mean the hearty breakfasts of great homely kitchens and welcoming Main Street diners just about everywhere else.

As well as bacon and eggs, there might be steaks and stacks of pancakes with syrups, wicked choices of spiced cakes and drooling pastries, peppery sausages or fried chicken with cream gravy, hashes and hams. In New York there'll be the famous smoked salmon and cream cheese on hot bagels, and perhaps oysters Kilpatrick or eggs Benedict. Baltimore offers Chesapeake Bay crab cakes; Honolulu feasts on fruit salads.

In the Southern States there'll be grits or hominy made from corn and New Orleans is famous for its hot rice cakes.

An American brunch will be the servant of the oven space you have to heat, bake and store. Choose accordingly from this menu or some of my suggested extras. The aim is a mixture of savoury, sweet and spiced.

Do it with style and generosity. Then everyone will have a terrifically nice day.

MENU

*

PINEAPPLE WITH MINT AND GIN

CORNED BEEF HASH

YUBA CITY PASTA SALAD

HASH-BROWN POTATOES

AMERICAN-STYLE SAUSAGE WITH VIRGINIA MOUNTAIN CREAM GRAVY

SNICKERDOODLE

CINNAMON BRIOCHE

*

Fruit Juices
Coca Cola
Beer
Californian White Zinfandel
Iced Tea/Coffee

PINEAPPLE WITH MINT AND GIN

Fresh pineapple is now available all year round and its wonderful sharp sweetness is a perfect stimulant for the unsuspecting breakfast palate. Pineapple also has an unexpected affinity with gin. Together they create a haunting new flavour and if your guests are not likely to be driving this would definitely give a flying start to your brunch. For a hot variation butter slices of pineapple and grill or cook over a moderate heat before pouring the gin into the pan; serve it with a sprig of mint.

3 or 4 large fresh pineapples (or enough to provide 1 thick slice per person)
600ml/1 pint gin
Large bunch of fresh mint
Sugar, to serve (optional)

Cut the skin from the pineapple from top to bottom, deeply enough to remove all the little eyes. Cut across into thick slices then into squares or segments, leaving in the core or not according to your taste. Place the pieces in a large shallow dish and pour on the gin. Add freshly torn (not chopped) mint leaves. Cover and allow to marinate at room temperature for several hours before refrigerating. Do not prepare this earlier than the previous evening or the texture of the pineapple will deteriorate. Some people might like a sprinkling of sugar, which is best added when serving.

CORNED BEEF HASH

An American hash can be made with any leftover cooked meat, but what Americans call corned beef and Britons call salt beef is considered by far the best. The flavour is considerably improved if the mixture is left to get to know itself overnight, but do not be prodigal with the onion or this is all the hash will taste of when cooked.

HASH-BROWN POTATOES, CORNED BEEF HASH, PINEAPPLE WITH MINT AND GIN

2kg/4lb cold salt beef or roast beef or lamb
2kg/4lb cold boiled potatoes
250g/8oz onion
2 dessertspoons chopped green pepper
½ teaspoon freshly grated nutmeg
20 eggs
8 tablespoons butter, fat or oil
300ml/½ pint water, double cream or stock
Chilli sauce, to serve (optional)
Black pepper

The above proportions are less of a guide than usual and may be adapted to your taste and what you have – the secret of a good hash is how it is cooked rather than what is in it.

Chop the meat finely and the potatoes roughly. The onion should be the finest of all and some might go to the trouble of grating it. Mix these ingredients together with the green pepper and then flavour generously with black pepper and nutmeg. Cover and refrigerate overnight.

Poach the eggs until they are as hard or runny as you like, with all due care for the current advice on eggs. You can prepare these the night before then slide them directly into cold water and store them like this in the refrigerator; tip them into hot water again in the morning and although they will heat through the yolks will not cook any more.

In the morning, heat enough butter, fat or oil to cover the base of a heavy-bottomed frying pan, add the meat mixture and press down firmly and evenly. (You will need to cook the hash in batches.) Once a crust has formed on the bottom, turn with a spatula so that most of the crust is lifted from the bottom and distributed. Press down again. Now add some cream, water or stock which will help form a better second bottom crust. Cook very slowly, turning from time to time until a good half of the mixture in the pan has been browned and mixed with the portion which has not. Then let the bottom crust get brown and crisp. Fold the hash in half, slide it carefully on to a warmed serving dish. Repeat with the remaining mixture and keep the hash warm until ready to serve. Reheat the eggs and top each serving with an egg and chilli sauce.

EXTRAS

Bacon, which should be sweet cure, would be appreciated and can be cooked in a roasting pan on the hob or in the oven. Fried eggs would always be welcome if you have the facilities, which usually means someone to do the eggs to order on the day.

If it is a nice day, put the barbecue in the garden and cook the eggs and bacon in pans on the barbecue. The same could go for the sausages and cream gravy. It's probably easier to cook scrambled eggs in batches, again over the barbecue, but make them a little 'southern' with chopped red and green pepper and the option of a dash of chilli sauce.

Slightly warmed bagels, quickly sliced and filled with cream cheese and a little smoked salmon, are astonishingly good for breakfast. If the bagels are really fresh they do not need to be heated.

Toast is nice if you can manage it for such numbers – it's far easier to offer Danish pastries, warm or cold, or croissants, perhaps with some of the fruit butters (see page 23).

And what would an American meal be without ice cream? A scoop of a good ice cream is fabulous with the snickerdoodle, or the cinnamon brioche, or the pineapple, or ...

If it is ice cream weather, you should also be serving iced tea, which is far easier than any other drink as it must be made in advance. The coffee should be South American for this is the most popular style in the US.

A selection of fruit juices is a must at brunch time since many people will not want alcohol, but will want a long refreshing drink. Cranberry juice and orange juice are usually liked. Possibly even Coca Cola.

YUBA CITY PASTA SALAD

Yuba City in California produces 70 per cent of the world's prunes. And within a few hours' drive you also find walnut and orange groves, entire towns devoted to the culinary exploitation of garlic, and plum tomatoes grown for fresh, dried and processed use. This salad, a designer mix of creams, browns and black with touches of bright colour, celebrates the produce of California. It may be served warm in the modern way or chilled.

16 or more whole cloves garlic
2 or 3 oranges
375g/12oz dried wholemeal or white pasta shapes
12 tablespoons or more walnut or olive oil
175g/6oz pitted black olives
175g/6oz walnut halves, toasted
24 pitted prunes, sliced
36 black grapes, halved and deseeded
20 red cherry tomatoes
Flat-leaved parsley or fresh coriander leaves, coarsely chopped
8 sun-dried tomato halves, sliced (optional)
Parmesan or Pecorino cheese, thinly flaked, to serve (optional)

First poach the garlic. Each clove should be left in its skin and looks better if the long thread attached to the top is still there. Large cloves take about 20 minutes to cook to a really soft and delicious mush inside their skins. Meanwhile slice off the skin and pith of the oranges then cut out the segments between the membranes and remove any pips. Cook the pasta in boiling salted water, drain and toss in just a little oil.

To serve warm, in a shallow frying pan warm about 8 tablespoons of the oil and add the cooked garlic, olives, toasted walnuts and prunes. Warm through thoroughly then pour the contents of the pan over the pasta and toss well. Add the grapes, oranges and tomatoes quickly with quite a lot of parsley or coriander. If you are using sun-dried tomatoes, scatter them on top.

To serve cold, toss the pasta in the full amount of oil then gently mix in or layer the remaining ingredients.

If you like, serve with thinly shaved flakes of hard, aged Parmesan or Pecorino cheese offered separately instead of salt and pepper.

HASH-BROWN POTATOES

Also called 'hashed brown potatoes', these are cooked in the same way as corned beef hash, that is they are tossed and turned during cooking so that the brown crisp bits are distributed through the mixture.

Melted butter or bacon fat, for frying
2·5kg/5lb peeled potatoes, roughly diced

Cover the bottom of a large heavy pan with the melted butter or bacon fat and add the potatoes, pressing them down evenly (you may need to do this in batches). Cook the potatoes until a crust has formed then, by tossing the pan and lightly stirring from time to time, cook all the potatoes and brown at least half of them. From time to time it helps to trickle melted fat through the potatoes.

Once they are in this state there are several ways to proceed. You may simply get the bottom well and truly browned and serve the potatoes from the pan. Or, having done one side, slide them on to a plate, invert and brown the other side, though I think this is better for smaller amounts. For a large number of guests, forget about keeping the hash-brown potatoes looking like big cakes and simply tip them into heated serving dishes.
SEE PAGE 25.

AMERICAN-STYLE SAUSAGE WITH VIRGINIA MOUNTAIN CREAM GRAVY

Sausages in skins are a rarity in the US. Instead you buy the sausagemeat in bulk and form it into patties which are then fried. Cream gravy is more generally served with fried chicken, but in West Virginia they enjoy it with their breakfast sausage.

1·5kg/3lb sausagemeat
6 tablespoons flour
900ml/1½ pints milk
Salt and pepper

Combine the sausagemeat and seasoning and form the mixture into small flat round patties. Fry in batches in a heavy-based pan over a low heat until cooked through and nicely browned on both sides. Pour off and reserve the fat after cooking each batch. Transfer the patties to a serving dish. Set aside and keep warm.

To make the gravy, heat 6 tablespoons of the reserved fat in the pan then stir in the flour, gathering the brown bits from the sausage as you do so. Let the flour brown slightly then stir in about a quarter of the milk off the heat. Add the rest of the milk and stir over a low heat until thickened. If the gravy seems too thick add more milk; if it is too thin cook a little longer. Season to taste.

If you make a second batch of gravy, crumble a cooked sausage patty into the pan with the fat and flour to ensure flavour and brown bits.

PLANNING AHEAD

In advance: The snickerdoodle and cinnamon brioche ring can be made several days in advance and stored in airtight containers. Serve them warmed through rather than hot.

Ensure you will have enough ice and containers for the fruit juice, beers and wine – yes, the baby's bath is still one of the best ideas for chilling things down. Double check you can supply enough coffee and tea. Two or three days ahead you can make the iced tea and keep it refrigerated.

The day before: Prepare the mixture for the corned beef hash, cover and refrigerate. Poach the eggs and store in cold water in the fridge. Prepare the potatoes for the hash-brown potatoes, put them in a large bowl and cover with cold water. Make up the American-style sausage patties, cover and store in the fridge.

If you are going to serve it cold, make the Yuba City pasta salad, cover, and refrigerate. If you are going to serve it warm, prepare the ingredients and cook the pasta; cover and refrigerate.

Prepare the chilled pineapple with mint and gin in the evening. Once it has marinated for several hours, refrigerate.

The day of the party: Finish preparing the pineapple in mint and gin if serving hot. Cook the corned beef hash. Cook the hash-brown potatoes. Cook the American-style sausage and make the Virginia mountain cream gravy. Reheat the poached eggs in hot water or cook them freshly. Finish making the Yuba City pasta salad if serving warm. Rewarm the snickerdoodle and the cinnamon brioche ring.

Above left **AMERICAN-STYLE SAUSAGE WITH VIRGINIA MOUNTAIN CREAM GRAVY, YUBA CITY PASTA SALAD**

PRESENTATION

The American party, brunch or otherwise, is always an opportunity to enjoy creative display. One of the easiest ways to make food look fabulous is to ensure everything is on different levels. This can be done simply by using a combination of bowls and stands. Otherwise the trick is to cover your table with a series of strong flat-bottomed objects – fat cans are good – and to put a large table cloth over the lot. You now have a series of peaks and dips on which to display the dishes.

Your brunch must look as colourful and generous as possible. Cook more than you expect to serve. Accept offers from others to bring something. American eating is about generosity and the enjoyment of others' enjoyment. It's a terrific example.

SNICKERDOODLE

This delicious name can refer to all sorts of cakes, cookies and cup cakes, which are sometimes also called 'snipdoodle'. What they have in common is speed of making and a topping of cinnamon and sugar. Generically snickerdoodle is a coffee cake, which in the US means the sort of sweet, usually spiced, cake eaten with breakfast. It is very much better warm than cold and doesn't mind being rewarmed on the day if made ahead. Serve with a scoop or two of ice cream.

125g/4oz sugar
125g/4oz plain flour
Pinch of salt
1 teaspoon baking powder
1 teaspoon cinnamon
1 egg
8 tablespoons milk
50g/2oz butter, melted
50g/2oz raisins (optional)
Granulated or demerara sugar and cinnamon, for topping
Vanilla ice cream, to serve (optional)

Butter a 23 × 32cm/9 × 13in cake tin. Stir the dry ingredients together then lightly beat in the egg and milk. Beat in the melted butter. A handful of raisins stirred into the mixture is a common and enjoyable variation, and you might also be more adventurous with the spicing, including mace, nutmeg or allspice, too. Pour into the tin and sprinkle the top with as much or as little granulated white or demerara sugar and cinnamon as you like. Bake in a preheated oven, 190°C, 375°F, Gas Mark 5, for 20–25 minutes. Turn it out and cut into squares while still warm.

Top **CINNAMON BRIOCHE, SNICKERDOODLE**

CINNAMON BRIOCHE

This more complicated breakfast cake requires more skill and is thus much more satisfying to make and infinitely more delicious than the simple snickerdoodle. It must be made in advance and may then be gently warmed on the day.

Brioche mixture:
500g/1lb strong white flour
Pinch of salt
2 tablespoons caster sugar
250g/8oz unsalted butter
1 packet easy-blend yeast
6 eggs (size 1), beaten

Filling:
125g/4oz unsalted butter
125g/4oz Muscovado sugar
2 teaspoons or more cinnamon
1 teaspoon vanilla essence
Pecan nut halves (optional)
Beaten egg, for glazing

To make the brioche, sift together the flour, salt and sugar and warm them gently in the oven. Melt the butter as gently as possible so you do not change its flavour then let it cool to room temperature. Mix the yeast into the dry ingredients thoroughly.

Add the butter and eggs and beat with a wooden spoon for 5 minutes until smooth and supple. The mixture will be somewhat sticky but should look as though it is making the effort to leave the sides of the bowl. If you are in doubt add more flour but do not make a dry, firm mixture. Cover with a damp cloth and leave to rise in the bowl in a warmish place until doubled in size. Lightly grease your hands with butter and knead the dough for a minute. If you have the time it gives a distinct improvement in flavour and texture if you let the dough prove again; indeed both provings should take as long as is practicable (about 1 hour each is acceptable).

To make the filling, cream together the butter and sugar then add the cinnamon and vanilla flavouring. If you are using pecans you might chop some and add to the mixture.

Butter a cake tin at least 25cm/10in diameter. Shape or roll the dough into two oblongs about 37 × 12cm/15 × 5in, greasing rather than flouring the rolling pin. Spread the filling evenly on both pieces, leaving only a small border untouched on all four sides. Form each into a roll by rolling from the long side. Seal well. Twist the two rolls together then into a circle. Transfer to the cake tin. Paint the top with a little beaten egg and dot with pecan halves if you like.

Bake in a preheated oven, 220°C, 425°F, Gas Mark 7, for 30–35 minutes. If the pecan halves are in danger of browning, spray lightly with water – but only do this after at least 20 minutes and with furious speed or the dough will collapse.

To serve *Allow to cool. Turn out, serve sliced, with or without butter.*

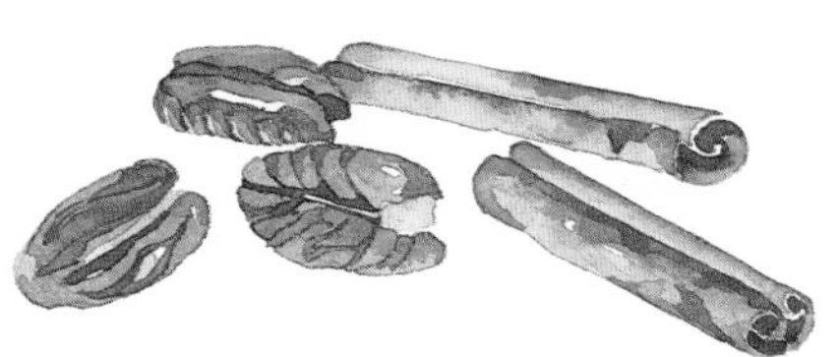

Oz Clarke's
WINE NOTES

Virginia mountain cream gravy, Yuba City pasta salad, and, oh I love it, snickerdoodle. Glynn, where did you find these wonderful names? Is Yuba City really Prune Paradise USA? Can you really call snickerdoodle snipdoodle? Or are you making it all up? I never realized how romantic basic American breakfast chow could sound. And now that I look at the menus again, I feel a distinct wanderlust coming on. Because I have eaten great patties of sausage with gravy in the wilds of West Virginia, I've eaten hundreds of snickerdoodles under less exotic names all across America, so much so that I began to get cinnamon and coffee withdrawal symptoms if I didn't stop and grab one by mid-morning. And as for corned beef hash and hash browns, whenever I have an early start on my American travels, I pass all these roadside shacks advertising franks, hash browns, easy-over eggs and as much coffee as I can drink – and I can never resist the temptation. I tell you, this is a party for trenchermen, because this kind of food just has to be eaten in piled-up platefuls.

I'm sure Glynn will have some good strong coffee on the hob, but by brunch time, I think we could maybe do a bit of drinking of a more serious kind. And an ice-cold beer might just about hit the spot. In America it would probably be the ubiquitous Budweiser, but I'm going to go for a Californian beer which really packs in the flavour – Anchor Steam. And I'll have some chilled bottles of White Zinfandel at the ready. This is actually pink and hardly tastes like wine at all – fresh, fruity and utterly gluggable, nothing challenging about it, which suits me just fine around brunch time.

Family Reunion Breakfast *for 8*

Reunions don't happen often in my far-flung family, yet when they do, the pattern is familiar. Someone has a new baby, someone has a new partner. Someone has just come back from the Orient or Himalayas, someone wants to go there. This wife is slimming, that husband is trying to put weight on, and there's someone new to the terrors of a breaking voice or teenage spots who would rather die than talk, eat or drink.

The trick with families is to lull them into a sense of getting what they expect, then to startle them out of any complacency. This achieved they may speak about what you want rather than what they intend.

This menu challenges from the start by offering dried peaches sumptuously plumped in fruit juice and fragrant with cardamom. Hot or cold, they'll break the ice and waken the tastebuds to a full appreciation of a proper kedgeree with a *gentle* Indian spicing and a toad-in-the-hole which has met a pig-in-a-blanket. Before the new vegetarian pipes up you'll pop down a platter of sweetcorn fritters with baked or grilled tomatoes on top.

Provided you remember who hates strawberry jam and who only eats coarse marmalade, that you have bought most newspapers, and have a couple of new jokes but no new carpets or upholstery, you should survive.

MENU

*

CARDAMOM PEACHES

MIXED-GRILL-IN-THE-HOLE

ORIGINAL KEDGEREE

SWEETCORN FRITTERS WITH BAKED TOMATOES

*

Fresh Orange Juice

CARDAMOM PEACHES

These spiced dried peaches sit in a rich sauce of mixed fruit juices and can be served hot or cold according to the season. In summer you might add some sliced fresh peaches or berries, in winter they are spectacularly good on top of porridge – either way yogurt or whipped cream and a little muscovado sugar or toasted nuts make them even more magical. Oh, all right, yes, they are marvellous with muesli too. But at a big breakfast they make a delicious chilled or warm first course all by themselves.

24 dried peach halves
300ml/½ pint freshly squeezed orange juice
600ml/1 pint apple juice
8 cardamom pods
1 cinnamon stick

Put the fruit and juices into a pan. Split the cardamom pods a little but do not let the seeds tumble out. Add the pods and the cinnamon stick to the mixture then bring slowly to the boil and simmer for just 2 minutes. Let cool and leave at room temperature overnight by which time the peaches should be plumped but not soft. Cover and refrigerate until needed; the peaches improve if they are allowed to rest a further day and night before serving.

To serve *These may be served warm on a cold morning. Thick yogurt would be good with them any day.*

MIXED-GRILL-IN-THE-HOLE

Toad-in-the-hole was originally a way to add interest to leftover steak or beef and is especially suitable for substantial breakfasts. If you like such things, coarsely chopped parsley and finely chopped garlic can be added to the batter mixture. If you insist on including onion, it should be chopped and boiled or microwaved into sweetness first and stirred into the batter before you fold in the egg whites. This recipe, which will remind many of pigs-in-a-blanket (sausages in batter) supposes there will be kedgeree and so everyone will not want one of everything. If only this dish is being served double the quantities.

4 lamb loin chops
4 beef sausages
4 lamb kidneys
4 rashers of bacon
4 eggs, separated
300ml/½ pint milk at room temperature
250g/8oz plain flour
Salt and pepper

Arrange the meats and bacon in a nice pattern in a shallow baking dish. Bake for 12 minutes in a preheated oven, 180°C, 350°F, Gas Mark 4. Increase the oven temperature to 220°C, 425°F, Gas Mark 7, and continue cooking for a further 5 minutes.

While baking at the higher temperature, make a batter by beating together the egg yolks, milk and flour. At the last minute whisk the egg whites until light and peaky but not dry and fold them into the batter.

Swiftly remove the baking dish from the oven (get someone else to close the door for you to conserve the heat), pour the batter evenly into the dish, then return it equally swiftly to the oven for 20–25 minutes until the batter is evenly risen and nicely brown. Serve at the table directly from the dish the moment it is ready.

ORIGINAL KEDGEREE, CARDAMOM PEACHES
SEE PAGE 33.

EXTRAS

The most important extras will probably have nothing to do with eating. If there are children you will need extra tissues. There should be a good range of newspapers, but firmness about when they can be read. You will probably need white and wholemeal toast and should certainly know enough about the family to have everyone's favourite jam, or marmalade, or peanut butter.

Like families, these events tend to go on a bit, so I should ensure a goodly tin of biscuits or a delicious cake for cutting into later in the morning, and a small stock of lightly chilled dry sherry, a sparkling wine and some beer in the refrigerator (although I wouldn't encourage alcohol before or with the breakfast itself). Have a packet of amusing sweeties and extra juice or cordial for youngsters, and maybe some iced lollies or individual ice creams, too.

To head off old battles, new clashes, or extended domination by an individual, keep your photograph albums handy. Serve generously.

PRESENTATION

This is what will smooth over the awkwardness which is endemic when families meet up after some time. You could use as many special and evocative things as you have or can. Find a special old tablecloth or eccentric teapot, family silver – anything which will stimulate exclamations of memory and exchanges of conversation.

So the occasion is not stiff, everything should be served in a homely family fashion with no pretence, no sprigs of parsley or silver service. Let them help themselves, in fact most of all ensure there is always something for everyone to do.

The orange juice should be in a jug and the peaches in a bowl.

ORIGINAL KEDGEREE

PLANNING AHEAD

Two days before: Prepare the cardamom peaches, cover and refrigerate.

The day before: Arrange the meats in a baking dish, cover and refrigerate. Cook the fish for the kedgeree, break it into generous pieces, cover and refrigerate. (Remember to keep the cooking liquid for the rice.) Hard-boil the eggs, shell and refrigerate. At a pinch the sweetcorn fritters could be made in advance for reheating but do not simply grate the sweetcorn in advance as it will lose flavour dramatically.

The day of the party: Remove the dish of meat, the fish and the hard-boiled eggs from the refrigerator so they come to room temperature by the time you want to complete the dishes.

30 minutes before, turn on the oven to preheat for the mixed-grill-in-the-hole. Prepare everything so you can offer coffee and tea quickly.

20 minutes before, put the meat into the oven and make the batter. Stand by to ask the first person through the door to help pour on the batter and rush the dish back into the oven.

Either make the kedgeree while the grill is cooking and keep it warm in a second oven or on a very low heat on the hob or make it while you chat to guests if your kitchen is big enough.

If you are eating in or close to the kitchen cook the fritters; if your kitchen is too small or remote for this you should have precooked the fritters and can now pop them, spread on a large plate and loosely covered with foil, into an oven *but* do not put them or the tomatoes in with the grill-in-the-hole unless it has cooked at least 15 minutes or it will collapse. Alternatively pop the tomatoes under the grill or in another oven. The peaches can be heated to warmth in a microwave oven, which will also help revive the kedgeree or bake the tomatoes.

Because this is one of the few genuinely new dishes created by the British occupation of India (the original *kidgeree* or *kitcheree* is a vegetarian dish of spiced rice and lentils topped with fried onions), it is properly made with a light spicing, and this is the way you will find it still in outposts of the former Empire. Like all Indian dishes it simply won't be right if you do not use basmati rice.

Those who like a real touch of the east might appreciate the addition of an inauthentic pinch or two of cayenne or the availability of Tabasco sauce. Hard-boiled quail eggs make a luxurious change and these should be halved lengthwise after shelling and scattered over the finished dish, substituting for some or all of the hens' eggs.

Other fish may also be used or a mixture. If the celebration is extra special, you might fold in a mixture of poached fresh and smoked salmon and top that with quail eggs. This would be a really marvellous breakfast to welcome family and friends on Christmas or New Year's Day. These quantities are generous for four people as a supper and thus just right for eight for breakfast if you are serving the mixed-grill-in-the-hole.

1kg/2lb smoked haddock or cod
1 bay leaf
125g/4oz butter
250g/8oz basmati rice
4 hard-boiled eggs
1 teaspoon ground coriander
½ teaspoon ground cumin
½ teaspoon ground turmeric

Unless the fish is uncoloured, cover it with boiling water and when cold drain that away. Then cover it with cold water, add the bay leaf and bring slowly to a gentle simmer; uncoloured smoked fish can be put straight into cold water with the bay leaf and treated the same way. Remove the pan from the heat once the water has simmered. Check with a fork that the flesh comes easily from any bones. If not, return to the heat for a few minutes. Once ready, remove the fish but reserve the water.

Wash the rice as instructed on the pack if you wish. Put it into a measuring jug and mark where it comes to. Melt a good knob of the butter in a saucepan and gently fry the rice in this until it goes milky and opaque. Now measure the water in which the fish was poached; you need twice the volume of liquid as you had rice – add extra water if necessary to make it up. Add that to the rice. Cook until bubbling holes appear on top of the rice. Cover with a clean tea cloth and jam on the saucepan lid. Leave over the lowest possible heat for about 10 minutes or until the rice has absorbed all the water.

While the rice is cooking, skin and bone the fish and pull into large generous pieces; shell the hard-boiled eggs and chop roughly into uneven pieces. Now you need yet another saucepan or frying pan which will be big enough to take all the ingredients.

Melt the remaining butter and in that sweat the three spices until they are strongly fragrant but not burning. Stir in the rice and mix until evenly coated with the spiced butter. Then fold in the egg followed by the fish. It is very important to be light-handed so you keep the shape and texture of the ingredients as contrasted as possible. Kedgeree may be kept warm in a low oven but is much the better for being served at once.

To serve *Kedgeree looks wonderful on silver so if you have just a single decent entrée dish of plate or silver use it now. Finish by scattering some currants or sultanas over the dish, if you wish.* *SEE PAGE 30.*

SWEETCORN FRITTERS WITH BAKED TOMATOES

Corn fritters are a delicious vegetarian way to start the day and because fresh corn is available for much of the year you can probably make these simple fritters, a recipe from the Shaker communities of the USA. Small red and yellow cherry tomatoes look prettiest if cooked just until the skins pop. If you can't find fresh corn, simply mix a small can of creamed corn with an egg or two and just enough flour to thicken the mixture a little and fry gently.

The fritters taste particularly good topped with a dollop of soured cream and, if liked, a dash of Tabasco sauce.

MIXED-GRILL-IN-THE-HOLE, SWEETCORN FRITTERS WITH BAKED TOMATOES

6 small fresh corn on the cob
2 eggs
1 tablespoon soft, salted butter
1 heaped teaspoon plain flour
Butter or vegetable oil, for frying
500g/1lb red or yellow cherry tomatoes
Soured cream and Tabasco sauce (optional), to serve
Salt and pepper

Peel off the husks and silk threads of the corn cobs and coarsely grate the corn kernels into a bowl, ensuring you collect all the juice. Then mix in the eggs, salted butter and flour. Fry the mixture in large or small spoonfuls in hot butter or vegetable oil until golden. Drain them on kitchen paper and keep warm.

Grill or microwave halved large tomatoes or whole cherry tomatoes until hot through but not collapsing.

To serve *Top each fritter with soured cream and a whole or halved tomato and Tabasco sauce.*

GERALDENE HOLT

Lunches

I always regard an invitation to lunch with particular pleasure. For a good lunch is a warm and friendly meal with little of the formality of a dinner party. It's an easy-going, relaxed event where people come together to eat and talk and truly enjoy each other's company.

Lunch is not the occasion for fussy food. I favour good, simple dishes, those that ideally can be made ahead or that will only improve if kept waiting – often because everyone is so busy exchanging their news that you start to eat a little later than planned.

How you arrange to serve food at lunch usually depends on the number of guests. For a large party it may well be easier to place serving dishes either in the centre of the table, or on one at the side – even in the kitchen – and ask everyone to help themselves. When the lunch party is small and intimate then it is easy enough to serve the food at the table.

The lunches I've chosen are the kind of meals I entertain with throughout the year. The Springtime Lunch I devised for friends and family one Easter. But the meal is just as delicious at other times. The Midsummer Lunch was first served to friends that we hadn't seen for ages. So I designed a menu that involved the minimum of last-minute cooking – so that I did not have to disappear into the kitchen for ages and miss some vital piece of news. The weather was glorious so we ate in the garden. But the meal would be equally nice served indoors – with the windows open and lots of fresh flowers to bring the summer inside.

The Mediterranean Seafood Lunch is a family favourite, especially in September when the weather is still warm enough to sit outside and the summery dishes bring back holiday memories.

The French Country Lunch is simply one of my favourite meals. It is ideal for a leisurely Sunday when lunch can last as long as you like. I never tire of the dishes and I don't mind a jot if lunch doesn't finish till seven. The Indian Lunch I devised one weekend for my student son and a crowd of his vegetarian friends; though the meat-eaters loved it too. I can never get over how good Indian food makes you feel: its blend of subtle spices and wonderful vegetables is always a delight. The cuisine induces such utter contentment that it somehow manages to make Monday seem a long way off.

Opposite **MEDITERRANEAN SEAFOOD LUNCH** *PAGE 40*

English Springtime Lunch for 6

The English spring with its lengthening days of bright sunshine and occasional showers has inspired poets and painters for centuries. The rest of us still welcome spring just as warmly for it is, above all, a time of renewal and of hope.

The countryside and the gardens soon begin to reflect the season. Spring flowers glow in hedges and borders, and young vegetables and herbs can be picked when they have a pure, intense flavour which is best left, as far as possible, unmasked.

For this lunch menu I have been inspired by some of the seasonal dishes of the past. Since the time of the seventeenth-century diarist and gardener, John Evelyn, the English have taken a pride in serving the earliest spring vegetables, so the first course is a dish of baby vegetables tossed in parsley butter. Then come some spring poussins with their delicate flavour, which make a fine main course at this time of year, and braised or stewed lettuce, a firm Victorian favourite which is well worth reviving.

The apricot flummery is derived from an eighteenth-century recipe from Hannah Glasse.

Menu

*

FILO PASTRY BASKETS OF BABY VEGETABLES

BRAISED LETTUCE

FONDANT POTATOES WITH SESAME SEEDS

POUSSINS IN NOODLE NESTS

*

APRICOT AND ORANGE-FLOWER WATER FLUMMERY

*

Alsace Tokay/Pinot Gris

Mosel Riesling Kabinett

BRAISED LETTUCE, FONDANT POTATOES WITH SESAME SEEDS, POUSSINS IN NOODLE NESTS

FILO PASTRY BASKETS OF BABY VEGETABLES

These light pastry baskets are quick and easy to prepare – they can be made ahead and filled with the vegetables at the last moment.

75g/3oz butter, melted
6 sheets filo pastry
500g/1lb mixed baby vegetables such as leeks, sweetcorn cobs, broad beans, broccoli florets, carrots, courgettes, mangetout peas, turnips
2 teaspoons finely chopped parsley

Reserve 50g/2oz of the butter for the vegetables and use the rest for buttering the pastry and the tins. Spread a sheet of filo pastry on a work surface. Brush the first sheet of pastry with melted butter. Cover with a second layer of pastry, brush with butter and cover with a third layer. Use a sharp knife to cut into three 12cm/5in squares. Place each square in a buttered patty tin, gently press the pastry into the base of the tin and allow the edges to spread out like a handkerchief. Repeat with the remaining pastry to make 6 cases in all and place a ball of crumpled foil in each pastry case to keep it in place. Use the pastry trimmings to make 6 curved handles for the baskets and place on a separate baking sheet.

Bake in a preheated oven, 200°C, 400°F, Gas Mark 6, for 8–10 minutes or until the pastry is golden brown. Cool the cases in the tins and set aside.

Prepare the vegetables, trimming as necessary. Place in a steaming basket over boiling water and cook until just tender or according to your taste.

Stir together the reserved melted butter and chopped parsley in a hot mixing bowl. Add the hot vegetables and toss them gently in the butter until coated.

To serve *Place each pastry case on a small plate, divide the vegetables among the cases, add a pastry handle to each basket and serve.*

BRAISED LETTUCE

Braised lettuce was a popular Victorian dish. The best variety to use for this dish is little gem lettuce with its firmly packed heart.

3 little gem lettuces
75g/3oz butter
2 tablespoons sherry or tarragon vinegar

Trim the stalks of the lettuces, discard any limp outer leaves and, if necessary, wash in cold water and drain well. Cut each lettuce in half lengthwise.

Melt 50g/2oz of the butter in a pan large enough to hold the lettuces in a single layer. When the butter is foaming, add the lettuces and turn over until coated with butter. Then place them cut side down and cover with a lid or a buttered paper.

Cook over moderate heat or in a preheated oven, 180°C, 350°F, Gas Mark 4, for 10–15 minutes or until they are cooked but not mushy.

Transfer the lettuces to a hot serving dish. Add the vinegar to the pan and mix with the cooking juices. Simmer for 1 minute, add the remaining butter and as soon as it is melted pour or spoon the sauce over the lettuces and serve.

FILO PASTRY BASKETS OF BABY VEGETABLES

EXTRAS

This menu provides a complete meal and does not require you to offer anything else in the way of extras.

Place a salt cellar with sea salt, and a pepper mill filled with black peppercorns on the table and have plenty of mineral water ready in the refrigerator.

Serve freshly brewed coffee after the meal. Hand sugar and cream separately. For a change serve whipped cream, sprinkled with a little ground cinnamon and grated dessert chocolate – it tastes delicious spooned into hot strong coffee served in small cups.

PRESENTATION

Since this is a springtime meal I like to keep to pastel colours in my table setting and flowers – yellows, white and mauve. At Easter you can make a pretty centrepiece for the table with pieces of wood and moss decorated with primroses, violets and polyanthus. Arrange some sugar or foil-covered chocolate eggs among the flowers to eat at the end of the meal.

PLANNING AHEAD

In advance: Make the filo pastry baskets 1–2 weeks ahead and freeze or make the day before and store overnight in an airtight box in the refrigerator.

The day before: Make the apricot purée for the dessert and refrigerate. Make the cream mixture and divide among the serving glasses.

The day of the party: Take the filo baskets out of the freezer. Finish making up the flummery and keep in a cool place until serving time. About 1¼ hours before lunch put the poussins in the oven. Prepare the vegetables for the filo baskets. Prepare the potatoes and lettuces. Reheat the filo baskets in a moderate oven just before serving and fill with vegetables. Just before serving the main course fry the noodles and braise the lettuce. Decorate the dessert at the last minute.

FONDANT POTATOES WITH SESAME SEEDS

This is a really delicious way of cooking very small new potatoes. There is no water – just butter.

750g/1½lb walnut-sized new potatoes
65g/2½oz unsalted butter
1 tablespoon sesame seeds
Coarse sea salt

Scrape the potatoes, rinse in cold water and dry them in a cloth.

Melt two-thirds of the butter in a wide, heavy-based pan with a tight-fitting lid. Add the potatoes and shake the pan to coat them with butter. Cover the pan and cook over low to moderate heat for 20–30 minutes, shaking the pan now and again to prevent the potatoes sticking to the bottom. When the potatoes are cooked, remove the lid and increase the heat to drive off any surplus moisture and give the potatoes a delicious crisp finish.

Add the remaining butter and, when it has melted, add the sesame seeds. Shake the pan until the sesame seeds are well distributed through the potatoes.

To serve *Tip the potatoes on to a hot serving dish and sprinkle with sea salt. Serve straight away with the poussins.*
SEE PAGE 36.

POUSSINS IN NOODLE NESTS

If you prefer, cook one larger chicken rather than individual poussins. Serve the chicken in the centre of a nest of noodles.

6 poussins
50g/2oz butter
½ clove garlic, lightly crushed
300g/10oz seedless white grapes
150g/5oz fine rice noodles
Sunflower oil, for frying
75ml/3fl oz medium-dry white wine
6 tablespoons double cream
Salt and black pepper

Place the poussins in a roasting tin and spread half the butter over the breasts, then season lightly with salt and pepper. Roast in a preheated oven, 190°C, 375°F, Gas Mark 5, for 45–50 minutes or until the juices run clear when birds are pierced with a skewer. Baste with the cooking juices now and again. When they are cooked, transfer the poussins to a hot serving dish and reserve the cooking juices.

Meanwhile, melt the remaining butter in a pan, add the garlic and cook until soft then discard. Gently sauté the grapes in the butter for 2–3 minutes and set aside. Deep-fry the noodles, in batches, in hot oil until crisp. Drain on kitchen paper.

To make the sauce, simmer the reserved cooking juices with the wine over high heat, stirring all the time, until reduced by half. Stir in the cream and add the grapes. Simmer for 2 minutes.

To serve *Arrange the poussins in the middle of a nest of the noodles and spoon the sauce over them.*
SEE PAGE 36

APRICOT AND ORANGE-FLOWER WATER FLUMMERY

A layer of fresh apricot purée covers a delicately scented cream to make a wonderfully light springtime pudding.

375g/12oz fresh apricots (or ready-to-eat dried apricots)
75–125g/3–4oz granulated sugar
300ml/½ pint hot water
1 tablespoon apricot brandy (optional)
3 teaspoons powdered gelatine
4 tablespoons cold water
450ml/¾ pint double cream
40g/1½oz caster sugar
1–2 teaspoons orange-flower water
6–12 small spring flowers such as primroses or violets or 1 tablespoon flaked almonds, toasted, for decoration

Halve and stone the apricots. Dissolve the granulated sugar in the hot water. Bring to the boil and simmer for 2 minutes. Add the apricots, fresh or dried, and cook gently for 8–12 minutes or until tender. Use a slotted spoon to transfer the fruit to a food processor or nylon sieve.

Boil the syrup steadily for 3 minutes to reduce by half, add to the fruit and process or sieve to make a thick purée. Stir in the apricot brandy (optional) and set the purée aside until cold.

Soften the gelatine in the 4 tablespoons of cold water in a saucepan then heat gently until dissolved. Add the cream and caster sugar and stir over low heat until dissolved. Remove from the heat and add the orange-flower water to taste.

Divide the cream mixture among 6 stemmed glasses and chill until set. Cover each with a layer of apricot purée and set aside in a cool place until ready to serve.

To serve *Decorate each glass with spring flowers or sprinkle some flaked almonds on top.*

Oz Clarke's
WINE NOTES

I love spring for all its promise of good things to come; long hazy days and a languid out-of-doors existence beckoning. And I love it for the freshness in the air, the star-burst of green in the trees and hedgerows, the carpets of wild flowers and the return of the birds. Geraldene's menu brilliantly captures this mood and the wines should reflect springtime in the same way.

Although spring is when we see the first crop of the most recent vintage's light reds, for this springtime lunch I'm going to stick to whites, because they better complement the food.

And my whites will have the dizzy fragrance of flowers – springtime flowers, mountain flowers, about them, but also something of the succulent richness of summer to come. So I've gone to Alsace, right on the German border; and to the beautiful cliff-hung Mosel valley in Germany, to villages like Wiltingen Klüsserath, Kasel or Serrig.

Mosel wines are as light and fresh as any wines in the world, and at the Kabinett level of ripeness, they have naturally low alcohol to go with their flowery fragrance and their green apple and lime acidity.

Alsace wines are fuller, in particular from the Tokay/Pinot Gris grape, gaining a honeyed fatness to go with their perfume of angelica and peach, lilies and freesias. If you want a lighter, simpler Alsace wine try a Pinot Blanc. For something more headily exotic, go for a Gewürztraminer – the co-ops are good and often terrific value.

APRICOT AND ORANGE-FLOWER WATER FLUMMERY

Mediterranean Seafood Lunch for 6

Each of us probably has our own image of Mediterranean food. It might be an Italian market stall piled high with yellow and red sweet peppers beside shiny purple aubergines and spiky dull-green globe artichokes. Or perhaps you think of a café table on a quayside in Greece or Spain, or a lunchtime picnic on a hillside in the South of France. All the pictures that one carries away from this unforgettable region are vivid and warm and colourful. The climate fashions the food and we relish its intense flavours of fruit and vegetables, herbs, lemons, garlic and olive oil.

Now that so much Mediterranean produce reaches us only a few hours after it is picked and packed we are able to recreate some of the splendid dishes of the region in our own kitchens. For the most authentic results it is always worth buying the best quality ingredients such as extra virgin olive oil or a piece of real Parmesan cheese.

Almost all of this menu can be prepared ahead. Only the ravioli is cooked at the last moment, and that does not take long. Just long enough, perhaps, for you to enjoy an aperitif – a cool glass of wine or some cloudy pastis – with your guests while you anticipate the meal to come.

Menu

*

PRAWNS WITH AÏOLI

FOUGASSE WITH PROVENÇAL HERBS

RAVIOLI STUFFED WITH MONKFISH AND MUSSELS IN A BASIL CREAM

*

FRESH LIME TART

*

Provence Rosé
or Côtes du Rhône Blanc

Muscat de Beaumes-de-Venise

SWEET PEPPER SALAD, RAVIOLI STUFFED WITH MONKFISH AND MUSSELS IN A BASIL CREAM

PRAWNS WITH AÏOLI

Traditionally the garlic mayonnaise known as *aïoli* is made with just the yolk of egg. However mayonnaise made with whole eggs is lighter in texture and is quick to make in a blender or food processor. All the ingredients must be at room temperature. Make the aïoli with just one clove of garlic to start with, and add a further crushed clove to the finished *aïoli* if you prefer a stronger flavour.

1 large (size 1) egg
1–2 cloves garlic
150ml/¼ pint extra virgin olive oil or a blend of olive and sunflower oils
Lemon juice to taste
1kg/2lb Mediterranean or King prawns, cooked but unpeeled
Bunch of flat-leaved parsley

Break the egg into a blender or food processor. Peel the garlic and cut the clove in half. If you can see the green-tipped growing shoot, remove it and discard because it can make the sauce bitter. Chop the garlic and whizz briefly with the egg. Gradually add the oil through the blender lid mixing all the time. Add lemon juice to taste.

To serve *Place a bowl of aïoli in the centre of a serving dish and surround with the unpeeled prawns and the parsley. Serve with the warm fougasse or French bread.*

FOUGASSE WITH PROVENÇAL HERBS

This loaf from the Midi is shaped like a pudgy-fingered hand. It is an easy bread to make at home and has a fine rich flavour. If you use easy-blend yeast, add it to the flour following the packet instructions. Do not soak in water. One loaf will be ample for six with the prawns, but another will allow for second helpings.

250g/8oz unbleached bread flour
½ teaspoon dried herbes de Provence, or dried mixed herbs
¼ teaspoon salt
15g/½oz fresh yeast or 1 teaspoon dried yeast
½ teaspoon sugar
175–200ml/6–7fl oz warm water
1 tablespoon olive oil
A little coarse sea salt
12 green olives, stoned

Sieve the flour into a bowl and stir in the herbs and salt. Set aside in a warm place. Blend the yeast with the sugar and stir in half the warm water. Set aside in a warm place for about 10 minutes until frothy.

Make a well in the centre of the flour and mix in half the oil, the yeast mixture and almost all of the remaining water. Work everything together to make a smooth dough adding more water if necessary. Knead on a floured surface for 4–5 minutes, then replace in the bowl and leave, covered with a plastic bag, in a warm place for about 1 hour until the dough has doubled in volume.

Transfer the dough to a floured surface and knead for 1–2 minutes. Roll out the dough to make an oval shape about 2·5cm/1in thick. Place the shape on a floured baking sheet and use a sharp knife to cut into the edge so that the loaf resembles a fat wide hand. Brush with the remaining oil and sprinkle with salt. Arrange olives on top, pressing them into the dough. Set aside in a warm place for about 30 minutes to rise. Bake in the centre of a preheated oven, 200°C, 400°F, Gas Mark 6, for 20–25 minutes until golden brown.

PRAWNS WITH AÏOLI, FOUGASSE WITH PROVENÇAL HERBS

EXTRAS

Both the prawns and the pasta are good with fresh lemon juice squeezed over them. Place a basket of lemons on the table so that guests can help themselves.

To accompany the ravioli serve an eye-catching salad of red, yellow and orange sweet peppers. You'll need about 1kg/2lb peppers. Place them under the grill until the skins are blackened, then put them inside a plastic bag and leave until cool for the skins to loosen. Peel off the skin, slice, discarding the seeds, dress with a lemony, herby vinaigrette and scatter with toasted pine kernels.

A cool finale to this Mediterranean meal could be a very simple extra dessert – chilled melon balls steeped in a thin sugar syrup made with a sweet white wine, such as Monbazillac, and flavoured with rosemary. Two medium-sized melons should be enough. Serve it in pretty glass dishes or in the hollowed-out melon shells, and decorate with rosemary flowers or mint leaves.

After the meal serve coffee made in a cafetière or by the filter method. A nice Mediterranean touch is to add 1–2 crushed cardamom seeds to the ground coffee before you pour on the water.

RAVIOLI STUFFED WITH MONKFISH AND MUSSELS IN A BASIL CREAM

PLANNING AHEAD

The day before: Bake the fougasse bread (reheat in the oven before serving).

The day of the party: Prepare the ravioli, lay it out on a large plate in a single layer, cover with a damp cloth, and refrigerate until needed. Make the sweet pepper salad, if liked.

Make the fresh lime tart no more than 2–3 hours in advance. Make the *aïoli*, cover and keep in refrigerator. Cook the ravioli no more than 30 minutes before the meal. Remember that the sauce needs to stand for 20–30 minutes for the flavours to infuse and allow time for this. Reheat the fougasse.

PRESENTATION

For this lunch I like to summon up the atmosphere of a sunny Mediterranean day. So an azure blue cloth with a jug of yellow sunflowers would make a beautiful background for the meal.

Because the prawns with *aïoli* are slightly messy to eat, provide fingerbowls with a slice of lemon or some small flowers floating in the water, and napkins to dry your fingers afterwards.

Even the Italians recognize that ravioli originated in the region of France around Nice. However this delicious form of stuffed egg pasta is highly popular in both countries. Ravioli with a fish stuffing and a herb cream sauce is particularly delicious. It is important to remember to chill all the ingredients for the stuffing before you start. The sauce is just as delicious made with freshly chopped tarragon instead of basil.

Pasta:

375g/12oz plain flour
1 teaspoon salt
3 eggs, beaten
1 tablespoon milk

Filling:

175g/6oz monkfish tail, boned and skinned
175g/6oz cod or haddock, boned and skinned
125g/4oz cooked shelled mussels or fresh salmon, boned and skinned
1 egg white
200ml/7fl oz double cream
½ teaspoon salt
A little grated nutmeg
1 teaspoon chopped chervil or parsley

Sauce:

300ml/½ pint double cream
2 tablespoons dry white wine (optional)
2 teaspoons basil leaves, chopped
2 teaspoons chives, chopped
1 egg yolk
75g/3oz freshly grated Parmesan cheese

To make the pasta, sieve the flour and salt into a large bowl or food processor. Beat the eggs with the milk and add to the flour. Mix until the dough forms a ball then cut the dough into 2 or 3 pieces. On a floured surface roll out one piece as thinly as possible – you are supposed to be able to read newspaper headlines through it. If you are using a pasta machine roll out on the thinnest setting. Cover the dough with a damp tea towel while you make the filling.

Cut the monkfish and cod into pieces and place in a food processor with the mussels or salmon, egg white, and a little of the cream. Whizz until finely chopped. Alternatively chop fish finely with a knife and beat in other ingredients. Add the remaining cream, the salt and nutmeg and whizz to a purée, but take care not to over-process. Stir in the chervil or parsley.

Use a toothed pasta wheel to cut strips of pasta 10cm/4in wide and place teaspoons of the filling 5cm/2in apart along the first half of the strip. Brush cold water along the long sides of the strip and between the fillings. Fold over the other half and press the layers together. Cut into square ravioli with the pasta wheel. Place on a floured plate or board and store in the refrigerator until ready to cook. Repeat with the remaining dough. The mixture makes around 60 ravioli, depending on how thin you roll out the pasta.

Prepare the sauce by heating the cream and wine with the basil and chives over moderate heat then allow to stand for 20–30 minutes to infuse the flavour. Whisk in egg yolk and heat gently, stirring, until slightly thickened but do not allow to boil.

Cook the ravioli in boiling salted water for 4–5 minutes. Do this in batches, depending on the size of your pan. The idea is not to let the water go off the boil by adding too many ravioli at one time. Drain well and transfer to one hot serving dish, or divide among individual gratin dishes. Sprinkle with Parmesan cheese and place under a hot grill until the cheese browns.

To serve *Spoon the warm basil cream over the pasta.*
SEE PAGE 40

FRESH LIME TART

Limes give a lovely golden green colour and a subtle tangy flavour to this delicious fruit curd tart.

Pastry:
150g/5oz plain flour
65g/2½oz caster sugar
75g/3oz butter, softened
2 egg yolks
1 drop of vanilla essence

Lime curd filling:
3 limes
100g/3½oz caster sugar
3 eggs
50g/2oz butter, melted

To make the pastry, sieve the flour and sugar on to a cold work-surface or into a chilled wide bowl. Make a well in the centre and add the butter and egg yolks mixed with the vanilla flavouring.

Use the fingertips to mix the butter with the egg yolks, gradually drawing in some of the flour all the time as you mix the dough. When the mixture starts to resemble bread-crumbs, press it together to form a ball. Rest the pastry in a cold place under the upturned bowl while you prepare the filling.

Wash and dry the limes. Cut a thin strip of rind from 1 lime and cut into long narrow shreds. Simmer in a little cold water for 5–7 minutes or until tender. Drain well, toss in a little of the caster sugar and set aside on a piece of kitchen paper in a warm place until dry.

Grate the remaining rind from the limes and mix with the strained juice of the fruit. Beat in the eggs, the remaining sugar and melted butter.

Roll out the pastry to fit a greased 23cm/9in flan tin and lightly prick the base all over. Bake on a hot baking sheet in a preheated oven, 200°C, 400°F, Gas Mark 6, for 8–10 minutes until the pastry is set and is starting to change colour. Remove the pastry case from the oven and lower the temperature to 180°C, 350°F, Gas Mark 4.

Pour the filling into the pastry case and bake for 20–25 minutes until set. Cool the tart in the tin, then transfer to a flat serving plate or board and arrange the shreds of lime on top of the tart.

Oz Clarke's *WINE NOTES*

If we were lazing on a sun-soaked beach at St-Tropez, or perched high on the cliffs above the bay of Naples, the quality of the wine we drank would definitely *not* be top of our list of priorities. Just so long as it was ice-cold, we'd be happy. Back home, though, without the benefit of the view, the wine does assume a more important role.

Simplicity is the secret. Fresh, bright, simple flavours to complement the heavenly yet simple flavours of the *aïoli* and fougasse, to provide pleasing refreshment with the ravioli. So we'll have Provence rosé, as young as possible, or a similarly young white Côtes du Rhône.

With that tangy lime tart, let's have the best of France's sweet golden Muscats – Muscat de Beaumes-de-Venise.

FRESH LIME TART, MELON WITH ROSEMARY SYRUP

MIDSUMMER LUNCH
for 4

When the composer Frederic Chopin first travelled to London, he wrote home that he found everything ruinously expensive, and complained that he didn't know enough about food to be able to eat cheaply. A century or so later, it's still true that knowing about food and how to prepare it is the most economical way of eating wisely and well.

High summer is the season when, for most of us, eating well is easiest and least expensive. Many fruits, vegetables and fish are in plentiful supply and therefore excellent value, but good, cheap eating requires one extra, vital ingredient – imagination.

So for this fairweather party I have juggled with some culinary conventions: fruit is served, not as dessert but as a first course, in a chilled soup. Serve it in frosted glasses or even in cups and saucers – and if you are lunching out of doors fill the saucers with ice to keep the soup delightfully cool.

Summer food can be simple: a salad of ripe tomatoes, freshly baked bread and some delicious cheese makes a fine meal. And the best summer cooking takes full advantage of the rich variety of fresh herbs, most of which never fail to lend distinction to a dish. So for the main course I recommend pink-fleshed rainbow trout for serving not hot, but cold, in a glaze of fragrant China tea flavoured with mint, and steamed small parcels of rice wrapped in lettuce leaves, with a red pepper sauce. For dessert there is a rich pudding of hazelnut cream sandwiched between layers of chocolate.

MENU

*

SUMMER FRUIT SOUP WITH TARRAGON

RAINBOW TROUT GLAZED WITH LAPSANG SOUCHONG AND MINT

GREEN RICE PARCELS WITH RED PEPPER SAUCE

*

HAZELNUT CHOCOLATE CREAMS

*

Mosel Riesling Spätlese
Asti Spumante

SUMMER FRUIT SOUP WITH TARRAGON

SUMMER FRUIT SOUP WITH TARRAGON

Make this lovely fruit soup no more than two hours ahead. An alternative garnish can be made with some of the melon and peaches or nectarines, finely diced.

½ ripe melon
3 or 4 peaches or nectarines
1 cucumber
Juice of 1 orange
25–50g/1–2oz caster sugar
A few drops of Tabasco sauce
Dash of dry sherry or white wine (optional)
1 teaspoon finely chopped tarragon
Salt
Tarragon sprigs, to garnish

Discard the melon seeds and scoop out the flesh. Wash and stone the peaches or nectarines. Peel one half of the cucumber but leave the peel on the other half. Cut both halves into chunks. Place the fruit, cucumber and orange juice in a food processor or blender and whizz to a purée.

Add the sugar, salt and Tabasco to taste. Stir in the sherry or wine, if desired, and the chopped tarragon. Pour the soup into a jug and chill.

To serve *Pour into chilled glasses or bowls and garnish with tarragon sprigs. Serve with breadsticks.*

RAINBOW TROUT GLAZED WITH LAPSANG SOUCHONG AND MINT

This very good cold fish dish can be made a day ahead. Keep it in the refrigerator until ready to serve.

1 Lapsang Souchong teabag
2 or 3 sprigs mint
150ml/¼ pint boiling water
4 rainbow trout fillets, about 150g/5oz each
1 lime
1 tablespoon finely chopped chives
4–8 bay leaves, fresh if possible
1 teaspoon powdered gelatine
Salt

Place the teabag and the mint in a heatproof jug and pour on the boiling water. Stir and leave to infuse for 10 minutes then strain into a bowl and cool by standing the bowl in cold water.

Place the fish in a shallow ovenproof dish and season lightly with salt. Cut some long strips of rind from the lime and add the strained juice and the chives to the tea. Pour over the fish and arrange bay leaves and strips of lime rind on each fillet.

Cover the dish with foil and bake in a preheated oven, 180°C, 350°F, Gas Mark 4, for 15–20 minutes until the fish is opaque.

Pour off the hot cooking liquid into a jug. Soften gelatine in 1 tablespoon of cold water, then stir into the hot liquid and pour over the trout. Chill the dish in the refrigerator until the liquid has set into a light jelly.

RAINBOW TROUT GLAZED WITH LAPSANG SOUCHONG AND MINT, GREEN RICE PARCELS WITH RED PEPPER SAUCE

EXTRAS

All you'll need to complete this simple budget menu is some breadsticks to accompany the fruit soup, and fresh crusty bread, or possibly dark rye bread or Pumpernickel, with the trout course. Before serving, pop the crusty bread in the oven for a few minutes until hot. Serve, cut into pieces, in a cloth-lined basket. Place sea salt and a pepper mill on the table and have ready plenty of mineral water. After the meal serve small cups of black coffee or, if the weather is hot, serve iced coffee in stemmed glasses with a tablespoon of vanilla ice cream and crushed ice.

GREEN RICE PARCELS WITH RED PEPPER SAUCE

If more convenient, the green rice can be made ahead and cooled. Then make the lettuce parcels and steam them until the rice is heated through just before serving. Red pepers have the sweetest flavour but the sauce can be made in just the same way with a green or yellow pepper, if you prefer. This dish can be served hot or cold.

175 g/6oz long grain rice
250ml/8fl oz water
1 clove garlic, chopped finely
50g/2oz butter
125g/4oz cooked spinach, puréed
Grated nutmeg
1 tablespoon finely chopped parsley
1 tablespoon finely chopped basil or coriander
1 egg, beaten
25g/1oz walnut pieces, chopped roughly and toasted lightly
1 round lettuce
Salt and pepper

Sauce:
1 sweet red pepper, cored, deseeded and diced
1 bay leaf
4 tablespoons water
2 tablespoons double cream

Put the rice in a nylon sieve and wash under cold running water for 4–5 minutes until the water from the sieve runs clear. Turn the rice into a pan with the water, garlic, half the butter and some salt and pepper. Bring to the boil, stir and cover with a tight-fitting lid. Turn the heat to its lowest setting and cook the rice for 15–20 minutes. Remove from the heat and spoon the rice into a mixing bowl.

Melt the rest of the butter in a pan, add the spinach and cook, stirring, over medium heat until all surplus water has evaporated. Season with nutmeg, salt and pepper. Stir in the parsley and basil or coriander and add to the rice with the egg and the walnuts. Mix well and check the seasoning.

Cut across the stalk of the lettuce and separate the leaves. Wash the leaves and shake dry. Place a spoonful of green rice on a lettuce leaf, fold in the sides and roll up like a parcel. Repeat until all the rice is used up. Pack the parcels into a steamer basket or colander and steam over boiling water for 3 minutes. Remove from the heat and keep hot until ready to serve, or cool to room temperature.

To make the sauce, put the red pepper in a pan with the bay leaf and the water and cook over medium heat for 6–8 minutes or until soft. Remove and reserve the bay leaf and purée the contents of the pan in a food processor or blender. Return the purée to the pan, add the bay leaf and the cream and simmer for 3–4 minutes. Discard the bay leaf and serve the hot sauce spooned over the green rice parcels, or cool the sauce and serve it cold with the parcels at room temperature.

SEE PAGE 45.

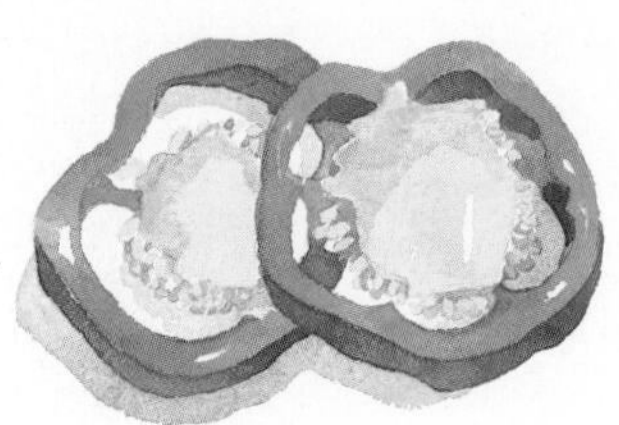

PLANNING AHEAD

In advance: Make the hazelnut and chocolate creams one or two weeks in advance and freeze them in a lidded container.

The day before: Prepare the trout fillets and refrigerate. If you have not made them in advance make the hazelnut and chocolate creams and refrigerate. Make up lots of ice cubes if you plan to arrange ice cubes around the soup bowls to keep the soup chilled.

The day of the party: Thaw the hazelnut and chocolate creams in the refrigerator if frozen. Prepare the green rice parcels to the point where they are ready to steam. If serving cold, steam them. Make the fruit soup and chill. Make the pepper sauce for the rice parcels. If serving cold, allow the sauce to cool. Otherwise keep the sauce hot and steam the rice parcels just before serving.

PRESENTATION

Fortunately it is fairly easy to make a midsummer meal look attractive. Lay the table with a summery cloth and have plenty of flowers around in colours to echo the cloth and napkins. Sometimes, instead of one vase of flowers in the centre of the table, I put a small posy – with the flowers arranged in an egg cup or a sherry glass – at each place setting, and guests are usually delighted to take the posy home afterwards.

To give added interest to this meal I like to serve the soup in chilled stemmed glasses or cups and saucers. Nicely garnished dishes look appetizing. The trout dish looks attractive when garnished with fresh bay leaves or other herbs.

HAZELNUT CHOCOLATE CREAMS

These rich chocolate creams can be made a day ahead and kept in the refrigerator or a very cold place until ready to serve. Or make them one or two weeks in advance and freeze them in a lidded container. Thaw in the refrigerator for two hours before serving.

125g/4oz dark dessert chocolate
40g/1½oz white dessert chocolate
4–5 tablespoons single cream or top of milk
200g/7oz full-fat soft cheese
40g/1½oz toasted hazelnuts
1–2 teaspoons rum or brandy (optional)

Break both kinds of chocolate into pieces and melt them in separate small bowls over hot water. Add 3–4 tablespoons of the cream to the dark chocolate to give a spreading consistency.

Draw eight 7cm/3in circles on a sheet of baking parchment. Spread a thin layer of dark chocolate over each circle. There will be a little chocolate left over: add the remaining cream to this and leave in a warm place. Take the melted white chocolate and trail thin lines across the dark chocolate discs to make an attractive pattern. Again there will be some leftover. If necessary use four of the discs to practise on because only the four best-looking discs will be on show. Place in the freezer or refrigerator to set.

Blend the cheese with the remaining melted chocolate, dark and white. Chop the hazelnuts finely and stir into the mixture with the rum or brandy if desired.

Carefully peel the paper from the chocolate discs and place four upside down on the paper or on a flat serving dish. Spread generously with the hazelnut cream and place the remaining discs on top. Store in a cold place until ready to serve.

Oz Clarke's
WINE NOTES

Everything about Geraldene's summer lunch positively sings out with optimism for the lovely lazy days of summer, when the sun rises in the east long before we're awake, and seems to hang endlessly in the sky from mid-morning to late-afternoon. The fruit soup and the rainbow trout are so fresh and so summery that they almost insist on being eaten out of doors, and I'm going to imagine a table set out under the oldest tree in the garden, the sunlight dappling the tablecloth as the branches sway imperceptibly in the breeze.

I think we'll eat languidly too. Since all the food can be prepared well in advance, there'll be no rushing in and out of the kitchen, and no pressure to eat dishes while they're hot. So my wines will be ones which are a delight to drink on their own as we lounge and chatter, as well as while we're eating.

There are no wines in the world which more brilliantly reflect the emotions, the scents, the flavours of early summer than the wines of the Mosel valley in Germany. They have an exhilarating green snap to their fruit, a lovely streak of lime and lemon acidity, and a dewy perfume redolent of flowers. Add to this a flicker of soft honeyed gentleness and even the merest hint of a sparkle and you have the perfect outdoor wine. If you go for a late-picked Riesling (Spätlese) from a village such as Ürzig, Wehlen, Graach or Bernkastel in the central part of the valley, you'll find a mildly sweet flavour too which will happily accompany the fruit soup as well as going superbly with the trout.

To stay in outdoors mood, have some grapy-sweet, sparkling Asti Spumante to finish off the meal.

HAZELNUT CHOCOLATE CREAMS

Indian Vegetarian Lunch for 10

To my mind, the best vegetarian food should be just as appetizing to carnivores as to confirmed vegetarians. Furthermore, good vegetarian food is wonderfully delicious and very healthy. Like many others, I find that Indian vegetarian cooking with its subtle spices and contrasts of textures and temperatures induces a feeling of pleasurable well-being and utter contentment towards the end of the meal. And I can imagine no nicer weekend lunch for up to 10 people than a table spread with this feast of oriental dishes.

Starting with rice or Naan bread everyone can compose their own menu by choosing the accompaniments from the dishes arranged before them. I include plenty of rice and bread because I find that guests continue to nibble them for some time – even at the end of the meal.

This lunch is the kind of meal for those who enjoy cooking. It takes 2–3 hours to prepare. However, this is a leisurely kind of cooking where precision is not a prerequisite. At the weekend, I like to work with family or friends in the kitchen – they chop herbs, crush spices or toast coconut to help out – or, if I'm cooking alone, it's a chance to listen to new tapes or the radio.

Menu

*

ROAST AUBERGINES WITH CUMIN AND FRESH GINGER

STUFFED NAAN BREAD

SPINACH WITH CURD CHEESE, CORIANDER AND CASHEW NUTS

DRY SPICED POTATO AND CAULIFLOWER

GREEN COCONUT CHUTNEY

RICE WITH RAISINS AND PINEAPPLE

OKRA WITH TOMATOES AND MINT

RED LENTILS WITH ONION RINGS

*

KULFI WITH MANGO SAUCE

*

Lassi *or* Apple Juice
Spiced Tea
Alsace Gewürztraminer

ROAST AUBERGINES WITH CUMIN AND FRESH GINGER
Baingan Bharta

The aubergines can be roasted in the oven or cooked on the hob in a heavy pan. Cooking the vegetable with no liquid gives a delicious intense flavour.

3 large aubergines
6 tablespoons sunflower oil
2 cloves garlic, chopped
1 teaspoon cumin seed
4cm/1½in piece of fresh root ginger, peeled and grated
2 tablespoons lemon juice, or to taste
Salt

Cut the aubergines into long strips and then pieces about 2·5cm/1in long. Heat the oil in a roasting tin and stir in the garlic and cumin seed. Cook for about 3 minutes over moderate heat then add the aubergines and stir until the vegetable has absorbed the oil. Roast in a preheated oven, 180°C, 350°F, Gas Mark 4, for about 30 minutes until the aubergine is cooked. Stir now and again during the cooking.

Season lightly with salt and stir in the ginger and lemon juice to taste. Cook in the oven for 5 minutes then transfer to a serving dish and keep hot until ready to serve.

STUFFED NAAN BREAD

This flat Indian bread is surprisingly easy to make. The unbleached flour gives a finer flavour and a nice warm colour to the dough.

1 packet dried yeast
300ml/½ pint warm water
750g/1½lb unbleached plain flour
1½ teaspoons salt
1 teaspoon black onion seed (optional)
150ml/¼ pint natural yogurt
2 tablespoons sunflower oil

Filling:
125g/4oz unblanched, shelled almonds
75g/3oz sultanas
75ml/3fl oz double cream

Sprinkle the yeast into half the water in a small bowl and set aside in a warm place for about 10 minutes until frothy.

Sieve the flour and salt into a warm bowl and stir in onion seed. Add the yeast mixture, the yogurt mixed with the remaining warm water and the oil and mix well to make a soft dough. Turn out on to a floured board and knead for 5–10 minutes until smooth and elastic. Shape into a ball, place in the mixing bowl, cover and leave in a warm place for about 1 hour until doubled in size.

Meanwhile, chop the almonds in a food processor until a little coarser than bought ground almonds, then mix with the sultanas and cream.

Turn the dough on to a floured surface, shape into a ball and divide into 8 pieces. Work on 2 pieces at a time and keep the remainder covered. Flatten or roll each piece into a 20–23cm/8–9in circle then spread ¼ of the filling over one circle and brush the rim with water. Cover with the other circle pressing the edges together firmly. Repeat with the remaining dough and filling.

Heat a baking tray in a preheated oven, 250°C, 475°F, Gas Mark 9, and place the Naan on the hot tray. Bake for 5–10 minutes until puffed up. Remove from the oven and place under a hot grill for up to 1 minute until the top is golden. Serve hot.

STUFFED NAAN BREAD, LASSI, ROAST AUBERGINES WITH CUMIN AND FRESH GINGER, SPINACH WITH CURD CHEESE, CORIANDER AND CASHEW NUTS, DRY SPICED POTATO AND CAULIFLOWER

GREEN COCONUT CHUTNEY, ONION PICKLE, RAITA

EXTRAS

Indian meals lend themselves to lots of delicious accompaniments such as chutneys and pickles and a wonderful array of breads. Some of these can be home-made, but many can be bought in. Two traditional and easy-to-make accompaniments are onion pickle – sliced onion mixed with tomato purée and lemon rind and juice – and raita, a mixture of natural yogurt, chopped mint, a little honey and some ground fenugreek.

The stuffed Naan provides the main bread component of this meal but puppodums are always popular and since they can be tricky to make you may as well buy them, either plain or spiced. The simplest way to cook these is in a microwave – they need no fat and take only moments to puff up and become crisp.

After meals many Indian restaurants serve *mukwa*, a digestif consisting of roasted spices, usually fennel seeds, often mixed with something sweet. Sugared almonds are sometimes used as a substitute.

PLANNING AHEAD

Indian vegetable dishes are usually at their best when freshly prepared and when both the flavour and nutritive value of the food are at their peak. However, some of the dishes in the meal can be cooked earlier.

In advance: Make the kulfi ice cream and keep in the freezer. The rice can even be cooked ahead and frozen, if you wish, but don't add the toasted coconut until just before serving.

The day before: Bake the Naan bread. Make the red lentil dish (leaving the onion rings until just before serving) and refrigerate.

The day of the party: Make the coconut chutney and the mango sauce for the kulfi and refrigerate. Prepare the rest of the vegetable dishes, leaving the spinach with curd cheese until last. Make the onion pickle and raita. Reheat the lentils and add the fried onion ring garnish. Reheat the Naan bread just before serving.

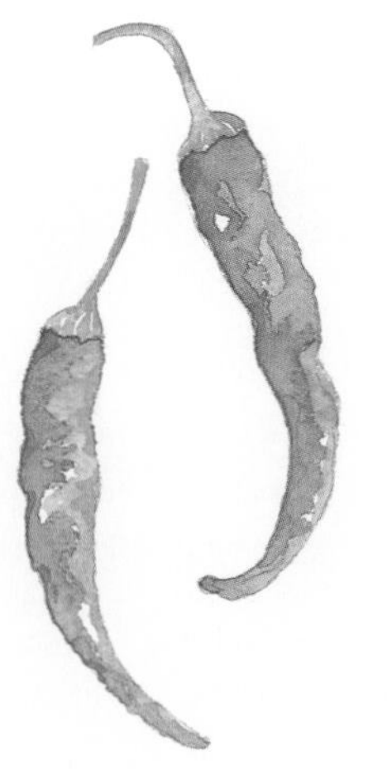

SPINACH WITH CURD CHEESE, CORIANDER AND CASHEW NUTS
Palak Paneer

If you prefer, the cashew nuts in this recipe can be replaced with peanuts which are cheaper but have a rather stronger flavour.

1kg/2lb fresh spinach
50g/2oz butter
2–3 tablespoons coriander leaves
¼ teaspoon ground fenugreek
125g/4oz curd cheese
125g/4oz unsalted cashew nuts
Salt

Wash and destalk the spinach. Melt half the butter in a pan and add the spinach. Cook gently until it has reduced to a bright green pulp and all surplus liquid has evaporated. Stir in the coriander leaves, fenugreek and cheese. Season with salt. Spoon into a hot serving dish. Melt the remaining butter and gently fry the cashew nuts until just turning colour. Spoon over the spinach.
SEE PAGE 48.

DRY SPICED POTATO AND CAULIFLOWER
Aloo Gobi

The fresh ginger and cumin in this colourful and very popular dish give a real fillip to ordinary potatoes and cauliflower.

750g/1½lb waxy potatoes, peeled
1 medium cauliflower
1 teaspoon salt
2 teaspoons ground turmeric
5cm/2in piece root ginger, peeled
1 small onion, peeled
1 small onion, peeled
4 tablespoons sunflower oil
½ teaspoon cumin seed
1 clove garlic, chopped
1 tablespoon chopped coriander leaves

Cut the potatoes into walnut-sized cubes. Cut florets from the cauliflower and discard the stem. Place the vegetables in a pan with the salt and turmeric and hot water to cover. Bring to the boil and cook for 6–8 minutes until almost cooked. Drain, reserving a little water; keep hot.

Finely chop the ginger and onion with a sharp knife or in a food processor. Add 3 tablespoons of the potato cooking water and purée.

Heat the oil in a pan, stir in the cumin seed and garlic and cook for 1 minute. Add the ginger paste and cook, stirring, for 5 minutes until the onion is cooked. Add the vegetables and reheat, gently turning them over in the mixture.

Turn into a hot serving dish and sprinkle with coriander.

GREEN COCONUT CHUTNEY

100g/3½oz fresh coconut
1–2 green chillies, chopped
2 tablespoons chopped mint leaves
1 clove garlic, chopped
1–2 teaspoons clear honey
75–125ml/3–4fl oz single cream
Salt

Have all ingredients at room temperature. Chop the coconut finely. Add the chilli, mint, garlic, honey and cream and whizz to a paste in a food processor or blender. Season to taste with a little salt. Spoon into a small dish for serving.
SEE PAGE 49.

RICE WITH RAISINS AND PINEAPPLE
Rajsehree Pulao

Basmati rice has a slim grain and a superb nutty flavour. If you have any of this savoury rice dish over it can be chilled or frozen and reheated in a steamer.

625g/1¼lb basmati rice
125g/4oz fresh coconut or half a coconut, grated or 50g/2oz unsweetened desiccated coconut
1·2 litres/2 pints hot water
50g/2oz butter
2 cloves garlic, chopped
2 teaspoons ground coriander
½ cinnamon stick
2 bay leaves
2–3 teaspoons salt
75ml/3fl oz double cream
125g/4oz seedless raisins
475g/15oz can crushed pineapple

Wash the rice in several changes of cold water and drain well. Reserve 2 tablespoons of the grated coconut and mix the rest with the hot water.

Melt half the butter in a flameproof casserole. Stir in the garlic and the ground coriander for 2 minutes over moderate heat. Add the rice, coconut and water, cinnamon, bay leaves and salt. Bring to the boil, stir and cover with a tightly fitting lid. Reduce the heat or place in a low oven and cook for 20 minutes.

Remove the rice from the heat, discard the cinnamon stick and the bay leaves and stir in the cream, raisins, pineapple and remaining butter, then reheat. Toast remaining coconut under a hot grill, turning often.

To serve *Spoon the rice into two hot serving dishes and sprinkle the toasted coconut on top.*

RICE WITH RAISINS AND PINEAPPLE, OKRA WITH TOMATOES AND MINT, PUPPODUMS, RED LENTILS WITH ONION RINGS

PRESENTATION

Indian food benefits from some scene setting. I like the effect of a grey tablecloth with black plates which makes the variety of Indian dishes glow like jewels in the candlelight of a dull winter day. Or serve the meal in individual small bowls like the traditional *thali*. If you enjoy them, light joss sticks, even play a tape of Indian music, and drape shawls over the chairs with lots of cushions around for lounging on while drinking spiced tea. It's well worth trying to create an air of Eastern opulence not only as a welcome respite from the hassle of everyday life but to make the lunch truly memorable.

Oz Clarke's *WINE NOTES*

Although there are some good non-alcoholic drinks suggested with this meal – and that's perfectly appropriate for Indian vegetarian food – I think that it might be nice to have something a little stronger than tea on the go especially if we're all going to be mucking in round the kitchen table.

No red wines will stand much chance against the delights of cumin and ginger, coriander and turmeric. Yet the fact that the dishes' highly spiced flavours are mild and aromatic rather than mouth-searingly hot means we can happily drink white wine or cold beer.

Fruity, even spicy, white wines will go best, nicely chilled, and a light dry Gewürztraminer would be excellent.

NON-ALCOHOLIC DRINKS

Spiced tea could be served. Simmer a cinnamon stick, 10 cardamom pods and 1 teaspoon of cloves in 2·5 litres/4 pints water for 10 minutes. Add 2–3 tablespoons tea and leave to infuse for 2–4 minutes. Strain into thin cups or glasses and provide milk and sugar.

Lassi is drunk with hot food in India. It is made with one-third natural yogurt to two-thirds iced water, served either sweetened or flavoured with a little salt, roasted cumin seed and sometimes dried mint. Enough lassi for ten people will require about 600ml/1 pint yogurt.

Apple juice is also excellent to accompany Indian food, especially served with herb-flower ice cubes.

Make the ice cubes by placing herb flowers and leaves in an ice tray. Use borage, lavender, lemon verbena, thyme, chives or sage. Fill with mineral water and freeze. Pour apple juice into a large jug and add some sparkling mineral water and a sliced lemon.

OKRA WITH TOMATOES AND MINT
Bhindi Masala

Garam masala means hot mixed spices. If you are keen on Indian cooking you may prefer to mix your own blend. This dish can also be served cold as a salad.

500g/1lb okra
2 tablespoons sunflower oil
1 onion, chopped
1 clove garlic, chopped
1 tablespoon garam masala
425g/14oz tomatoes, peeled and chopped
300ml/½ pint natural Greek or set yogurt
1 tablespoon chopped mint
Salt

Rinse the okra in cold water and trim the stalk ends taking care not to cut into the pods.

Heat the oil in a wide pan and stir in the onion and garlic. Cook for 4–5 minutes until they are soft but not browned. Stir in the garam masala and tomatoes. Add the okra to the pan, spooning the tomato mixture over to coat them. Cook, covered, over medium heat, for 25–30 minutes, stirring now and again to make sure the okra cook evenly. The dish is done when the okra are tender and the sauce is reduced and not watery.

Check the flavour of the dish and add salt to taste.

To serve *Transfer to a hot serving dish and, just before serving, spoon the yogurt on top and sprinkle with the chopped mint.*
SEE PAGE 51.

RED LENTILS WITH ONION RINGS
Masoor Dhal

Red Egyptian lentils cook to a lovely soft purée. This dish can be made ahead and reheats extremely well but is nicer if the onion rings are fried at the last moment.

2 onions
2 tablespoons sunflower oil
2 cloves garlic, chopped
1–2 tablespoons curry paste or powder
6 cardamom pods, bruised
375g/12oz red lentils
900ml/1½ pints vegetable stock or water
1–2 teaspoons salt
2 tablespoons chopped fresh coriander

Chop one of the onions. Heat half the oil in a pan or flameproof casserole and stir in the chopped onion, garlic and curry paste or powder. Cook for 4 minutes then add the cardamom pods, lentils and stock. Bring to the boil, stir and cover with a tightly fitting lid. Cook over low heat for 45 minutes or until the lentils are mushy, adding the salt towards the end of the cooking time. Stir and if the *dhal* is too liquid, stir over high heat for a few minutes to evaporate some of the liquid.

Slice the remaining onion into rings and fry in the rest of the oil until slightly browned.

Sir the chopped coriander into the *dhal* and transfer to a hot serving dish. Arrange the fried onion rings on top and keep it hot until ready to serve.
SEE PAGE 51.

KULFI WITH MANGO SAUCE

This kulfi ice cream is delectable. Don't be put off by the fact that it takes some time to prepare. It is firmer, more granular and less sweet than western ice cream. It can be made several days ahead and kept in the freezer until you are ready for it. It looks wonderfully exotic if made in a decorative mould, such as a Victorian jelly mould. Turn it out on to a plate and serve with the mango sauce.

KULFI WITH MANGO SAUCE, SPICED TEA, MUKWAS

3 litres/5 pints milk, fresh or UHT
12 cardamom pods, bruised
75g/3oz caster sugar
65g/2½oz unblanched, shelled almonds

Sauce:
2 ripe mangoes
25g/1oz caster sugar
Juice of 1 sweet orange or 2 tangerines

Pour the milk into a wide pan. I find a heavy-based preserving pan works best. Use the handle of a wooden spoon to measure the depth of the milk. Add the cardamom pods and bring the milk to the boil. Reduce the heat and simmer the milk for about 1 hour until it is reduced to 1·8 litres/3 pints which is just over half its original depth.

Strain the milk into a large bowl or mould and stir in the sugar. Finely chop the almonds with a sharp knife or in a food processor and stir into the milk. Cool, then cover and freeze overnight.

The kulfi can be turned out of the bowl and served straight away. It will be granular but delicious. Alternatively, to make a smoother ice cream, chop the kulfi into pieces and beat well or whizz in a food processor. Spoon back into the bowl or mould and freeze again until firm.

To make the sauce, peel the mangoes and chop the fruit into a food processor or large sieve. Add the sugar and orange juice and whizz to a smooth purée or press through the sieve. Pour into a jug and chill until ready to serve.

To serve *Dip the bowl or mould briefly in hot water and turn out the kulfi.*

French Country Lunch
for 6

A country lunch in France is a relaxed, even lengthy meal when family and friends share the considerable pleasure of eating good food together. Sunday lunch, in particular, can last for as long as three hours with each course served at a leisurely pace, accompanied by a local wine and lively conversation.

Simplicity is the hallmark of French country cooking in which the best quality ingredients are prepared in a way that enhances their true flavour. This is my favourite kind of cooking and it leads to an unhurried, informal style of entertaining where the cook is absent from the table simply to bring in the next course. The dishes I've chosen can all be prepared ahead and will come to no harm if kept waiting a short time until you are ready to serve them.

This relaxed style makes the meal more flexible: lunch can be served outside on a warm autumn day or indoors around a dining table – even in the kitchen if it's large enough.

Because this is a fairly rich meal, there is no need for large portions. In fact, you may prefer to serve fresh fruit, such as grapes or pears, rather than snow eggs for dessert.

MENU

*

RAW VEGETABLES WITH WALNUT SAUCE FROM TOULOUSE

BEEF COOKED IN RED WINE

MARINATED GOAT'S MILK CHEESE WITH CHIVE BREAD

POTATOES WITH BUTTON MUSHROOMS

*

SNOW EGGS

*

Côtes de Provence Rouge
or Côtes du Rhône Rouge

Sauvignon de Touraine
or Sancerre

BEEF COOKED IN RED WINE, POTATOES WITH BUTTON MUSHROOMS

RAW VEGETABLES WITH WALNUT SAUCE FROM TOULOUSE
Aillade Toulousaine aux Crudités

This walnut and olive oil sauce from the south of France makes a delicious and nutritious alternative to mayonnaise as an accompaniment to raw or cooked vegetables.

75g/3oz shelled walnuts
2–3 cloves garlic, peeled
150ml/¼ pint olive oil
50–75ml/2–3fl oz hot water
1 tablespoon chopped coriander leaves or fresh parsley
Salt
625g/1¼lb mixed raw vegetables cut into finger-size pieces: celery, carrot, chicory, bulb fennel, sweet peppers, florets of cauliflower, watercress, etc
1 French loaf to serve

Cover the walnuts with boiling water, drain and rinse in cold water. If you wish, peel the thin brown skin from the walnuts but unless they are bitter I leave them unskinned.

Place the walnuts in a food processor or blender with the garlic and process until finely ground. Gradually mix in the oil and hot water and process to make a thick sauce. Season with salt to taste and spoon into a bowl. Sprinkle coriander or parsley on top.

To serve *Arrange the vegetables on a large plate or wooden board, making small heaps of each kind of vegetable, and place the bowl of sauce in the centre. Serve with chunks of French bread.*

FINGERS OF RAW VEGETABLES WITH WALNUT SAUCE FROM TOULOUSE

BEEF COOKED IN RED WINE
Daube Provençale de Boeuf

The wonderful, full-bodied flavour of this classic dish from Provence results from marinating the beef in red wine with herbs for two days before slow-cooking the meat until beautifully tender.

300ml/½ pint Côtes du Rhône red wine
3 tablespoons olive oil
1–2 cloves garlic, crushed
1 teaspoon dried herbes de Provence
½ teaspoon salt
½ teaspoon black peppercorns
1kg/2¼lb topside of beef
125g/4oz smoked streaky bacon, diced
1 onion, chopped
250g/8oz tomatoes, peeled and chopped
A strip of orange peel
2 anchovy fillets, chopped
100g/3½oz black olives

Place a plastic bag in a bowl large enough to hold the beef. Pour the wine into the bag and add the olive oil, garlic, herbs, salt and peppercorns. Put the meat in the bag and seal with a knot or a twist-tie – this bag method helps to marinate the beef more effectively. Store in a cold place or the refrigerator for two days. Turn the meat over now and again.

Cook the bacon with the onion in a flameproof casserole over a moderate heat until the bacon fat runs. Add the beef and sear lightly all over. Pour in the marinade, add the tomatoes, orange peel and anchovies and bring to the boil. Cover the casserole with a tightly fitting lid and cook in a preheated oven, 160°C, 325°F, Gas Mark 3, for 2–3 hours until tender. Add the olives 10 minutes before the end of cooking time.

To serve *Transfer the meat and the olives to a hot serving dish and reduce the cooking liquid over high heat until slightly thickened. Carve the meat into fairly thick slices and spoon the sauce over the meat and the olives.*

EXTRAS

This menu has five courses and the food is substantial and filling so all you will need in the way of extras is perhaps, a simple green salad such as frisée dressed with a fruity vinaigrette, which I would offer with the main course.

Serve a large baguette loaf of French bread cut into chunks with the *crudités*.

If you serve fruit for dessert a bunch of grapes or six fine pears would make a perfect conclusion to the meal. On the table place sea salt and a pepper mill filled with black peppercorns and have plenty of sparkling mineral water on hand. At the end of the meal serve strong filter coffee, with sugar and cream handed separately.

PRESENTATION

I like to serve this on a scrubbed wooden table but the French prefer lily-white tablecloths which do, I admit, give meals more of a sense of occasion.

French country food is usually served from the hefty pottery dishes and bowls in which it is prepared, brought straight from the oven to the table. So it's a good idea to provide heatproof table mats on which to stand the hot pots. I like to use dark, glazed plates and rough weave napkins for this meal. As well as wine glasses provide tumblers for water.

MARINATED GOATS' CHEESE WITH CHIVE BREAD

PLANNING AHEAD

Two days before: Put the beef to marinate. Turn it over a few times in the next two days.

The day before: Prepare the chive bread to the foil stage and set aside. Put the goats' cheese to marinate in the evening.

The day of the party: Make the walnut sauce for the crudités. Prepare the snow eggs and store in a cold dry place until ready to serve. Prepare the beef in red wine and put it in the oven about 3 hours before serving time. Prepare the potatoes and mushrooms. Cut up the raw vegetables for the first course, cover and refrigerate until the guests arrive. Make the frisée salad but don't dress it until the last minute.

Just before the guests arrive arrange the crudités and bowl of walnut sauce on a large platter. Put the chive bread in the oven 10 minutes before serving.

POTATOES WITH BUTTON MUSHROOMS
Pommes de Terre aux Champignons

You can use larger size caps as an alternative to button mushrooms. Cut them into quarters before cooking.

1kg/2lb waxy potatoes such as Desirée
65g/2½oz butter
2 shallots, finely chopped
1 small clove garlic, crushed
250g/8oz button mushrooms, wiped and stalks trimmed
1 tablespoon plain flour
300ml/½ pint single cream
Freshly grated nutmeg
Splash of dry sherry (optional)
Salt and pepper

Peel the potatoes and cut into pieces about the size of a walnut. Cook in salted water for 10–15 minutes or until just cooked. Drain off the cooking water and set the potatoes aside in the pan under a folded tea towel.

Meanwhile, melt the butter in a pan and cook the shallots and garlic for 3–4 minutes until soft but not coloured. Add the mushrooms and cook, stirring, until they have softened and almost all their liquid has evaporated.

Stir in the flour and cook for 1–2 minutes then add the cream. Cook, stirring, for 4–5 minutes until the sauce has thickened. Season to taste with salt, pepper, nutmeg and sherry. Transfer the potatoes to a hot oven dish and pour the mushrooms and sauce over the top. Cover with a lid and place in a preheated oven, 180°C, 350°F, Gas Mark 4, for 10–15 minutes until piping hot.

SEE PAGE 54.

MARINATED GOAT'S MILK CHEESE WITH CHIVE BREAD
Fromage de Chèvre Mariné aux Herbes, Pain de Ciboulette

Several other soft French cheeses such as Brie and Camembert taste excellent if marinated for a few hours in a mixture of walnut oil and fresh herbs.

200g/7oz log-shaped chèvre or goat's milk cheese
3 tablespoons fine-flavoured oil such as walnut, hazelnut or virgin olive oil
1 teaspoon lemon juice
½ teaspoon chopped thyme
½ teaspoon chopped marjoram
75g/3oz butter
1 tablespoon chopped chives
½ teaspoon finely grated lemon rind
1 French loaf
Salt and pepper

Cut the cheese into 6 slices and place them cut side down on a shallow plate. Mix the oil with half the lemon juice, the thyme, marjoram and some salt and pepper and spoon over the cheese making sure that all sides are coated. Cover with a plate and leave the cheese in a cold place for 8–12 hours.

Soften the butter and blend in the chives, lemon rind and remaining lemon juice until the mixture is soft and spreadable. Make a series of diagonal cuts, 2·5cm/1in apart, not quite through the loaf. Spread the chive butter on each side of the slices and wrap the loaf tightly in foil. Set aside until 10 minutes before you are ready to serve the loaf.

Place the loaf in a preheated oven, 200°C, 400°F, Gas Mark 6, for 10 minutes.

To serve *Place each portion of cheese on a small individual plate with a chunk of the hot chive bread.*

SNOW EGGS
Oeufs à la Neige

This fluffy pudding of poached meringue and vanilla-flavoured egg custard can be made several hours ahead if kept in a cold, dry place until ready to serve.

600ml/1 pint milk
2 egg whites
75g/3oz caster sugar
3 egg yolks
1½ tablespoons kirsch
Few drops of vanilla essence
50g/2oz granulated sugar
2 tablespoons cold water

Pour the milk into your widest pan and heat gently.

To make the meringue, whisk the egg whites until stiff then whisk in 25g/1oz of the caster sugar. Bring the milk almost to the boil and place rounded dessertspoons of the meringue in the milk. Poach three or four meringue 'eggs' at a time, and very gently spoon hot milk over them for about 1 minute until they are cooked. Lift out each meringue with a slotted spoon and place in a large shallow dish. Repeat until all the meringue has been poached.

Whisk the remaining caster sugar into the egg yolks in a bowl and stir in the milk. Strain the mixture back into the pan, add any milk that has drained from the meringue eggs and, over a very low heat, cook the custard carefully, stirring all the time and never allowing it to boil, until just thickened.

Remove from the heat and add the kirsch and vanilla essence according to taste. Cool the custard until lukewarm by standing the pan in a bowl of cold water, then gently pour into the shallow dish so that the 'eggs' float.

To make the caramel topping, dissolve the granulated sugar in the cold water in a pan, then boil fast until the mixture turns a golden brown caramel (don't let it get too dark or the flavour will be bitter). Remove the pan from the heat and quickly spoon the caramel over the meringue 'eggs' in a criss-cross of fine lines.

SNOW EGGS

Oz Clarke's
WINE NOTES

It's easy to imagine Paris as the heart of France with its street cafés, its wide boulevards, its brawling riot of people and traffic, its sophistication and glamour.

But none of this is the *heart* of France. France's heart beats louder and stronger the further you remove yourself from Paris, in particular as you fan out to the south and the west. And whereas in Paris, the whole gamut of French wines would be on offer at a restaurant, in the rest of France, the local food will always be served with the local wine.

Provençal reds have not been among France's most brilliant – usually having a rather lumpish, broad quality to them. But things are changing. The new reds from Provence are showing richer, ripe fruit, less abrasive tannins, and sometimes a hint of sweet oak. The wines of the nearby Coteaux des Baux-en-Provence, on the other hand, are rapidly becoming stars in France's southern firmament, precisely because of the gentle lush softness of their fruit. Domaine de Trévallon is an outstanding example. Geraldene uses a neighbouring Côtes du Rhône to marinate her beef, and a fresh young ripe raspberry Rhône red, especially a Rhône-Villages, would be an excellent alternative accompaniment; and either wine can be served through the first course also.

Interestingly, for the cheese, red wine is *not* the best accompaniment. Much of France's best goat's milk cheese comes from the Loire valley, where the tangy, gooseberry-flavoured Sauvignon grape makes a dry white which goes perfectly with the mildly acid cheese. Sancerre is excellent but expensive, and a good Sauvignon de Touraine will cost you half as much and give you just as much flavour.

NIGEL SLATER

TEA & COFFEE PARTIES

There is something slightly decadent about eating and drinking in the afternoon. Anything more elaborate than just a cup of tea turns tea-time into a treat, an indulgence even. It is the perfect time of day for a party. Tea is the traditional drink at this time of day, but many people nowadays prefer coffee or tisanes and these menus cater for all tastes.

A tea or coffee party can be a very grand affair, where everyone dresses up and drinks from elegant china, or it can be an informal laid-back party round the kitchen table. Whichever way you like to serve it, the food's the thing. Everyone loves a home-made cake. Freshly baked biscuits, cakes, toasted crumpets, and generously-filled sandwiches must be on everybody's list of comfort-food. Perhaps it is the association of tea parties with childhood that makes them so enjoyable.

Some of my most successful parties have been held in the afternoon. In the summer, the garden is the place for celebrating. Under the trees, sitting among the apple blossom, or lazing on the lawn in the sun. For a garden party, the weather is all-important. Usually, I don't mention that I am planning to eat in the garden, I simply invite people to a party, and only decide to have the event outdoors if the weather turns out really fine on the day.

In winter family celebrations around a roaring fire are so enjoyable. Any afternoon, however cold and wet, will be cheered up when the entire family gathers at the fireside. The food can be a little richer in chilly weather, with lots of toasted snacks and piping-hot boozy coffee.

Certainly Champagne and caviar make for a wonderful time, so long as there is enough of both, and there rarely is. Extravagance, though, is not a prerequisite of a good party. The best are often the cheapest ones to give, where someone has splashed out with effort rather than money. Frugal food is often the tastiest, and makes exceptionally good party food, and if one of the dishes is hot, it somehow seems to make the party that much more special and memorable.

Opposite **TEA IN THE GARDEN** *PAGE 68*

Farmhouse Tea

for 8

This is a simple party menu with an eclectic choice of china and natural table decorations. The food is easy home cooking, much of which can be done in advance. This party will not break the bank, none of the ingredients is expensive and most are kitchen staples. Although there is nothing extravagant about these dishes, far from it, the effect as the table fills with homemade goodies is both welcoming and generous.

Home baking is always popular, particularly when it involves cakes and tarts. Here there is an unusual baked custard topped with a layer of fruity malt loaf, a rich wholemeal cake full of pears, and a chocolate mousse enclosed in a deliciously crumbly hazelnut pastry.

Mushrooms come stuffed with a mixture of grated vegetables and cheese, and the cheapest of all meats, chicken livers, are potted and eaten with a peach chutney and crisp wholemeal toast.

To me, this is the quintessential family celebration tea. The menu has something for everyone, the recipes are so easy that all the family can lend a hand, and its heart is in the traditional home baking always firmly associated with luscious farmhouse teas.

MENU

*

HOT MUSHROOMS STUFFED WITH CHEESE AND WALNUTS

POTTED CHICKEN LIVERS WITH WHOLEMEAL TOAST AND PEACH CHUTNEY

*

CHOCOLATE MOUSSE TART WITH HAZELNUT ORANGE PASTRY

MALT LOAF PUDDING

WHOLEMEAL PEAR AND GINGER CAKE

*

Traditional Teas

HOT MUSHROOMS STUFFED WITH CHEESE AND WALNUTS, POTTED CHICKEN LIVERS WITH WHOLEMEAL TOAST AND PEACH CHUTNEY

HOT MUSHROOMS STUFFED WITH CHEESE AND WALNUTS

The stuffing for these mushrooms can be used for all manner of vegetables, such as peppers, courgettes or large tomatoes. Use any type of cheese you like, Caerphilly or Wensleydale are just suggestions. A blue cheese would be good too.

24 large open mushrooms, about 7cm/3in in diameter
8 tablespoons vegetable oil
2 small parsnips, coarsely grated
2 small turnips, coarsely grated
4 medium carrots, coarsely grated
6 spring onions, chopped
125g/4oz Caerphilly or Wensleydale cheese, grated
4 tablespoons shelled walnuts, roughly chopped
2 thick slices brown bread, crumbed
Salt
Pepper

Wipe the mushrooms, remove their stalks and reserve for a soup or stock. Cook them in 6 tablespoons of the vegetable oil in a large shallow pan. You may need to do this in batches. Transfer the mushrooms to a large roasting tin, placing them in rows. In the same pan that you cooked the mushrooms, heat the remaining oil and add the grated vegetables. Fry, stirring occasionally, for 3 minutes, until they start to sweat. In a large bowl, mix the grated vegetables with the onions, cheese and walnuts. Reserve a small handful of bread-crumbs and add the remainder to the mixture.

Season with salt and pepper. Place 1 heaped tablespoon of vegetable stuffing in each mushroom cup. Scatter over the reserved breadcrumbs and cook in a preheated oven, 180°C, 350°F, Gas Mark 4, for 15 minutes. Remove from the oven and serve while still hot.

POTTED CHICKEN LIVERS WITH WHOLEMEAL TOAST AND PEACH CHUTNEY

Sieve the chicken livers after blending if you prefer a smooth pâté. I tend to simply mash them with a fork, as I like the coarse texture. This pâté is also good served on oatcakes. Choose a fruity, spicy chutney, such as peach, apple or gooseberry to serve with it.

175g/6oz butter, softened
250g/8oz chicken livers
2 tablespoons brandy
Salt and pepper
Peach chutney, to serve

Melt a third of the butter in a shallow pan, and stir in the chicken livers. Cook them, stirring occasionally, for 4–5 minutes. The livers should be brown on the outside, but still pink inside. Remove them with a draining spoon and place them in a blender or food processor. If you don't have either, the livers can be rubbed through a sieve or even mashed with a fork which will produce a coarser paste.

Add the brandy to the pan juices, let this bubble a little then pour it over the livers. Purée with the remaining butter, using the machine or by hand, until smooth; add salt and pepper, being generous with both. Pour into an earthenware pot and leave in the fridge overnight to set.

To serve *Serve with crisp wholemeal toast and a dish of chutney.*

EXTRAS

You won't need much in the way of extras with this menu – some fruity chutney and wholemeal bread for the toast to serve with the potted chicken livers and cream to accompany the puddings.

An alternative pudding to the chocolate tart, say with a fruity base, will be appreciated by some. Perhaps a fruit fool, made in the modern way, with fromage frais or thick yogurt replacing the more traditional custard.

To make a fool, gently stew fruit, such as blackberries, gooseberries or blueberries, with a little sugar to taste if you wish, until the berries start to burst. Purée the berries, and when cold, stir them into half their quantity of cold fromage frais or thick yogurt.

Spoon the fool into stemmed glasses and leave in the fridge for an hour. Add a flower, leaf or berry to the top of each fool just before serving.

I like to eat thick yellow cream with the pear cake, but Greek-style yogurt or a purée of apples or pears is also good. Don't peel the fruit, just core and chop it up. Cook slowly with a little water until the fruit is fluffy. Sieve it if you wish, but I think it is best eaten, skin and all, as a tart accompaniment to the dark wholemeal cake.

If you prefer, make a fruity cumberland sauce to spoon over the chicken liver pâté instead of the chutney. Put 6 tablespoons of redcurrant jelly in a small saucepan with a glass of port. Add the finely pared rind of 1 orange and 1 lemon cut into the thinnest possible shreds. Simmer for 10 minutes, until the citrus rind is soft.

Let the sauce cool a little, then place it by the pâté in a little pot with a spoon.

Serve traditional teas in a big china pot, with milk, sugar and lemon.

CHOCOLATE MOUSSE TART WITH HAZELNUT ORANGE PASTRY

PLANNING AHEAD

This is one of those party menus where almost everything can be done the day before, leaving very little last-minute fiddling.

In advance: Make the pear and ginger cake a couple of days before the party if you want to. Wrap it in clingfilm or foil and store it in a tin. Make the chicken liver pâté a day or so before, and keep it in the fridge.

The day before: Make the hazelnut tart shell and keep it in a tin. Don't be tempted to fill it until the day of the party. You should bake the malt loaf pudding today so that it will be thoroughly chilled for tomorrow.

The day of the party: Make the chocolate mousse and fill the tart shell. Prepare the stuffing for the mushrooms, and fill them ready to go into the oven later in the afternoon. At the last minute prepare the wholemeal toast for the chicken liver pâté.

As the guests arrive: Put the kettle on for the tea.

Any crisp, nutty pastry is a perfect base for this chocolate tart, but especially one made with almonds or hazelnuts.

50g/2oz butter
125g/4oz plain flour
50g/2oz hazelnuts, skinned and finely chopped
1 tablespoon caster sugar
Grated rind of 1 orange
1 small egg (size 5 or 6), beaten
200g/7oz plain chocolate
4 eggs, separated

To finish:
125g/4oz plain chocolate
125ml/4fl oz double cream
2 tablespoons cocoa powder

For the pastry, rub the butter into the flour then add the skinned and chopped nuts, the sugar and the orange rind. Bind the mixture with the egg and bring together with your hands to form a ball.

Press the mixture lightly over the base and sides of a 20cm/8in loose-bottomed sponge tin. Bake in a preheated oven, 200°C, 400°F, Gas Mark 6, for 20 minutes, until golden and slightly shrunken away from the tin. Cool on a rack.

For the filling, melt the chocolate in a bowl over a pan of simmering water. Beat the egg whites until stiff. Remove the chocolate from the heat and stir in the yolks. Quickly fold a third of the egg white into the chocolate mixture. Fold the chocolate mixture into the remaining egg white. Pour into the pastry case tapping the sides of the tin to spread the mixture evenly. Place in the refrigerator for 3 hours to set.

To finish, melt the chocolate as before. Spread it smoothly about 1·5mm/$\frac{1}{16}$in thick over a clean smooth work surface. Allow to cool to setting point. Holding a large flexible knife at an angle of 45°, press the blade firmly against the surface, pushing away from you, rolling the chocolate as you go, to make thin rolls, rather like chocolate cigarettes. Set aside.

Whip the cream until it stands in soft peaks. Spoon roughly over the top of the tart. Scatter the rolled chocolate over the cream and sieve the cocoa powder over the chocolate rolls. Remove the sides from the tin and serve.

MALT LOAF PUDDING

This is a special version of bread and butter pudding, but with lots of custard and only a little bread. It is best served chilled.

900ml/1½ pints milk
300ml/½ pint double cream
125g/4oz raisins
9 eggs
125g/4oz caster sugar
1 teaspoon vanilla essence
1 malt loaf
Butter for spreading
Nutmeg

Heat the milk and cream together until tepid. Scatter the raisins over a large shallow oven-proof dish. Crack the eggs into a mixing bowl and add the sugar, milk and cream mixture, and vanilla flavouring. Whisk it all together and pour over the raisins.

Cut the malt loaf into thin slices and butter each piece. Float the bread on top of the egg custard mixture; the pieces should be touching, but not overlapping. Grate a little nutmeg over the top. Place the dish in a larger, metal roasting tin. Pour in enough hot water to come halfway up the sides of the dish.

Place in a preheated oven, 160°C, 325°F, Gas Mark 3, and cook for about an hour, or until the custard is set, but still wobbly when shaken.

WHOLEMEAL PEAR AND GINGER CAKE

One of the simplest cakes to make, this dark, moist cake will keep for a few days in a tin. It is just as successful with apples, and if served warm, with thick cream, it makes an admirable family pudding.

4 pears
325ml/11fl oz vegetable oil
375g/12oz soft brown sugar
3 eggs
375g/12oz wholemeal flour
1 tablespoon bicarbonate of soda
½ teaspoon grated nutmeg
2 tablespoons grated fresh root ginger
Butter for greasing
Brown sugar, to finish

Butter a deep 25cm/10in cake tin. Line the base with greaseproof paper and butter it. Halve and core the pears, but do not peel. Chop them into small dice.

Beat the oil and sugar together with an electric whisk until thoroughly combined. Beat in the eggs, one at a time; don't worry if the mixture curdles a little at this point. Fold in the flour, bicarbonate of soda, spices and pears.

Spoon into the cake tin and smooth the top. Bake in a preheated oven, 160°C, 325°F, Gas Mark 3, for 1½ hours until firm in the centre.

Cool for 10 minutes, then turn out on to a rack.

To serve *Sprinkle with a little brown sugar and serve warm or cold with cream or thick yogurt.*

MALT LOAF PUDDING, CHOCOLATE MOUSSE TART WITH HAZELNUT ORANGE PASTRY, WHOLEMEAL PEAR AND GINGER CAKE

PRESENTATION

My favourite way to present the food at this party is on bright colourful china on a gingham cloth. The effect is fun if the china does not match.

I sometimes set a shallow wicker basket in the centre of the table and fill it with anything I can find in the garden or in the lanes and fields. Don't pick wild flowers; instead gather any interesting leaves and twigs, bits of bark and dried thistles. Acorns or fir-cones look wonderful in a big pile. A big basket of hips, haws and berries – or, in spring and summer, flowers from a cottage garden – would make an admirable centrepiece for the table.

Vegetarian High Tea for 6

This is an informal high tea party for friends or family. An abundance of fresh green leaves and clean-tasting herb teas balances the rich and substantial cakes and pastries. The overall effect is fresh and cheerful with good, simple food for healthy appetites.

The strudel with its crisp, flaky pastry is served with a leafy salad. Wheatgerm and raisin scones filled with a cheese and herb pâté can be made in the round and then split and stuffed or cut with small cutters for a more elegant effect. The lemon cake, both light and rich at the same time, is a traditional tea-time cake but layered to double height and decorated with crystallized fruit. Heart-shaped shortbreads filled with cream and sliced apricots go well with a selection of herbal tisanes such as rosehip, fennel or elderflower.

Some of the freshly baked scones, unfilled and served warm with butter, and a plate of heart-shaped shortbreads without the cream and fruit would make a simpler, less rich meal.

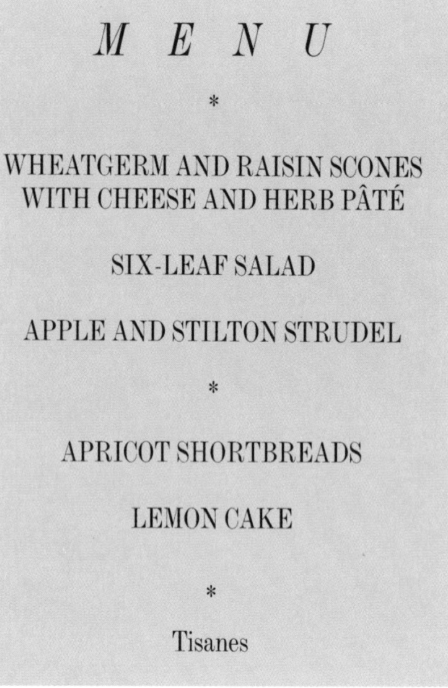

MENU

*

WHEATGERM AND RAISIN SCONES WITH CHEESE AND HERB PÂTÉ

SIX-LEAF SALAD

APPLE AND STILTON STRUDEL

*

APRICOT SHORTBREADS

LEMON CAKE

*

Tisanes

WHEATGERM AND RAISIN SCONES WITH CHEESE AND HERB PÂTÉ, SIX-LEAF SALAD, APPLE AND STILTON STRUDEL, TISANES

WHEATGERM AND RAISIN SCONES WITH CHEESE AND HERB PÂTÉ

An alternative less rich spread can be made by mixing equal quantities of butter and chopped mushrooms and seasoning with lemon juice and black pepper. Fill the scones with a little of the mushroom butter and some watercress.

Cheese and herb pâté:
225g/8oz half-fat soft cheese
2 tablespoons each finely chopped parsley, chervil and tarragon
1 garlic clove, peeled and crushed with a little salt

Scones:
175g/6oz plain flour
50g/2oz plain wholemeal flour
2 tablespoons wheatgerm
1 tablespoon baking powder
½ teaspoon bicarbonate of soda
125g/4oz butter
50g/2oz raisins
2 eggs
Milk to mix
Wheatgerm for rolling

To make the pâté, thoroughly mix the cheese and the herbs with a wooden spoon. Beat in the crushed garlic and keep the pâté, covered, in the refrigerator until needed.

To make the scones, put the flours, wheatgerm, baking powder and bicarbonate of soda into large mixing bowl. Rub the butter into the mixture with your fingertips. The mixture should resemble breadcrumbs. Scatter in the raisins. Beat the egg and stir into the mixture with a fork. Add enough milk to bind the dough, mixing it into a ball with your hand.

Dust your hands with flour and sprinkle the work surface with wheatgerm then remove the dough from the bowl and pat it out into a round on the work surface. Gently roll it out into a round 2·5cm/1in thick. Score the round into wedges with a large knife, cutting halfway down to the base. Bake the round on a greased baking sheet in a preheated oven, 200°C, 400°F, Gas Mark 6, for 20–25 minutes.

To serve *Split the scone into wedges, either straight from the oven or when cool, then cut through horizontally and sandwich them together with the cheese and herb pâté.*

SIX-LEAF SALAD

There is now a dazzling selection of salad leaves available. Highlight the different flavours and textures by making a herby dressing. Use finely chopped tarragon instead of chervil for a dressing with a stronger aniseed flavour.

8 handfuls assorted salad leaves (choose from quattro stagioni, chicory, radicchio, lollo biondo, feuille de chêne, frisée)
1½ tablespoons white wine vinegar
7 tablespoons virgin olive oil
2 tablespoons each finely chopped parsley and chervil
Salt and pepper

Wash the salad leaves carefully and shake them dry.

In a large salad bowl, mix the seasonings with the vinegar and stir in the olive oil. Throw in the chopped herbs and mix well.

Add the leaves, torn into smaller pieces if you wish, and toss no more than 15 minutes before serving.

PLANNING AHEAD

In advance: Make the wheatgerm and raisin scones and the sponges for the lemon cake and freeze them. Make sure to wrap them thoroughly before storing in the deep freeze and take them out to thaw the night before.

The day before: Make the shortbread biscuits and store them in an airtight tin. Prepare the cheese and herb pâté. Cover it tightly, and keep it in the refrigerator. Make the salad dressing and store in a screw-top jar in a cool place.

The morning of the party: Prepare the strudel and keep it in the fridge, uncooked. Whip the cream and store it, covered, in the fridge. Assemble the cake no more than two hours before serving. Fill the biscuits next and lastly split the scones and stuff them with the pâté. That leaves only the baking of the strudel. Toss the salad leaves in the vinaigrette when the guests arrive.

PRESENTATION

Use lots of white linen for this party. Decorate the tables with swags of crisp cloths, butter-muslin or white sheets. A profusion of flowers, such as huge clutches of white lilac or anemones, or bowls of sweet-smelling cream hyacinths, would be so pretty. Keep the colours fresh and bright, and the cutlery and china simple.

The centre of the table should be reserved for the golden strudel. It will need a sharp knife. If you have a long serving hotplate, use it to keep the strudel warm during the party.

The easiest way to serve the tisanes is to bring the kettle into the room along with a little wicker basket of tisane sachets. Heat-proof glasses, to show off the lovely colours of the herbal teas, are an alternative to cups. Offer a pot of runny honey for sweetening the tisanes.

TISANES

Tisanes are herb-flavoured drinks made by infusing finely chopped dried herbs in nearly boiling water. They can be made from the flowers, roots or leaves of plants. Strictly speaking, they are not 'teas' as they are not made from the leaves of the tea bush.

They do not contain caffeine and many are believed to possess therapeutic properties. Some, such as rosehip and hibiscus, a favourite of mine, are blended and are usually, though not always, bought in easy-to-use sachets with strings attached for dunking the bags in freshly boiled water.

Among the most common tisanes are camomile which is said to relax you (its appeal is sadly lost on me as its association with shampoo is too strong), elderflower which is said to soothe the nerves, and lime blossom which is reputed to relieve headaches.

A tea infuser is a help when making drinks from loose tisanes. Use an infuser made from stainless steel and leave plenty of room in it for the leaves to expand and give up their flavour to the brew. Remove the infuser, which is often on a thin chain, when the drink is as strong as you like it.

Served quite weak and without milk, they can sometimes benefit from a thin slice of lemon. Honey or sugar can be added to sweeten.

APPLE AND STILTON STRUDEL

Strict vegetarians will want to substitute a non-rennet blue cheese, such as Danish Blue, for the Stilton. Any mature cheese can be used, and this would be a suitable dish to finish up ends of assorted cheese from the cheese board.

500g/1lb apples, preferably Cox's
2 tablespoons lemon juice
250g/8oz Stilton cheese
1 teaspoon fresh thyme
½ teaspoon ground nutmeg
8 sheets filo pastry
125g/4oz unsalted butter, melted
125g/4oz dry breadcrumbs
Black pepper

Peel, core and chop the apples into 1cm/½in cubes. Place in a bowl and sprinkle with the lemon juice. Crumble in the cheese and add the thyme and nutmeg. Mix well and season with pepper.

Lay a damp tea towel on a flat surface and place 2 sheets of filo pastry on it. Brush with a little melted butter and sprinkle on a few breadcrumbs. Place another 2 sheets of pastry on top and repeat the process. Continue layering until the pastry is used up, reserving a little butter and some breadcrumbs to finish.

Spread the apple mixture over two-thirds of the pastry, leaving a strip uncovered. Using the tea towel, roll up the strudel into a large sausage. Transfer to a lightly greased baking sheet. Brush the top with the remaining melted butter and sprinkle over the last of the breadcrumbs. Bake in a preheated oven, 180°C, 350°F, Gas Mark 4, for 30–35 minutes. Serve warm.

APRICOT SHORTBREADS

Apricots and cream are just one of the fillings you can use with these shortbreads. Try strawberries and clotted cream instead.

75g/3oz butter
125g/4oz caster sugar
1 egg
1 egg yolk
225g/8oz plain flour
500g/1lb fresh apricots
175ml/6fl oz double cream, whipped to soft peaks
8 tablespoons apricot jam, warmed and sieved
Icing sugar, to decorate

In a mixing bowl, cream the butter with a wooden spoon until it lightens in colour. Add the sugar and beat until light and fluffy. Mix in the egg and egg yolk and gradually add the flour, stirring it in thoroughly but gently. The dough will start to stiffen as you add the flour; you may find it easier to incorporate the last of the flour by hand.

Dust a little flour over the work surface, then roll out the biscuit dough with a rolling pin to 5mm/¼in thick. Don't roll too much or the dough will toughen. With a heart-shaped cutter, cut out as many biscuits as you can. Using a palette knife transfer the biscuits to a baking sheet. Bake in a preheated oven, 180°C, 350°F, Gas Mark 4, for 10–12 minutes until golden.

Allow the biscuits to cool slightly before placing them on a rack. If you are not eating the biscuits immediately, store them in a biscuit tin when quite cool.

Halve the apricots and remove the stones. Cut the apricots into thick pieces. Place a tablespoon of thick cream on to half of the shortbreads then add a slice or two of apricot and a spoonful of apricot jam. Place the remaining biscuits on top and dust with a little icing sugar.

LEMON CAKE

If you prefer, sandwich the sponge layers together with lemon or orange curd and a thin spreading of thick Greek-style yogurt. Alternatively, do not fill the cake – just halve the recipe and serve wedges of lemon cake with poached fruits, such as apricots.

375g/12oz butter
375g/12oz caster sugar
Rind and juice of 3 lemons
6 eggs, beaten
375g/12oz self-raising flour
175g/6oz icing sugar
600ml/1 pint double cream
Icing sugar, to dust
Crystallized fruits, to decorate

Butter and line the bases of four 20cm/8in sandwich tins.

Cream the butter and caster sugar until fluffy. Add the lemon rind and beat the eggs into the mixture, a little at a time. Fold in the flour. Divide the mixture equally among the 4 tins. Bake in a preheated oven, 180°C, 350°F, Gas Mark 4, for about 25 minutes, 2 on the top shelf and 2 on the middle shelf, swopping them over half-way through cooking. They are cooked when they are firm to the touch and have shrunk slightly from the sides of the tins.

Remove the cakes from the oven and leave to cool for 5 minutes before turning them out on to cooling racks. When the cakes are cool, place them on four plates and, using a knitting needle, make holes all over them.

Over a gentle heat, dissolve the icing sugar in the lemon juice. Pour the hot syrup over the cakes and leave them, covered, for an hour or so until they have absorbed the juice.

Whip the cream to soft peaks and use it to sandwich the cakes together, lifting each layer very carefully on top of the others.

To serve *Dust the top of the cake with icing sugar. Place it on a serving plate and decorate it on top and around the base with a selection of crystallized fruits.*

LEMON CAKE, APRICOT SHORTBREADS

Tea in the Garden for 8

What could be a more perfect setting for a party, especially a tea party, than a garden at the height of summer? Sunshine seems to bring out the best in everyone, and a party in the open air gives the chance for friends and family to get together.

Flowers are used in the food and for decorating the table. Use soft pastel-coloured flowers rather than anything vivid which will not flatter the food in quite the same way.

Little bunches of green vegetables are tied up with long chives and accompanied by a fresh herb dip. Chicken sandwiches always seem to go down well, and here they are given a surprise addition of nasturtium flowers. Salmon can be used instead of chicken. Poached peaches with almonds and honey is a refreshingly fruity dessert. A lightly alcoholic punch is served as well as tea.

The table centrepiece is a cake in the shape of a summer boater. You can decorate this simply or really go to town with ribbons, bows and flowers. If the weather breaks, just pick up the food and run for cover.

Menu

*

GREEN CRUDITÉS WITH HERB DIP

CHICKEN AND NASTURTIUM FLOWER SANDWICHES

*

RASPBERRY SPONGE CAKE

POACHED PEACHES WITH HONEY AND ALMONDS

*

Tisane Fruit Punch
Tea

CHICKEN AND NASTURTIUM FLOWER SANDWICHES, GREEN CRUDITÉS WITH HERB DIP

GREEN CRUDITÉS WITH HERB DIP

All manner of green vegetables work well served as crudités. Asparagus, dwarf green beans and broccoli are particularly good whether used raw or briefly blanched. Sieving the cream or cottage cheese is not essential, but it does give a lighter texture to the dip. Add a tablespoon of yogurt or cream if you like a softer consistency.

2kg/4lb mixed asparagus, dwarf green beans and broccoli
Long chives for tying bundles of vegetables

Dip:
500g/1lb half-fat cream or cottage cheese, sieved
5 tablespoons finely chopped fresh herbs, such as parsley, dill and tarragon
2 cloves garlic, finely crushed
Freshly ground black pepper
Sprigs of herbs, to garnish

Wash the vegetables. Break off the asparagus spears, reserving the stalks for a soup or stir-fry. Cut the broccoli into florets. Don't be tempted to top and tail the beans – it takes hours and you have enough to do. Blanch the vegetables for 1 minute in boiling water. Divide them into small bundles containing some of each vegetable. Tie the chives neatly around the bundles.

Mix the cheese, chopped herbs, garlic and pepper together in a bowl or use a food processor.

To serve *Spoon the dip on the side of each individual plate and arrange several bundles of vegetables alongside. Garnish with sprigs of herbs. Alternatively, pile the dip into serving bowls.*

CHICKEN AND NASTURTIUM FLOWER SANDWICHES

The bright orange colour of nasturtium flowers adds a cheerful note and the leaves a gentle peppery flavour to both salads and sandwiches. You can save time by buying a ready-roasted chicken but I prefer to use chicken that has been poached, and allowed to cool in its stock which keeps the meat juicy. Substitute the same quantity of cooked salmon if you wish.

500g/1lb cooked chicken, roughly chopped
4 tablespoons strained natural yogurt
1 tablespoon chopped chives
16 slices of bread cut from a brown sandwich loaf
Butter, for spreading
8 nasturtium flowers
Nasturtium leaves and flowers, to garnish (optional)
Salt

Mix the chopped chicken with the yogurt, chopped chives and salt to taste. Lightly butter the bread. Spread the chicken mixture evenly on to eight slices of bread. Remove the petals from the nasturtium flowers and scatter them over the chicken mixture. Place a slice of bread on top of each one, press down lightly and cut the sandwiches into neat quarters with a sharp knife.

To serve *Place the sandwiches on plates lined with nasturtium leaves. Scatter nasturtium flowers or petals on top.*

SANDWICH FILLINGS

Long gone are the days when sandwiches were filled with soggy tomatoes and potted fish paste. Summer sandwiches can now benefit from the new varieties of salad ingredients and interesting breads available. Instead of chicken and nasturtium, try one of the following:
– Dark rye bread with smoked salmon and chopped dill.
– Thin slices of white bread with sliced cucumber, strawberries, a little fresh mint.
– French baguette split and stuffed with tomatoes, black olives and anchovies, drizzled with garlicky vinaigrette.
– Fruit bread with grated carrots and raisins dressed with lemon juice, and seasoned with toasted cumin seeds.
– Sliced crusty bread with goats' cheese and sliced ripe figs.
– Wholemeal bread with cottage cheese, alfalfa sprouts, shredded fennel and toasted flaked almonds.

PLANNING AHEAD

In advance: The sponge cakes can be baked well in advance, carefully wrapped and then frozen. Thaw them overnight. Make ice for the punch.

The day before: Prepare the poached peaches. Keep them covered in the fridge until you are ready to serve them. Roast or poach the chicken for the sandwiches and keep in the refrigerator. Make the herb dip and cover.

The morning of the party: Blanch the vegetables early in the day. Tie them up with the chives and store in the fridge. Make the punch up to the point before the Champagne is added.

An hour before: Make the sandwiches and cover with clingfilm. Fill and decorate the cake. Pour the Champagne in the punch just before serving.

RASPBERRY SPONGE CAKE

PRESENTATION

As this is a garden tea why not make use of flowers growing there? Petals of lupins, peonies, sweet peas and especially roses scattered over the cloth make a beautiful table decoration. Use nasturtium leaves to line the sandwich plates – or instead of them.

Serve the dip in small bowls or tall glasses. If you have no time for tying up the vegetables you can always arrange them in small baskets or bowls.

Let's hope there will be plenty of sunshine for this party. Glass dishes and plates will sparkle in the sunlight, and would be most suitable for the peaches and the punch. Set fruit such as strawberries and raspberries into ice cube trays to make fruit-filled ice cubes.

RASPBERRY SPONGECAKE, POACHED PEACHES WITH HONEY AND ALMONDS

This is a very simple all-in-one sponge cake which can be assembled to look like a wonderful summer boater, complete with satin ribbon and flowers. Ring the changes with strawberries or blackberries as they come into season, and sprinkle *kirsch* instead of rosewater over the raspberries if you prefer.

Cake:
300g/10oz self-raising flour
2 teaspoons baking powder
300g/10oz butter, softened
300g/10oz caster sugar
5 large eggs (size 1)

Filling and decoration:
250g/8oz raspberries
1 tablespoon rosewater
600ml/1 pint double cream, whipped to soft peaks
3 tablespoons icing sugar
Pink ribbon, 5cm/2in wide

Lightly grease and line one 25cm/10in and two 18cm/7in sponge tins. In a large mixing bowl, sift 125g/4oz of the flour and 1 teaspoon of the baking powder together. Add 125g/4oz of the butter, 125g/4oz of the sugar and 2 eggs to the flour and whisk using an electric mixer for 3–4 minutes or until the mixture is light and fluffy. Spoon into the large cake tin and bake in preheated oven, 160°C, 325°F, Gas Mark 3, for 30 minutes.

Repeat using the remaining cake ingredients. Divide the mixture between the two smaller sponge tins and smooth level. Bake in the preheated oven for 30–35 minutes.

When the cakes are cooked, run a knife around the edge and turn out on to a wire rack. Peel off the greaseproof paper lining from the bottom of each cake and set them aside to cool.

Reserve half the raspberries for decoration (optional), and sprinkle the remainder with the rosewater.

When the cakes are thoroughly cool, place the large cake, top side down, on a cake board. Spread one third of the whipped cream over the surface of the cake, levelling it and smoothing it with a palette knife. Spread the remaining cream on the top side of one of the two smaller cakes. Sprinkle the raspberries in rosewater over the cream and lay the remaining sponge on top.

Place the cream and raspberry sandwich on top of the larger cake. The cake will now resemble a hat shape. Dust the top of the cake thickly with icing sugar. Tie the ribbon around the cake in a bow. Dot the reserved raspberries around the edge of the base sponge (optional).

To serve *Serve on the cake board, or on a large flat glass plate, and decorate with fresh roses if desired.*

POACHED PEACHES WITH HONEY AND ALMONDS

Peaches or nectarines poached with honey and rosewater make a refreshing summer dessert. Apricots, with their lovely orange-pink blush, can be used instead. Allow three or four per person and don't bother to skin them.

2 tablespoons lavender or orange blossom honey
1 tablespoon rosewater
250ml/8fl oz water
4 large ripe peaches, or 8 smaller ones
2 tablespoons peach liqueur (optional)
1 tablespoon flaked almonds, toasted

Place the honey in a small saucepan with the rosewater and water. Bring the mixture up to boiling point and add the whole peaches (with their skins still on). Simmer the peaches for 5–10 minutes. To test if they are cooked, insert the point of a sharp knife – they should be tender through to the stone.

Remove the saucepan from the heat and leave the peaches to cool in the liquid for 5 minutes. Carefully remove the skin of each peach by rubbing it gently, and if large halve them and remove the stones. Add the peach liqueur, if used, to the syrup, stir well and return the fruit to the syrup. When cool leave in the refrigerator to chill for at least an hour.

To serve *Place the peaches on a large deep serving plate and spoon over the syrup. Scatter the toasted almond flakes over them.*

TISANE FRUIT PUNCH

There is no reason why clear honey cannot be used to sweeten this punch if you wish. Use pink Champagne if you are feeling extravagant, but a dry sparkling white wine will work just as well. Mixed fruit teas, such as apple and blackcurrant or raspberry, make a change from rosehip, but avoid flower tisanes such as camomile.

1·2 litres/2 pints rosehip tea
Caster sugar
Summer fruits, for decoration
Ice cubes
2 bottles sparkling dry white or rosé wine or Champagne

Make the rosehip tea, sweetening to taste with a little caster sugar. Chill thoroughly in the refrigerator. When you are ready to serve the punch remove the rosehip tea from the fridge, pour it into a large punch bowl and throw in lots of ice cubes.

Add summer fruits – fresh raspberries, stoned cherries or sliced strawberries – to the tea, then pour in the thoroughly chilled sparkling wine or Champagne.

To serve *Ladle into glasses, making sure that each glass gets a few fruits.*

TISANE FRUIT PUNCH

TEAS

It needs more care than is often realized to make a good pot of tea. It is essential to make tea with freshly drawn cold water; water that has been sitting for a while has a flat taste. China teapots seem to make a better tea than metal ones.

Scald the teapot with boiling water then put in one teaspoon of tea per person, and one for the pot. Pour boiling water on to the tea and put on the lid. Leave the pot to stand for 2–3 minutes before pouring. Provide milk, lemon and sugar to allow for all tastes.

There are many teas to choose from but here are a few of the most famous:

Darjeeling is grown in the foothills of the Himalayas. There is a fruitiness to this tea, a light Muscat flavour which makes it one of the most popular.

Assam is another Indian tea, this time with a strong mature character.

Lapsang Souchong, a well-known tea, is a large-leaf variety from China. It has a slightly 'tarry' flavour.

Jasmine is a fragrant tea from China. Dried jasmine flowers are mixed with the black or green tea. It is usually drunk without milk or lemon.

Earl Grey is a black tea scented with oil of bergamot and is best drunk alone.

Fireside Coffee Party for 6

I like to think of this party as particularly suited to brightening up chilly autumn and winter days. The colours of the food, the rosy pink smoked salmon, the glowing sweet wine and the dark, aromatic coffee, are a warming sight. The flavours are rich and comforting, especially the dark, nutty chocolate squares and the spicy potted ham.

The toasted muffins and the boozy fruits are all the more enjoyable by a roaring fire. If you have a long-handled fork, the muffins can be toasted by the fire – and the coffee can be kept warm in a jug at the fireside.

Decorate the table with warm tones, rich red tartans and deep brown dried flowers and leaves. Occasionally I am tempted to dress up, and I might suggest that the guests came in Victorian costume, which suits the traditional character of the food.

MENU

*

SMOKED SALMON AND DILL MOUSSE

TOASTED MUFFINS WITH POTTED HAM

*

WINTER FRUITS IN MUSCAT DE BEAUMES-DE VENISE

CHOCOLATE NUT SQUARES

*

Spiced Coffee

TOASTED MUFFINS WITH POTTED HAM, SMOKED SALMON AND DILL MOUSSE, SPICED COFFEE

SMOKED SALMON AND DILL MOUSSE

If time is short, you can omit the covering layer of thinly sliced smoked salmon, and serve the mousse straight from the dish, in large spoonfuls. Either way, serve it with thin slices of crisp brown toast and wedges of lemon or halves of lime.

175g/6oz smoked salmon, thinly sliced
175g/6oz smoked salmon trimmings
225ml/7½fl oz double cream
2 teaspoons finely chopped fresh dill
4 teaspoons gelatine
75ml/3fl oz hot fish stock
2 tablespoons lemon juice
Freshly ground black pepper
Lemon slices and fresh dill, to garnish

Line a 25cm/10in terrine dish with clingfilm or greaseproof paper, leaving enough excess over the edge to fold over when the dish has been filled.

Overlapping each slice as you go to make sure there are no gaps, lay the slices of smoked salmon over the base and up the sides of the terrine, forming a thin lining of fish. Leave enough hanging over the edge of the dish to cover the filling.

Mix the smoked salmon trimmings to a coarse paste in a food processor. Transfer the paste to a large mixing bowl. Softly whip the cream and fold into the smoked salmon. Season with black pepper and blend in the chopped dill.

Dissolve the gelatine in the fish stock, cool and stir into the fish cream with the lemon juice. Pour into the lined terrine, cover with a plate, and place in the refrigerator. Remove the plate after half an hour, and fold over the loose ends of the smoked salmon to cover the mousse filling, then wrap the overhanging clingfilm or greaseproof paper over the salmon. Refrigerate for a further 1½ hours or overnight until set.

To serve *Turn the mousse out on to a large dish. Remove the clingfilm. Garnish with lemon slices and dill.*

TOASTED MUFFINS WITH POTTED HAM

Any cooked ham, such as traditional York or the spicier Bradenham, can be used. It is an original way to use up the end of a ham joint that is no longer suitable for serving in slices.

250g/8oz cooked ham, diced
50g/2oz unsalted butter
1 teaspoon coarse grain mustard
6 juniper berries, crushed
1 tablespoon Worcestershire sauce
50g/2oz butter, melted (optional)
Whole juniper berries and small bay leaves, to garnish
12 English muffins
Butter for spreading

In a food processor, make a thick purée of the ham, unsalted butter, mustard, crushed juniper berries and Worcestershire sauce. Place the mixture in one large pot or 6 individual pots and cover with clingfilm if you are using it the same or the next day, or with a layer of melted butter if you are making it in advance. It will keep for 3 or 4 days in the refrigerator. Before serving garnish the potted ham with whole juniper berries and bay leaves.

To serve *Toast the muffins, spread them with butter, and spread spoonfuls of potted ham on top.*

SMOKED SALMON AND DILL MOUSSE

MUFFINS AND CRUMPETS

There is much confusion over muffins – of which there are two types, English and American – and crumpets, pikelets and Scotch pancakes.

English muffins are soft, white and round, with a light, open texture inside. Made from flour, milk and yeast, they are cooked on a flat 'griddle' giving the traditional golden top and white sides. Nowadays, muffins are often bought ready-cooked. Split them open around the centre and toast them. They are traditionally served at teatime.

American muffins resemble English fairy cakes in shape and texture. Fruit, such as blueberries, and jam or marmalade are often added to the mixture before cooking. They usually appear on the breakfast table, and are eaten warm straight from the oven.

Crumpets, made from batter rather than a dough, are flat and round with a honeycomb texture. Savoury toppings, such as cheese, work better than jam or honey.

Pikelets are similar in texture and flavour to crumpets, but slightly flatter in appearance.

Scotch pancakes are small, flat, golden-brown cakes made by dropping spoonfuls of batter on to a hot griddle. When bought ready-made they are best toasted and served with butter and honey.

WINTER FRUITS IN MUSCAT DE BEAUMES-DE-VENISE

PLANNING AHEAD

This is one of those parties where most of the preparation can successfully be done in advance. All of the principal dishes can be made a day or more before the party, leaving just a few odds and ends to do as the guests appear.

In advance: The chocolate nut squares will keep well in the fridge for up to a week. Store them as a whole cake, wrapped in greaseproof paper and foil, in the lower part of the fridge.

The day before: Make the smoked salmon and dill mousse. Wrap it well, in its dish, in clingfilm and store at the top of the fridge. Make the potted ham and keep it, covered, at the top of the fridge. If you need to make it further in advance, melt some butter and pour it over the top to seal. It should then keep for several days. The night before the party, steep the fruits in the sweet wine.

The day of the party: Cut the chocolate cake into squares and put in paper cases. Mix the Cognac and spices for the coffee and set aside. At the very last minute make the coffee, toast the muffins and the wholemeal toast for the mousse.

WINTER FRUITS IN MUSCAT DE BEAUMES-DE-VENISE

Macerating fruits in wine is one of the simplest of all desserts. In summer, ripe strawberries or peach slices can be put in a glass and topped up with chilled Sauternes. With Muscat de Beaumes-de-Venise, any fruit is suitable, but lychees, figs and fresh dates are particularly good. The contrast between the sweetness of the wine and the tartness of kumquats, limequats and carambola comes as a pleasant surprise.

12 lychees, shells removed
12 kumquats
12 limequats
12 whole satsumas, peeled, pith removed
2 carambola (star fruit), sliced
1 bottle of Muscat de Beaumes-de-Venise (or any other sweet white dessert wine)

Place the lychees, kumquats, limequats, satsumas and carambola in a glass dish. Pour the Muscat de Beaumes-de-Venise over the fruit. Leave in a cool place for at least four hours or preferably overnight.

To serve *Spoon into individual dishes. Use cocktail sticks to spear the fruit.*

CHOCOLATE NUT SQUARES

The better the quality of the chocolate you use, the richer the flavour of the finished cake will be. You may also find that cheap chocolate, because of its high sugar and low cocoa butter content, is difficult to melt. Use walnuts or pecan nuts instead of brazils if you prefer, and substitute stoned dates for the large raisins if you have some.

50g/2oz shelled hazelnuts
50g/2oz shelled almonds
50g/2oz shelled brazil nuts
175g/6oz plain chocolate
100g/3½oz unsalted butter
1 egg
50g/2oz large raisins

Line a 15cm/6in square cake tin with greaseproof paper. Spread the nuts on a baking sheet or grill pan and toast under a hot grill until the skins start to blister. Rub the nuts with a cloth, discard any of the skins which have flaked off and return the nuts to the grill to toast until they are golden brown. Allow to cool then chop coarsely or leave whole as required.

Melt 125g/4oz of the chocolate and all the butter together in a heavy-based saucepan over a low heat. Remove the chocolate from the heat when completely melted and stir in 125g/4oz of the toasted nuts, keeping the remaining nuts on one side. Beat the egg lightly with a fork and add to the chocolate and nuts along with the raisins. Spoon the mixture into the lined cake tin and leave to set in the fridge for 4 hours, or preferably overnight.

When completely set, remove from the tin and peel off the paper. Melt the remaining chocolate in a basin over simmering water. Pour the chocolate over the cake, sprinkle over the remaining nuts, and return to the fridge for 10 minutes until set.

To serve *With a large heavy knife, cut the cake into small squares. Place in paper cases on a serving plate.*

SPICED COFFEE

A ground coffee, medium or high roast, is best for this warming winter drink. Try to allow ten minutes to infuse the spices and aromatics with the cognac to give the flavours time to blend.

12 sugar cubes
Rind of 2 small oranges
3 short strips lemon rind
2 cinnamon sticks
6 cloves
6 tablespoons Cognac
1 vanilla pod
750ml/1¼ pints hot black coffee
Sugar and 6 cinnamon sticks, to serve (optional)

Mix the sugar, orange and lemon rinds, 2 cinnamon sticks and cloves in a stainless-steel pan. Pour on the Cognac and add the vanilla pod. Leave to infuse for 10 minutes. Heat the pan gently and ignite the Cognac. Pour on the coffee and stir.

To serve *Strain into mugs or glasses. Stir with cinnamon sticks.*

PRESENTATION

There is nothing to beat a crisp white cloth on a table, it so flatters the food. You can, though, take advantage of the colours in this menu to use a rich, dark wooden surface such as a polished table. The shining wood reflects the flames from the fire and looks particularly welcoming.

Candles are a must here – creamy white ones look elegant without being fussy. Ribbon is a cheerful accessory and cheap enough to throw around generously. Look out for tartan ribbon, or a deep, wine-red colour; scatter it over the table, wrap it round the candlesticks, and use it to tie up little bundles of cocktail sticks that guests can use to spear pieces of wine-soaked fruit.

Make a centrepiece for the table by filling a dark wicker basket or garden trug with fircones, sprays of rosehips, hawthorns and teasels. Twigs with crisp leaves and dried thistles make economical table decorations and they, too, look good tied up with some more of that bright tartan ribbon.

Glass will reflect the colours of the fruits and the Muscat wine. If you don't have a large dish then put single portions of the fruits in individual glasses, crystal if you have them.

Provide a sharp knife to cut the salmon mousse and some butter for the muffins.

Pop the toaster, with a mat underneath, on the table so that your guests can help themselves to muffins as they want them.

WINTER FRUITS IN MUSCAT DE BEAUMES-DE-VENISE, CHOCOLATE NUT SQUARES

FRANCES BISSELL

Dinner Parties

I think more people would give dinner parties if they had another name. 'Dinner party' sounds so formal, conjuring up visions of heavy damask, cut crystal glasses and a fine china dinner service, not to mention exquisitely arranged flowers, an immaculately coiffed hostess and a jovial host. Well, dinner parties are not like that in our house. My 'dinner service' consists of mixed white plates, some black glass octagonal bowls and a large bowl for pasta or salad, glass plates for individual salads or fruit desserts and glass bowls for sorbets. Cutlery is similarly assorted. Yet somehow it all works together, whatever the style of meal, whether modern 'plate' service, where each dish is arranged in the kitchen, or family style where guests help themselves from dishes placed on the table.

There is no fixed number of courses for a dinner party. Four or five smallish courses, including cheese and salad, is the pattern of most of my meals. You do not have to 'cook' every course either. A platter of cold cuts, *crudités* or smoked fish all make excellent starters. And perfectly ripe, fragrant luscious fruit in season is one of the best desserts you can serve.

A dinner party does not have to be expensive. Inexpensive ingredients can be made into tasty dishes with a little care and imagination. As with any meal it is important to achieve balance and harmony of taste, colour, temperature and texture. Contrast soft-textured dishes with a crisp, crunchy salad before or after. Plan the meal to include some hot and some cold dishes. This is much easier on the cook too.

Think about what wines you want to serve and leave yourself enough time to chill them sufficiently, or to bring them to room temperature. Above all, serve the wines that you like, no matter what the rule books tell you. My suggestions are based on wines that we have enjoyed with the food I describe. That is what a dinner party is about, enjoyment and pleasure, for the cook as well as the guests.

Opposite **SPRING DINNER PARTY** *PAGE 86*

Italian Dinner Party for 8

I need very little excuse to cook Italian dishes and most of our friends like to eat them, so a dinner party with an Italian flavour is certain to be a great success.

Pasta is one of our favourite dishes but when I want to cook something really special, I make risotto, a lovely creamy rice dish, cooked in a well-flavoured stock. What you put in a risotto is up to you, but simple, inexpensive vegetables or herbs, rather than meat or shellfish, work best. I usually follow the risotto with a fish or a meat dish, and if I want it to be a lengthy, elaborate meal then I might serve both. But an Italian meal is not an expensive meal: it depends on fresh flavours and ingredients, simply cooked and served.

There are lots of marvellous Italian wines. The light, elegant and bubbly Prosecco is well worth tracking down. Follow it with the cherry-red fruity Dolcetto from Alba. With its slight dry hint of almonds, it is a perfect foil to the pale, rich pork dish. And for pudding a sweet wine made from the luscious Moscato grape. Moscato Naturale is low in alcohol.

Menu

*

TOMATO AND BASIL RISOTTO

MILK ROAST PORK WITH GARLIC AND FENNEL SAUCE

or

FISH PARCELS BAKED WITH MINT AND ORANGE

*

APRICOTS IN VANILLA SYRUP

ALMOND DIPPING BISCUITS

*

Prosecco *or* Chardonnay dell' Alto Adige

Dolcetto d'Alba *or* Frascati

Moscato Naturale *or* Marsala

MILK ROAST PORK WITH GARLIC AND FENNEL SAUCE, GREEN BEANS

TOMATO AND BASIL RISOTTO

Risotto is such a delicious dish that it is worth leaving your guests for the half hour or so that it takes to make.

3 shallots or 1 onion, peeled and chopped
2 tablespoons olive oil
500g/1lb risotto rice, such as arborio
1·2–1·6 litres/2–2½ pints chicken or vegetable stock, boiling
½ bottle Prosecco wine
375g/12oz firm ripe tomatoes, peeled, deseeded and chopped
50g/2oz fresh basil, shredded
50g/2oz butter
50–75g/2–3oz freshly grated Parmesan cheese
Salt and pepper

Gently fry the shallots or onions in the olive oil until wilted. Do not let them brown. Stir in the rice until it is well coated with oil. Pour on about 150ml/¼ pint of the stock and stir until it has been absorbed. Add a similar quantity and stir until it too has been absorbed. Continue to add stock gradually, stirring continuously. Meanwhile, heat the wine and add it alternately with the stock, leaving one-third of the liquid to add at the end.

After about 30 minutes, the rice will be getting tender. Don't overcook it, but it should have a nice creamy consistency. Stir in the tomatoes, season to taste and add the rest of the wine. Let it be absorbed, then stir in more stock if necessary.

To finish the risotto, stir in the basil, butter and Parmesan. Serve immediately.

MILK ROAST PORK WITH GARLIC AND FENNEL SAUCE

This simple rustic dish will look after itself once you put it in the oven. And yes, I do mean three heads and not three cloves of garlic! When cooked slowly for a long time, the garlic loses its pungency becoming mild and creamy. This dish does not produce crackling because the pork is pot-roasted.

1·5–1·7kg/3–3½lb boned loin of pork
3 heads garlic, peeled
1 fennel bulb, trimmed and sliced
1 onion, peeled and sliced
12 allspice berries
1 cinnamon stick
1·2 litres/2 pints milk
Salt and pepper

Remove the skin from the pork, and most of the fat under the skin. Tie the pork at intervals into a neat roll. Fry the meat all over to brown it on the outside. Scatter half the vegetables in the bottom of a lidded flameproof casserole that is just big enough to hold the meat, vegetables and liquid. Put in the allspice and cinnamon and lay the pork on top. Pack the rest of the vegetables over and around the pork. Bring the milk to the boil, pour it over the pork, cover and place in the centre of a slowish oven, 170°C, 325°F, Gas Mark 3, and bake for 2 hours or until the meat juices run clear when a skewer is inserted into the centre of the joint. Remove the meat from the casserole and keep it warm while you prepare the sauce. Boil the remaining liquid to reduce it then pour the liquid and vegetables into a sieve. Rub through, to make a thick, flavoursome purée-like sauce, discarding the cinnamon and allspice as you work the mixture through.

To serve *Slice the pork and serve with the sauce and a fresh green vegetable such as spinach, broccoli or green beans.*

TOMATO AND BASIL RISOTTO

EXTRAS

Before the meal you might like to serve a platter or basket of raw vegetables with a dip. One of my favourite dips is also one of the easiest to prepare. All you do is pour some sea salt into a small bowl, and into another pour some extra virgin olive oil, the vegetables are dipped into the oil, then the salt.

Crisp breadsticks will also be very good to eat with that first glass of Prosecco, as will a few olives.

A crisp green vegetable will provide the best contrast with the pork. Choose whatever looks the freshest, broccoli, green beans or mangetout. Savoy cabbage is also extremely good with this particular pork dish.

For salad try some of the red lettuces and chicories whose agreeable bitterness will follow the smooth, succulent pork dish very well. Look for lollo rosso, feuille de chêne and radicchio.

You may want to stay with the Italian theme and choose a creamy Taleggio or Fontina, or a blue cheese such as Dolcelatte or Gorgonzola for the cheese board. With it serve some crusty farmhouse-style bread instead of biscuits. In fact, I would be inclined to have a basket of such bread on the table throughout the meal for mopping up sauces and salad dressings.

Have sea salt and a mill of black peppercorns on the table, and plenty of mineral water in the fridge.

FISH PARCELS BAKED WITH MINT AND ORANGE

The Roman gourmet, Apicius, recommended using mint with fish and it is truly an excellent combination.

4 large plaice or Dover sole, filleted and skinned
4 tablespoons dry vermouth
Finely grated rind of 1 orange
Juice of 1 orange
1–2 tablespoons extra virgin olive oil or hazelnut oil
8 sprigs fresh mint
25g/1oz butter, melted, or 2 tablespoons olive oil
Salt and pepper
Orange slices, to garnish (optional)

Cut 8 large heart-shaped pieces of greaseproof paper. Cut each fillet in two lengthways so that you have 16 pieces. Mix together the vermouth, orange rind and juice and oil. Remove the mint tips for garnish; chop the rest finely and mix with the vermouth and oil. Brush this over the fillets, on both sides, and roll them up.

Paint the paper hearts with butter or oil and place two rolled fillets together on one side of each heart. Fold over the other side of the paper as if you were making a pastry turn-over so that the edges meet and fold them over once, and once again, twisting the paper slightly each time to crimp it so that the parcel is well sealed. Put the parcels on a baking sheet so they are not touching and bake in a preheated oven, 180°C, 350°F, Gas Mark 4, for 12–15 minutes, or 5 minutes longer if they have been refrigerated.

To serve *Serve the parcels on heated plates, garnished with mint sprigs and a few twists of orange if liked.*

PLANNING AHEAD

Two days before: Bake the almond biscuits and store in an airtight container.

The day of the party: Prepare the fish parcels and the apricots in vanilla syrup earlier in the day (up to 8 hours in advance) and refrigerate.

Start cooking the pork $2\frac{1}{2}$ hours before required.

By accident I discovered that it is, just, possible to do the first cooking of the risotto in advance which can be useful if you don't want to leave your guests too long. An hour or so before eating sweat the vegetables, stir in the rice and add the first then the second 150ml/$\frac{1}{4}$ pint of liquid before leaving it. After that cook it continuously, using boiling liquid. This method will not find favour with the purists.

PRESENTATION

There is a simplicity about Italian dining that I like very much. Each course is served separately and is on usually a single dish, unadorned with vegetables or potatoes, or indeed much garnish of any kind. I would echo this simplicity in the table setting.

It is important for the risotto to be served in well-heated soup plates, so do make sure that your china is heatproof up to a certain point.

The pork, when it is cooked, is not a particularly picturesque joint and I would therefore carve it in the kitchen and arrange the slices on a platter with some of the sauce to keep the meat moist. Serve the rest of the sauce separately.

FISH PARCELS BAKED WITH MINT AND ORANGE

APRICOTS IN VANILLA SYRUP

When fresh apricots are unavailable you can poach whole dried apricots in apple juice with a vanilla pod and honey and then let them soak up the syrup for a day or two. Alternatively, use fresh peaches or nectarines. Skinning by dunking in boiling water is easier than peeling, but it cooks the outer layer of the fruit and you lose the lovely fresh flavour.

2 tablespoons clear honey
900ml/1½ pints clear apple juice
1 vanilla pod
20 fresh ripe but firm apricots

Mix the honey and apple juice and bring to the boil with the vanilla pod. Boil for 5 minutes, then allow to go cold. Split the pod, scrape out the vanilla seeds and stir them into the syrup.

Peel the apricots with a very sharp knife, halve them and discard the stones. Place the fruit in a large glass bowl or individual glass dishes. Pour the syrup over the apricots, cover and leave them for 2–3 hours in the refrigerator.

ALMOND DIPPING BISCUITS

These are very brittle, hard biscuits, indeed another name for them is 'dead men's bones'. For an even simpler dessert serve them as they do in Tuscany as *cantuccini Vin Santo*. Vin Santo is a sweet raisiny wine in which you dip the crunchy *cantuccini* before eating them.

200g/7oz unblanched almonds
150g/5oz granulated sugar
125g/4oz plain flour
1 teaspoon baking powder
40g/1½oz butter, melted
1 egg, lightly beaten
1 egg yolk
4 tablespoons milk

Spread the almonds on a baking sheet and toast in a preheated oven, 190°C, 375°F, Gas Mark 5, for 7–10 minutes until pale golden. Stir occasionally to prevent burning. Grind a quarter of them with a quarter of the sugar and put in a large bowl. Stir in the rest of the sugar and the dry ingredients. Coarsely chop half the remaining almonds, leave the rest whole and add all of them to the bowl. Stir in the melted butter and beaten whole egg and knead lightly until all the ingredients are thoroughly combined.

Divide the dough into 2, and using your hands, roll out each piece like a log. Flatten, again with your hands, to about 2cm/¾in thick. Transfer the dough using two spatulas or palette knives to a buttered, floured baking sheet, leaving room for the mixture to spread. Beat the egg yolk with the milk and brush the biscuits with the glaze. Bake in the top half of a preheated oven, 190°C, 375°F, Gas Mark 5, for 20–25 minutes until golden brown and a warmed skewer inserted into the centre comes out clean.

Cut into diagonal slices about 2cm/¾in wide. Switch off the oven and put the biscuits back for about 15 minutes, to dry off thoroughly. Transfer the biscuits to a rack and allow them to cool completely. Store in an airtight container.

Oz Clarke's *WINE NOTES*

By deciding to drink Prosecco Frances has put her finger on one of the best bargains in sparkling wine today. Or should I say frothing wine, because Prosecco froths, rather than explodes with a raging spume. The Italians don't need any celebratory excuse for drinking fizz. It's a café drink, an end of the day drink, a picnic drink or just a having a drink drink. Since this is a dinner party, I'll have several bottles of this chilled right down as cold as you dare, to offer my guests as soon as they arrive.

With the risotto, I'll go for a fresh Chardonnay from northern Italy, either the Tyrolean Alto Adige or Friuli, because the soft young Chardonnay fruit does seem to complement the creaminess of risotto particularly well, and the citrus and mint flavour of the fish course will either bring out the lemon and apple fruit of Chardonnay or accentuate the nutty fatness of a really good Frascati.

Much as I love Dolcetto, I'm in a white wine mood with the pork in such a creamy sauce, so I'll stick to Frascati. And with the apricots in that vanilla syrup I'll have the rich, smoky flavours of a good Marsala from western Sicily.

APRICOTS IN VANILLA SYRUP, ALMOND DIPPING BISCUITS

Vegetarian Dinner Party for 6

*F*or me a balanced diet means that some meals during the week will include neither fish nor meat. From there it is a small step to create meals that are suitable for vegetarian friends. However one does need to be particularly aware of ingredients. I was about to put Worcester sauce in the dressing for the four-bean salad before being reminded that it contains anchovies.

Cheese can sometimes be a problem too since many vegetarians are not prepared to eat cheeses which are made with rennet, a coagulating agent extracted from the stomach lining of a calf or lamb. Non-rennet 'vegetarian' cheeses should be substituted.

An alternative way of serving this menu would be to offer slices of tomato tart with pre-dinner drinks, and an extra bottle of the Pinot Gris, perhaps. This crisp fragrant white wine from the Alsace region of France is one of our favourites, and one that we find goes particularly well with vegetables.

There's lots of gulpable fruitiness in the red wine too. Red wines from the Loire Valley, such as the Chinon and Saumur are delightful served in summer slightly chilled to enhance that rich raspberryish quality.

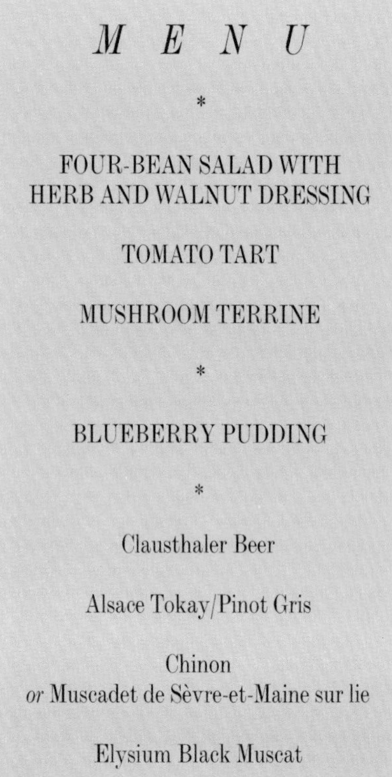

MENU

*

FOUR-BEAN SALAD WITH HERB AND WALNUT DRESSING

TOMATO TART

MUSHROOM TERRINE

*

BLUEBERRY PUDDING

*

Clausthaler Beer

Alsace Tokay/Pinot Gris

Chinon
or Muscadet de Sèvre-et-Maine sur lie

Elysium Black Muscat

FOUR-BEAN SALAD WITH HERB AND WALNUT DRESSING, TOMATO TART

FOUR-BEAN SALAD WITH HERB AND WALNUT DRESSING

A mixture of fresh and dried beans makes a substantial tasty salad. You could substitute chick peas and fresh peas for some beans.

250g/8oz fresh runner beans
250g/8oz dwarf green beans
425g/14oz can flageolet beans or 250g/8oz dried flageolet beans, soaked and cooked
425g/14oz can haricot beans or 250g/8oz dried haricot beans, soaked and cooked
2 shallots, peeled and chopped
3 cloves garlic, peeled and crushed
125g/4oz walnuts, roughly chopped
75ml/3fl oz walnut oil
2 tablespoons sherry vinegar or balsamic vinegar
2 dashes Angostura bitters
¼ teaspoon tomato purée
Dash of soy sauce
2 tablespoons finely chopped herbs
Salt and pepper
Radicchio leaves, to serve

Top and tail the fresh beans and cook until just tender. Break them into bite-sized pieces. Drain and rinse the canned beans and put all the beans in a large bowl. Mix in the shallots, garlic and walnuts.

To make the dressing, mix the rest of the ingredients, season with salt and pepper and pour over the beans. Stir thoroughly to make sure the salad is well coated. Serve in a large bowl lined with radicchio leaves, which provide an excellent contrast to the pale green and white of the beans.

TOMATO TART

Fresh, sweet, ripe tomatoes, baked in the oven with garlic and olive oil, give off one of the most appetizing smells imaginable. A more elaborate tart can be made with courgettes and aubergines.

Dough:
150ml/¼ pint skimmed milk
1 teaspoon dried yeast
250g/8oz strong plain flour
¼ teaspoon salt
Extra flour for kneading

Filling:
75ml/3fl oz extra virgin olive oil
6 cloves garlic, peeled and thinly sliced (optional)
750g/1½lb firm ripe tomatoes, sliced
Finely chopped parsley (optional)
Salt and pepper

Heat the milk for the dough to blood heat, pour into a bowl and sprinkle on the dried yeast. Allow it to work for 15 minutes. Sift the flour and the salt together, pour on the yeasty liquid and mix thoroughly. Once a mass is formed, turn out on to a floured work surface and knead until smooth. Put the dough in an oiled bowl covered with a clean damp tea-towel and let it rise for a couple of hours.

When the dough has risen sufficiently, knock it back and knead it once more. Again working on a floured work surface, roll and stretch it to fit an oiled shallow tart tin about 25–30cm/10–12in diameter, pressing the dough up the sides as well to form a wall. Brush the dough all over with olive oil and scatter slices of garlic on the bottom if using it. Arrange the tomato slices on top in overlapping circles and brush with the remaining oil. Lightly season with salt and pepper, cover and let the dough prove once more for about 45 minutes. Bake in the top half of a preheated oven, 200°C, 400°F, Gas Mark 6, for 20–25 minutes.

To serve *This tastes best warm or just cold but not refrigerated.*

EXTRAS

Fortunately for vegetarians there are now many more cheeses being made with vegetarian 'rennet', including some Cheddars, and some blue cheeses as well as goats' milk cheese and ewes' milk cheese. I would serve two or three such cheeses with this meal, perhaps one hard, one blue and one soft cheese.

With no potatoes, rice or pasta in this meal, there is a place for a basket of crisp, fresh bread rolls. Depending on the time of year, I would also serve a bowl of mixed nuts and tangerines or a bowl of fresh or 'wet' walnuts with some Muscat grapes. If you cook this meal in summer, you might serve a bowl of ripe cherries with some fresh Ricotta cheese.

A salt cellar filled with sea salt and a pepper mill for freshly ground black pepper would be a good idea for those who might like extra seasoning on the salad and tomato tart.

PLANNING AHEAD

In advance: If you like you can make the pancakes for the mushroom terrine in advance. Layer them with greaseproof paper and freeze or keep in the refrigerator for up to 3 days. Make the blueberry pudding at least one day before required –it *can* be made 2–3 days ahead.

The day before: If you are using dried beans for the salad, put them to soak the night before.

The day of the party: Make the mushroom terrine in the morning and refrigerate when cool. Take out of the refrigerator 30 minutes before serving. Make the dough for the tomato tart several hours ahead, cover and refrigerate for its first proving. Cook the soaked dried beans. Assemble the bean salad. Finish the tomato tart.

MUSHROOM TERRINE

PRESENTATION

For a long time, vegetarian food and meals were associated with tweedy homespun rusticity; brown food in brown pots served on wooden tables. In fact, vegetarian food can look as light, delicate and attractive as any other sort of food and it certainly can stand glamorous, even elegant treatment.

A crisp, white linen or damask cloth with thin, clear glassware are what I would choose to show these dishes and wines off beautifully.

The rich purply reds of the blueberry pudding look absolutely jewel-like on glass plates.

MUSHROOM TERRINE

Sliced terrines look very impressive with their different-coloured layers and this one is not at all difficult to make. Your meat-eating friends would be delighted to be served it as a starter, I'm sure.

Batter:
125g/4oz plain flour
2 eggs, lightly beaten
300ml/½ pint milk
Pinch of salt

Filling:
8 baby leeks
250g/8oz button mushrooms
150g/5oz oyster mushrooms
150g/5oz shiitake or open-cap mushrooms
3 tablespoons olive oil
3 firm ripe tomatoes, peeled, deseeded and diced
4 eggs
300ml/½ pint milk
1 teaspoon finely chopped fresh tarragon (optional)
1 tablespoon finely chopped fresh parsley
Salt
Pepper

Mix together the flour, eggs, milk and salt to form a smooth batter. Let it stand for about 40 minutes, then make eight 20cm/8in thin pancakes. Use 7 of them to line a well-oiled 1kg/2lb loaf tin, letting them overhang the edges and keeping back one pancake to cover the terrine.

Trim and thoroughly wash the leeks. Lay them in a frying pan, pour boiling water over them and boil until just tender. Drain, rinse under cold water, pat dry and put to one side. Trim the mushrooms and wipe them. Fry them separately in the olive oil for 2–3 minutes until slightly softened and coloured. Place half the button mushrooms in the bottom of the terrine, some tomato dice on top, then the shiitake or open-cap mushrooms, the leeks, the oyster mushrooms, more tomato dice, then the remaining button mushrooms.

Beat the eggs and milk together and stir in the herbs and seasoning. Gently pour the mixture over the vegetables. Fold the overlapping pancakes over the top using the last one to cover it completely. Cover with buttered foil and stand in a deep roasting tin. Pour boiling water into the tin to come halfway up the sides of the loaf tin. Bake in a preheated oven, 160°C, 325°F, Gas Mark 3, just below the centre of the oven, for 50–60 minutes. When done, a knife point or warmed skewer inserted into the centre will come out clean.

Allow the terrine to rest, in a cool place but not the refrigerator, for 30–60 minutes before serving

To serve *A homemade tomato sauce, leek sauce, watercress sauce or garlic sauce are all delicious with the mushroom terrine.*

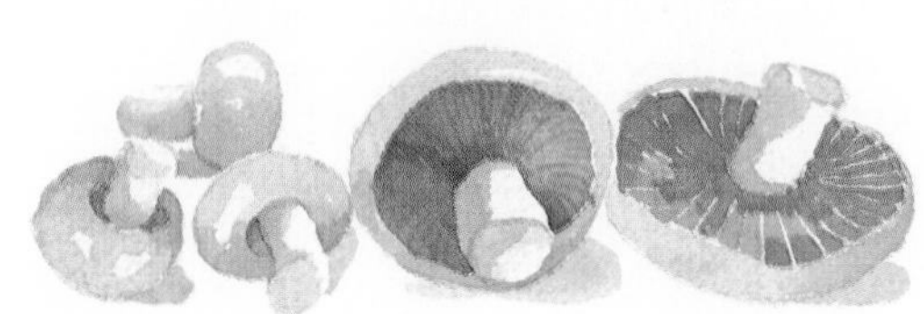

BLUEBERRY PUDDING

This is our old friend the summer pudding with a different filling. The filling can be varied with the seasons: soft berry fruits in the summer, apples and blackberries in the autumn, and in the winter months you can use up fruit you have carefully stored in the freezer.

1kg/2lb blueberries
125g/4oz sugar
2 tablespoons lemon juice
150ml/$\frac{1}{4}$ pint water
3 tablespoons crème de cassis
8–10 slices crustless bread
Clotted cream, crème fraîche, fromage frais, natural yogurt, double cream or whipped cream, to serve

Put the berries in a saucepan with the sugar, lemon juice, water and *crème de cassis*. Heat until the sugar has dissolved and then cook until the juices run.

Cut a circle of bread to line the base of a 1·2 litre/2 pint pudding basin and then cut the rest of the slices each into wedge-shaped pieces and use them to line the sides of the basin.

Spoon in the fruit, holding back some of the juice. Cut more bread to fit the top of the pudding and press this well down. Spoon on more juice then cover the pudding with clingfilm and a saucer weighted down with a heavy can. Refrigerate overnight. Turn out on to a plate and pour over any remaining juice.

Top **BLUEBERRY PUDDING**

Oz Clarke's *WINE NOTES*

One of the encouraging things about how our eating habits have changed in the last few years is the way that cooks have made a genuine effort to break vegetarian food out of the nut cutlet and brown rice straitjacket which used to mean that when you genuinely didn't want to eat meat – or fish for that matter – you had almost no chance of finding an enjoyable as well as a healthy meal.

Three ingredients in particular help create the variety of textures which make such food interesting and also give the depth of savoury flavour which makes your mouth water in anticipation of the next forkful. Fresh and dried pulses can go from being as soft and floury as overcooked potato through the full spectrum of sensation to the crisp crunchiness of stir-fried mangetout.

Mushrooms, in all their fabulous variety, provide splendidly deep, penetrating savoury flavours. And ripe tomatoes, raw, lightly cooked or stewed to within an inch of their life give a wonderful intensity of sweetness and acidity.

Despite this, the wines which go best are relatively simple ones. Frances has gone for the lushness of Tokay/Pinot Gris and the crisp juiciness of a red Chinon. I've decided to rely upon the light creamy texture streaked with lemon that you get in a really good Muscadet bottled straight off its yeasty lees (look for *sur lie* on the label). I've also included a Clausthaler non-alcoholic beer because it actually tastes *real*, allowing the non-drinkers to enjoy their non-intoxicating brews for once.

And I wholeheartedly agree with the choice of Elysium: tasting of rosehip syrup and sloes and treacly grapes, it is sheer delight with blueberries, a match rather than a contrast.

Spring Dinner Party *for 6*

This is the kind of dinner I would serve around Easter time, or perhaps on a weekend in early May. Certainly the lamb and the eggs give it an Easter theme. At this time of year I like to include plenty of spring vegetables in my meals, even to the extent of serving them in two courses before the main course. These are especially good served freshly cooked and still warm.

The fresh sharp flavour of rhubarb is a springtime thing too, either in a simple rhubarb fool or, as here, in a more elaborate tart flavoured with ginger.

The sappy vigour of a Sauvignon Blanc from Touraine or from New Zealand makes for a perfect springtime wine. I love its herbaceous character which reminds me of the smell of flowering currant bushes as you brush past them. With the lamb, back to the classics and a wine from Bordeaux – a *cru bourgeois* from a good year such as 1982 or a grander name from a lesser vintage such as 1987. I would stay in Bordeaux for the sweet wine, too, and choose a Monbazillac or Loupiac, light and full of luscious sweet fruit.

MENU

*

ASPARAGUS AND QUAIL EGGS

COURGETTE AND SKATE SALAD WITH TOMATO VINAIGRETTE

ROAST RACK OF LAMB WITH A HERB AND MUSTARD CRUST

CREAMY DAUPHINOISE POTATOES

*

RHUBARB AND GINGER TART

*

Sauvignon de Touraine *or* Sancerre
Cru Bourgeois Claret *or* Coonawarra Cabernet Sauvignon
Loupiac *or* Australian Liqueur Muscat

ROAST RACK OF LAMB WITH A HERB AND MUSTARD CRUST, CREAMY DAUPHINOISE POTATOES

ASPARAGUS AND QUAIL EGGS

This is a quick and easy alternative to the skate salad or could be an additional course served before it. However, it is only quick and easy if you serve the eggs in their shell and let your guests deal with them themselves. If you have ever tried to shell a dozen and a half quail eggs for a warm salad you will understand why.

500–750g/1–1½lb asparagus
18 quail eggs
Fingers of buttered brown bread or toast, to serve

Trim the asparagus so that just 12–15cm/5–6in of tender green tip remains. Boil or steam until just tender. Meanwhile boil the quail eggs for 2 minutes.

Drain the asparagus and arrange a few on each plate. Drain the eggs and put 3 on each plate with bread or toast fingers. Everyone shells their own eggs, or breaks them open to dip the asparagus into the yolk.

COURGETTE AND SKATE SALAD WITH TOMATO VINAIGRETTE

Skate is one of my favourite fish, with a firm sweet flesh. Because it has no tiresome small bones and, when cooked, comes away from its web of cartilage very readily, it is easy to handle and lends itself perfectly to recipes such as this.

1kg/2lb skate wings
150ml/¼ pint white wine
10 black peppercorns
2 teaspoons sea salt
6 sprigs parsley
500g/1lb courgettes
1 firm ripe tomato, skinned, deseeded and diced, to garnish

Dressing:
250g/8oz ripe tomatoes, chopped roughly
6–8 tablespoons extra virgin olive oil
2 tablespoons finely chopped parsley
2 or 3 cloves garlic, peeled and crushed
Salt and pepper

Put the skate wings in a large, deep frying pan or roasting tin. Pour on the white wine and enough water to cover the fish. Add the peppercorns, sea salt and parsley sprigs. Bring slowly to the boil, let the liquid bubble for about 2 minutes then remove the pan from the heat. The fish will continue to cook in the very hot water.

Top and tail the courgettes and slice very thinly, or shave into strips with a potato peeler. Blanch the courgettes in boiling water for 1 minute.

To make the dressing, rub the ripe tomatoes through a sieve. Whisk in the olive oil and season with salt and pepper to taste. Stir in the parsley and garlic.

Carefully remove the skate from the cooking liquid. Peel off and discard the skin. Carefully remove the shreds of skate and arrange in a pile on individual plates. Place the courgettes around the fish and pour the dressing over both. Garnish with the tomato and serve immediately.

ASPARAGUS AND QUAIL EGGS, COURGETTE AND SKATE SALAD WITH TOMATO VINAIGRETTE

EXTRAS

Depending on what is available, a green vegetable goes well with the lamb – perhaps spring greens or cabbage which can be shredded and cooked quickly, either by stir-frying or steaming.

A selection of goats' milk cheeses would suit this meal. Select them in various stages of ripeness, from fresh, mild and soft, to firm, dry and tangy.

If you have time make some plaited saffron bread rolls to serve with the meal. The dough recipe for the tomato tart on page 83 is a standard recipe and that quantity will make six bread rolls. To make more, simply double or triple all the ingredients. It will not need any extra proving or rising time. For a saffron bread, put a pinch of saffron threads in a tea cup and pour on 3 tablespoons of boiling water. Let it steep for 20–30 minutes and then mix it in with the yeasty liquid.

I do not like mint sauce with lamb, nor most mint jellies. I prefer to serve a homemade redcurrant or other sharp fruit jelly that acts as a better foil for the rich lamb than does the vinegar in mint sauce.

Sugared almonds are very good served with the coffee instead of truffles.

ROAST RACK OF LAMB WITH A HERB AND MUSTARD CRUST

Although the meat is trimmed of much of its fat, a protective layer is formed by the herb and mustard crust and this keeps the meat moist and imparts some of its subtle flavours to the meat. Lavender with roast lamb is as nice a combination as lamb and rosemary.

3 racks of lamb (best end), with 6 or 7 chops on each
1 tablespoon finely chopped rosemary or lavender flowers (optional)
1 teaspoon finely chopped thyme
125g/4oz fresh white breadcrumbs
3 tablespoons olive oil
3 tablespoons powdered mustard
9 cloves garlic, peeled
2 tablespoons lemon juice
6 sprigs rosemary or lavender
Salt and pepper

Trim the meat of its skin and most of the fat. Mix the chopped herbs, breadcrumbs, olive oil, mustard, 6 of the garlic cloves, crushed, lemon juice and some salt and pepper and spread this paste over the smooth surface of the joints.

Slice and sliver the remaining 3 garlic cloves and insert the slivers at various points in the meat between the bones and the flesh. Place the herb sprigs on a rack in a roasting tin and lay the meat on top. Roast in a preheated oven, 200°C, 400°F, Gas Mark 6, for 25–35 minutes depending on whether you like the meat pink or well done.

To serve *Divide each rack into cutlets and serve 3 or 4 per person with creamy dauphinoise potatoes.*
SEE PAGE 86.

CREAMY DAUPHINOISE POTATOES

This classic recipe from France is a perfect accompaniment to roast meats. Variations on the theme can be created by adding chopped parsley and thinly sliced onion, and replacing the cream and egg mixture with meat stock. The cheese can be omitted if you prefer.

500ml/17fl oz milk or use half milk and half single cream
750g/1½lb potatoes
Freshly grated nutmeg
1 egg
50g/2oz butter
1 clove garlic, peeled
125g/4oz freshly grated Gruyère cheese
Salt and pepper

Scald the milk and then let it cool. Peel the potatoes and slice them to the thickness of a 50p piece or slightly more. Season the potato slices with salt, pepper and nutmeg. Beat the egg and milk together.

Using half the butter grease an ovenproof dish. Rub over with a clove of garlic and layer the potatoes in it. Sprinkle three quarters of the grated cheese over the potatoes and strain the egg and milk mixture over them. Scatter the rest of the cheese on top and bake in a preheated oven, 180°C, 350°F, Gas Mark 4, for 20 minutes. Then turn the oven up to 200°C, 400°F, Gas Mark 6, and move the potatoes to the bottom half of the oven while you put the lamb in; continue cooking for 25–30 minutes.
SEE PAGE 86.

PLANNING AHEAD

The day before: Prepare the lamb for roasting. Trim it. Make the mustard mixture, spread it on and spike the lamb with garlic. Closely cover with clingfilm to hold in place and then refrigerate. The tomato vinaigrette for the skate salad can be made in advance. Everything else for the starters tastes much better if freshly cooked.

The day of the party: Poach the rhubarb and make the syrup and the pastry cases in the morning. Assemble the tarts an hour or two before you sit down for the first course.

Prepare the potatoes just before putting them into the oven (a little under an hour before serving). Put the lamb in the oven 20 minutes later. In the meantime prepare the skate salad.

Any other green vegetables you intend to serve with the lamb should be cooked just in time to serve.

PRESENTATION

A roast served at the table is the centrepiece of probably the most formal and traditional meal that I cook. Since a rack of lamb is easy to carve, serve the whole thing and carve it at the table. Serve the potatoes and vegetables from bowls in the centre of the table on to the main plate or on to side plates as you prefer. I prefer to use the main plate.

The salads look best if they are arranged on individual plates and for six people this does not take long to do in the kitchen. This is one of the few occasions when I can bring out my Edwardian asparagus tongs, designed for those elegant days when ladies used to dine in gloves and would not want to soil them by eating asparagus in their fingers.

Perhaps for this meal I would also bring out the antique table cloth and napkins, the best glasses and even a candelabra. And, of course, whatever fragrant spring flowers I could find.

RHUBARB AND GINGER TART

The ginger-flavoured pastry echoes the ginger in the filling. If you want to fill a pastry case with a soft, moist filling, brush the tart with melted chocolate first to provide a seal keeping the pastry crisp.

Pastry:
40g/1½oz icing sugar
175g/6oz plain flour
1½ teaspoons ground ginger
Pinch of salt
50g/2oz full-fat soft cheese
40g/1½ unsalted butter
Iced water, to mix

Filling:
1kg/2lb rhubarb
50–75g/2–3oz light muscovado sugar or to taste
125g/4oz white chocolate
1 heaped tablespoon finely chopped stem ginger
3–4 tablespoons stem ginger syrup
450ml/¾ pint thick Greek yogurt or whipped double cream

To make the pastry, sift the icing sugar, flour, ground ginger and salt into a mixing bowl. Cut in the cheese and butter then rub lightly with the fingertips until the mixture resembles crumbs. Stir in enough iced water to make a firm dough. Knead lightly, cover and put it in the refrigerator for 30 minutes. Roll out the pastry and line 6 individual 10cm/4in loose-based tart tins. Prick the pastry all over, line it with foil and weight down with baking beans or crumpled foil. Bake for 30–35 minutes in a preheated oven, 180°C, 350°F, Gas Mark 4, until crisp.

Meanwhile, trim the rhubarb and cut into 5cm/2in lengths, halving or quartering the stalks if they are very thick. Put the rhubarb in a saucepan with the muscovado sugar and a couple of tablespoons of water and cook gently until the rhubarb is just tender. Drain the fruit, reserving the liquid, and leave to cool.

Allow the pastry cases to cool then melt the chocolate and brush over the insides. Chill briefly to set the chocolate. Boil the rhubarb-cooking liquid until syrupy then remove from the heat and add the stem ginger and ginger syrup. Stir half the mixture into the yogurt or whisk it into the cream. Spread this over the base of the tarts, arrange the rhubarb on top and brush with remaining syrup.

Top **RHUBARB AND GINGER TART**

Oz Clarke's WINE NOTES

The worst thing about an early Easter is that Lent seems to start in the depths of winter. When I think about renouncing all my indulgences for 40 days, which isn't *so* difficult if you've gone completely berserk on pancakes the day before, I do find considerable solace in the thought that by the time Easter comes wild flowers will be carpeting the countryside, the days will be bathed in sunshine and I shall be busy dusting down the garden furniture and de-mothing my cricket whites. So I'm going to assume that Frances has chosen a late Easter for our dinner – as late as possible, please.

Even so, despite the warm days, the evenings are still cool, and a dinner still needs to be reassuringly based round hot food. So Frances' warm salads are doubly welcome; yet the fresh vegetables and fish beckon you towards summer. And the snappy, green-field flavours of the Sauvignon Blanc grape are quite the best accompaniments for asparagus, and pretty good with slightly sweet skate. In a fit of celebration I'll choose a ripe young Sancerre, France's top Sauvignon wine.

I do get a bit worried about eating lamb when I see the woolly little bundles gambolling about the meadows – still, in hard-hearted mood, I must admit spring lamb is absolutely yummy, and the sweetness of the meat, and the perfumy fragrance of the herbs will go brilliantly with Cabernet Sauvignon reds. Frances chooses a classic from Bordeaux's Médoc; I'll go for the blackcurrant and cedar ripeness of a Cabernet from Coonawarra – the area they call Australia's Médoc. And for that wonderfully rich, yet palate-tingling tart – I'll stay in Australia with a luscious sweet Muscat from Victoria.

A Taste of the East for 6

The inspiration for this dinner party comes from my experiences in the Far East where I have been lucky enough to travel widely and also to spend enough time to get to know the markets and cooks there and learn about Oriental ingredients. Many of these ingredients are now available in the West, such as the various types of Chinese cabbages, Sichuan pepper, fresh root ginger, star anise, chilli, lemon grass, coriander and the different types of soy sauces, oils and vinegars.

It is not necessary to be a Chinese cook to use them. The following are not, strictly speaking, Chinese dishes although they are based on dishes I have seen being prepared in Oriental restaurants and homes.

The flavours are subtle and delicate rather than fiercely overpowering so that classic fine wines accompany them perfectly. I serve the steamed salmon wonton or parcels as canapés with Champagne at many of my dinner parties, Eastern-inspired or not.

For the main wine try a white Burgundy, especially the 'quieter' wines of Rully or Montagny rather than the more celebrated wines of the Côte d'Or; we have often found Chardonnay to be the grape variety most suited to Oriental food.

MENU

*

STEAMED SALMON PARCELS OR WONTON WITH DIPPING SAUCE

WARM BEEF SALAD

POACHED CHICKEN WITH ORIENTAL HERBS AND SPICES

*

ROSE 'BEAN CURD' WITH ALMOND SAUCE

*

Champagne *or* Gewürztraminer

White Burgundy *or* Italian Chardonnay

Italian Rosenmuskateller

POACHED CHICKEN WITH ORIENTAL HERBS AND SPICES, DIPPING SAUCE, BOILED RICE, STEAMED SALMON PARCELS, GINGER AND HORSERADISH SAUCE

STEAMED SALMON PARCELS OR WONTON WITH DIPPING SAUCE

A salmon and vegetable mixture can be wrapped up and steamed in leaves or, if you can get them, in wonton wrappers. You can make a different filling by chopping prawns or scallops, or a mixture of both, with a little white fish such as plaice or whiting.

750g/1½lb salmon fillet, skinned
6 spring onions, finely chopped
50g/2oz bean sprouts, blanched and chopped
75g/3oz button or oyster mushrooms, wiped and finely chopped
3 cloves garlic, peeled and crushed
2 tablespoons soy sauce
1 tablespoon toasted sesame oil
2 teaspoons sherry vinegar or rice vinegar
Pinch ground black pepper or Sichuan pepper
18–24 leaves – quite large and a mixture of spinach, lettuce, chard, tender cabbage and Chinese leaf – or 36 wonton wrappers

Dipping sauce:
4 tablespoons soy sauce
6 tablespoons water
2 tablespoons toasted sesame oil
2 tablespoons rice or sherry vinegar
3 spring onions, finely chopped
1 tablespoon finely chopped coriander
1 small chilli, finely chopped (optional)

Run your fingers lightly over the cut surface of the salmon and remove with tweezers any fine bones you can feel. Chop the salmon finely. This can be done in a food processor or with a knife but be careful not to over-process the fish so that it has a pasty texture. Mix together the fish, vegetables and seasoning.

If using leaves for wrapping, remove any central stalks which would make it difficult to roll them. Blanch the leaves either by dipping them in boiling water or by draping them over a colander a few at a time and pouring boiling water over them. Drain and refresh under cold water. Dry the leaves on kitchen paper and carefully open them out. Spoon some of the fish mixture on to each leaf and roll up into neat parcels, making sure the filling is enclosed. Place in a lightly oiled steamer basket and steam for 6–8 minutes.

If using wonton wrappers, spoon a little of the fish mixture on to a wonton wrapper and moisten round the filling with your finger or a brush dipped in water. Draw the edges of the wonton over the filling and pinch together to seal it in the form of a bundle or money bag. Repeat with the remaining wrappers and filling. Lightly oil a steamer basket and steam the wonton for 8–10 minutes.

Meanwhile mix together all the ingredients for the dipping sauce, adjusting the quantities to your taste.

To serve *Serve the parcels or wonton hot with a small bowl of dipping sauce. If preferred the dipping sauce can be spooned over the parcels.*

EXTRAS

If you like, make a very simple delicious ginger and horseradish cream sauce to serve with the chicken. Mix together a tablespoon each of freshly grated root ginger, grated horseradish and Greek yogurt. Season with salt and pepper and gently fold into about 150ml/¼ pint whipped cream.

For an unusual accompaniment make mixed vegetable noodles. Using a swivel-headed peeler, shave 2 or 3 carrots and a mooli into long thin ribbons. Cut 2 or 3 celery sticks and leeks into long strips. Steam, boil in salted water or stir-fry them as you wish.

Plain or boiled rice is the most suitable accompaniment to these dishes. Fried rice is another possibility, but plain rice is just as good and much easier to prepare.

Japanese rice crackers could be passed around with drinks when your guests arrive. They are crisp and crunchy with an intensely savoury flavour which is most appetizing.

One of the finest Oriental teas would be a very agreeable alternative to coffee after dinner. Jasmine tea, Rose Congou and Formosa Oolong are some of my favourites.

PRESENTATION

Although this is not a Chinese meal you can make it feel as Oriental as you like. Chopsticks look very attractive and sometimes I put them on the table together with chopstick rests. If I am serving a dinner with a particular ethnic mood to it, I might try to pick up that theme in the table setting, say with a piece of batik in place of a tablecloth, or a Chinese embroidered shawl.

VEGETABLE NOODLES, WARM BEEF SALAD

PLANNING AHEAD

Two days before: Make the ginger and horseradish sauce and refrigerate.

The beef can marinate for a day or two but it and the chicken should be cooked as required.

The day before: Make the rose bean curd and almond sauce and refrigerate. Put them together just before serving.

The day of the party: The salmon mixture for the steamed salmon parcels can be made in the morning or afternoon and refrigerated. Leaves can be blanched at the same time. Alternatively, leaves or wonton can be stuffed in the morning. Prepare the vegetable noodles but don't cook them until the last minute. Cook the chicken and beef. Boil the rice and noodles. Fill the wonton wrappers or stuff the leaves if not already done and steam just before serving.

POACHED CHICKEN WITH ORIENTAL HERBS AND SPICES

In China, chicken poached with ginseng root is widely regarded as a fortifying and healing dish.

1 chicken, about 1·6kg/3½lb
6 cloves garlic, peeled
2 stems lemon grass
6 sprigs fresh coriander
2·5cm/1in piece fresh root ginger, peeled and sliced
1 or 2 pieces young ginseng root (optional)
4 star anise pods
Rind of 1 orange
1 leek, sliced
1 celery stick, sliced
1 carrot, sliced
1 turnip, sliced
1 onion, sliced

Cut the wing pinions from the chicken and remove any fat from the cavity. Put the garlic, herbs, spices and orange rind inside the cavity. Arrange the vegetables in the bottom of a stock pot or large saucepan, lay the chicken on top and cover with water. Bring slowly to the boil and skim any scum from the surface then cover and poach very gently for 1 hour.

Serve the chicken whole, chopped into small pieces to take with chopsticks, or jointed and served on individual plates. The broth with some of the vegetables should be served separately in soup bowls and a bowl of fluffy boiled rice is the best accompaniment.

SEE PAGE 90

WARM BEEF SALAD

The Oriental style is to serve meat well-cooked rather than rare, but with such a tender cut of meat I like to cook it so that it is still pink in the centre and the meat juices blend with the glorious dressing.

500g/1lb tail end of fillet steak
150ml/¼ pint rice wine or dry Amontillado sherry
5cm/2in piece fresh root ginger, peeled
3 or 4 cloves garlic, peeled and crushed
2 tablespoons fermented black beans or 2 tablespoons soy sauce
2 tablespoons finely chopped fresh coriander leaves
1 tablespoon toasted sesame oil
1 tablespoon olive oil
1 tablespoon rice or sherry vinegar

Trim excess fat and gristle from the meat then put it in a bowl and pour over the rice wine or sherry. Slice half the ginger and grate the rest. Cut the slices into shreds and put to one side. Mix the grated ginger and garlic with the black beans or soy sauce and add to the sherry. Marinate the beef for 2–3 hours, or overnight. Remove it from the marinade and dry it thoroughly. Strain and reserve the marinade. Flatten the thicker end of the steak with a rolling pin. Dry-fry the steak on both sides until done to your liking. Remove from the pan, transfer to a plate and keep it warm.

Pour the marinade into the pan and bring to the boil, scraping up any cooking residues. Reduce it slightly then strain into a jug. Stir in the coriander, oils, vinegar and shredded ginger and check for taste.

To serve *Slice the beef in thin diagonal slices and pour the dressing over it.*

ROSE 'BEAN CURD' WITH ALMOND SAUCE

This is not, of course, real bean curd, but more like a jelly or even a Turkish delight, although it slightly resembles bean curd in texture and, if it is not coloured, in colour.

3 teaspoons powdered gelatine
4 tablespoons water
450ml/¾ pint milk
65ml/2½fl oz double cream
3 tablespoons rosewater
2 or 3 drops red food colouring (optional)
125g/4oz ground almonds
175g/6oz sugar
300ml/½ pint water

Soak the gelatine in the water. When it is soft, put it in a saucepan with half the milk and heat, stirring until the gelatine has dissolved. Mix in the cream, the rest of the milk, the rosewater and colouring (optional) and pour it into a wetted square-sided shallow tray to set. A clean Swiss roll tin is perfect for this. Refrigerate until set.

To make the almond sauce, mix together the almonds, sugar and water. Heat gently until the sugar has melted then bring to the boil. Remove from the heat and let stand for a couple of hours. Chill and serve as it is, or press through a sieve for a smooth sauce. Cut the rose jelly or 'bean curd' into squares, lozenges or other shapes and serve in glass bowls on a little of the sauce.

Oz Clarke's
WINE NOTES

So many of the most thrilling taste experiences in food today can be traced directly to Oriental influences. But much as I adore the flavours, they do make the job of choosing suitable wines a great deal more difficult since Oriental cuisines rarely attach much importance to table wine. Apart from religious strictures against alcohol in some parts of the Far East, there is another reason why wine is not of great importance: the climates would make it extremely difficult to grow decent grapes. Thailand, Vietnam and most parts of India and China just can't grow wine grapes, and Japanese efforts have only met with very limited success. With Oriental influences very much on Frances' mind in this menu, we shall have to improvise.

Many of the most individual flavourings used are highly aromatic, often seeming either sweet, or sour, or both at once, sometimes heating up your palate, until a balancing herb cools it down again. Most wine flavours disappear against such a background, and few are complementary. However both the Gewürztraminer and the Muscat grape have a tropical fruit quality and a citrus acidity which is positively called for. Torres Esmeralda is a combination of Gewürztraminer and Muscat and will go brilliantly with all these dishes. The sweet vanilla of oak is also called for, so for my Chardonnay, I'll choose one of the ultra-modern, oak-aged Italians – Il Marzocco from Tuscan producer Avignonesi – not as fruity and overpowering as some from the New World, but beautifully softened by oak.

With the rose 'bean curd', a rose-flavoured Rosenmuskateller from Italy's Alto Adige will be absolutely delicious.

ROSE 'BEAN CURD' WITH ALMOND SAUCE

AUTUMN DINNER PARTY *for 8*

Lots of good smells, rich flavours and steaming hot food make this a perfect meal for a cold autumn day. I was always taught that one should never serve soup and pasta at the same meal. Then one day in Rome in a small family-run *trattoria* near the river, we saw a table of elegantly dressed Italians order huge bowls of minestrone, followed by plates of ravioli.

If serving a meal with one more course, I would slip in a cold dish such as marinated smoked haddock fillets between the soup and the lasagne.

An Italian Chardonnay with its firmness and balance of fruit and acidity would be a perfect match for the rich soup and also for smoked fish. A robust red, with lots of peppery fruit, is just right for the lasagne. I have a soft spot for Corsican wines and have found that this simple country wine is excellent with game.

To serve with the intense flavours of the dried fruit compote, I would chose an equally intense wine: the Pedro Ximenez sherry is thick, dark, syrupy and concentrated, to be drunk in rather small sips.

MENU

*

PUMPKIN AND CHEESE SOUP

ROSEMARY POPOVERS

HARE AND CHESTNUT LASAGNE

*

DRIED FRUIT COMPOTE

*

Chardonnay Alto Adige *or* Deidesheimer

Vin de Corse Rouge *or* Crozes-Hermitage

Pedro Ximenez Sherry *or* Moscato d'Asti Naturale

HARE AND CHESTNUT LASAGNE

PUMPKIN AND CHEESE SOUP

Add chunks of cooked ham or sausage to this soup for a substantial lunch or supper dish. Sage can be used instead of bay leaves.

3 rashers smoked streaky bacon
1 large Spanish or other mild onion
1·5kg/3lb piece pumpkin
900ml/1½ pints milk
2 bay leaves
3 cloves
432g/14oz can borlotti beans
900ml/1½ pints vegetable or chicken stock or water
75g/3oz Lancashire or white Stilton cheese, crumbled
75g/3oz Gruyère cheese, diced
2 tablespoons finely chopped fresh parsley
50g/2oz freshly grated Parmesan cheese
Salt and pepper

Remove and discard the rind and cut the bacon into matchsticks. Put it into a heavy flameproof casserole and cook gently until the fat runs. Peel and thinly slice the onion and cook it with the bacon until soft and translucent but do not let it brown.

Discard any seeds and stringy filaments from the pumpkin and cut the rind away. Cut the flesh into 2·5cm/1in chunks and add to the pan. Pour on the milk and add the bay leaves and cloves. Cover and simmer gently until the pumpkin and onion are tender. The pumpkin will start to collapse but this does not matter since that is what gives body to the soup. Remove the bay leaves and cloves.

Drain the beans and add them to the soup, together with the stock or water. Bring to the boil, then remove from the heat, stir in the Lancashire or white Stilton and Gruyère cheese and season the soup.

To serve *Just before serving, scatter the parsley and freshly grated Parmesan on top and serve immediately with the rosemary popovers. An alternative accompaniment would be triangles of bread fried in butter or olive oil and then dipped in chopped fresh parsley.*

ROSEMARY POPOVERS

This recipe uses basically the same batter as Yorkshire puddings, and it shows you just how versatile a mix it is. Flavour the popovers with fresh or dried herbs, spices or grated cheese, for example. Popovers can also be made for dessert, filled with fruit such as poached bilberries and served with syrup and cream.

3 eggs
125g/4oz plain flour, sifted
300ml/½ pint skimmed milk
Good pinch of salt
1 teaspoon finely chopped rosemary
Groundnut or sunflower oil, for greasing

Lightly beat the eggs in a bowl and gradually beat in the flour. Then thin the mixture down with the skimmed milk, beating continuously until the batter is smooth and the texture that of thick cream. Stir in the salt and rosemary. Leave the batter to stand, covered, for at least 30 minutes to let the starch granules swell.

Brush 24 bun tins lightly with the oil and place in the top half of a preheated oven, 200°C, 400°F, Gas Mark 6. Leave there for 5 minutes until the baking tin is very hot. Stir up the batter, remove the bun tins from the oven and pour in the batter to fill them two-thirds full. Put back in the oven and bake for 15–20 minutes until well risen and golden-brown. Serve immediately with the soup.

PUMPKIN AND CHEESE SOUP, ROSEMARY POPOVERS

EXTRAS

As an alternative first course (or as a second course, if guests are likely to be really hungry), I serve slices of marinated smoked haddock. Two or three hours before the meal slice smoked haddock fillets thinly and dribble over some hazelnut oil and the sieved juice of fresh tomatoes. Cover with onion rings, and sprinkle lightly with salt and pepper. Serve on a plate with a few salad leaves or with some shreds of cucumber, or quartered, deseeded cherry tomatoes, and decorate with herbs. Wholemeal bread or pumpernickel goes very well with the fish.

Vegetable accompaniments never seem quite right with pasta dishes and with the lasagne I would serve a large crisp green salad with a garlicky dressing. And do not forget some crusty bread to mop up the juices.

Rather than serve a selection of cheeses, I often like to present just one cheese, say a large piece of Farmhouse Cheddar or Lancashire, or the mild yet flavoursome French Cantal. Accompany the cheese with a bowl of ripe pears.

Place sea salt and black pepper on the table.

PLANNING AHEAD

In advance: If you have time make some light, crisp biscuits to accompany the compote – they should be lightly spiced and not too sweet. Make them about half as thick as you would normally make biscuits. Store in an airtight tin. You could make up the dipping biscuit recipe on page 81 for this.

Two days before: Make the dried fruit compote.

The day before: Add more liquid to the compote if necessary. Make the batter for the rosemary popovers and store in the fridge. Make the hare sauce and refrigerate.

The day of the party: Make the pasta and assemble the lasagne. Make the pumpkin soup, stirring in the Gruyère cubes at the last moment. If you are serving marinated haddock, begin preparing this two or three hours before the meal.

PRESENTATION

I have a rectangular earthenware dish in which I always cook my lasagne. This plain rustic pottery usually inspires the rest of the meal which will be presented in equally simple fashion, perhaps with table mats instead of a cloth. If I use a cloth, it will be a bright and cheerful one, rather than a white one.

Another way of serving the pumpkin soup is to take a whole pumpkin, remove the flesh and cook the soup in the oven inside the pumpkin shell. It looks quite spectacular.

HARE AND CHESTNUT LASAGNE

Prepare the hare sauce the day before it is needed so that the flavours have a chance to develop, making the sauce altogether tastier. Use meat from the legs and shoulders for the hare sauce, reserving the saddle for another dish.

Hare sauce:
750g/1½lb boneless hare
3 tablespoons olive oil
1 onion, sliced
2 celery stalks, sliced
1 leek, sliced
3 cloves garlic, crushed
1 tablespoon vegetable or tomato purée
600ml/1 pint red wine or hare stock
15g/½oz bitter dessert chocolate
1 bay leaf, 1 sage leaf and a sprig of thyme, tied together
Salt and pepper

Pasta:
275g/9oz strong white flour
2 eggs
1 egg white
50g/2oz unsweetened chestnut purée

White sauce:
25g/1oz butter
25g/1oz plain flour
900ml/1½ pints milk
Grating of fresh nutmeg
Salt and white pepper

Cut the meat into fairly even 1cm/½in dice. Fry in 2 tablespoons of the olive oil until nicely browned, remove from the pan with a slotted spoon and put in a clean flameproof casserole or saucepan. Fry the onion, celery and leek in the remaining oil until just turning golden brown but without burning them. Put the vegetables into the pan with the hare, together with the crushed garlic. Fry the vegetable purée in the remaining pan juices until it begins to darken a little then deglaze the pan by pouring on a little wine or stock and stirring and scraping up any residues stuck to the bottom. Add the chocolate and the rest of the liquid, bring to the boil and pour over the meat and vegetables. Tuck in the bouquet of herbs. Cover and simmer very gently until the meat is tender – about an hour or so at least. Season lightly. Remove from the heat, cool quickly and refrigerate.

To make the pasta, put the flour into a food processor, add the eggs and egg white and process, in short bursts, for about 30 seconds, or mix well in a large bowl. Add the chestnut purée and process, or mix in, briefly so that it combines with the dough. The texture will be crumbly but soft and probably still streaked cream and brown. Scoop the dough together and form it into a ball. Let it rest, covered with a damp cloth, in a cool place for 10–15 minutes.

Cut off a piece of dough the size of an egg and roll it out as thinly as possible. Cut it into rectangles about 15 x 10cm/6 x 4in and place on a board covered with a tea towel to dry flat. Repeat with the remaining dough.

To make the white sauce, melt the butter in a heavy saucepan and stir in the flour. Cook gently for 5 minutes before removing the pan from the heat and adding a quarter of the milk. Blend in, return to the heat and stir continuously until the mixture thickens. Again off the heat, blend in half the remaining milk then return to the heat and cook gently. Blend in the rest of the milk and cook the sauce for about 10 minutes, stirring it to ensure that it is smooth. Season with nutmeg, salt and white pepper.

To assemble the lasagne, cook the pasta sheets in boiling salted water until just tender. Drain on a clean tea towel. Spoon a little of the white sauce on the bottom of a 30 x 20cm/12 x 8in, deepish ovenproof dish. Cover with a layer of pasta, then a layer of hare sauce and a little more white sauce. Place a layer of pasta on top and continue in this way finishing with a layer of white sauce. Bake in the centre of a preheated oven, 190°C, 375°F, Gas Mark 5, for 50–60 minutes. *SEE PAGE 94.*

DRIED FRUIT COMPOTE

Prepare this a day or two before required. This recipe makes plenty, and I always make more than I need because it is very good with yogurt for breakfast. As a dessert, compote does not need cream but is very good served with some kind of crunchy biscuit.

1kg/2lb mixed dried fruit – apricots, prunes, pears, peaches, apple rings, mango, figs, muscatel raisins
1 cinnamon stick 7–10cm/3–4in long
Seeds from 8 cardamom pods
6 star anise pods (optional)
6 cloves
1 bay leaf
2·3 litres/4 pints freshly brewed Earl Grey or jasmine tea
Sweet dessert wine (optional)

Rinse the fruit thoroughly and place it in a large glass bowl with the spices. Pour on the tea, cover and allow to soak for one or two days.

Depending on how dry the fruit is, you may need to add more water or tea while it is soaking so keep an eye on it. You could also add some sweet wine such as a Muscat or a Moscato d'Asti which you have brought to the boil first.

Serve chilled, straight from the bowl. I like to keep the spices in the fruit mixture rather than removing them as they look very attractive.

Top **DRIED FRUIT COMPOTE**

Oz Clarke's WINE NOTES

If Frances was always taught that you weren't supposed to serve soup and pasta at the same meal, I was always taught that you shouldn't serve wine with soup. Well, I suppose I can see that wine's role as an aid to digesting the food might seem a little superfluous when faced with a spoonful or two of unambitious consommé, but Frances' pumpkin and cheese soup isn't just a soup, it's a feast! So long as you don't get stingy with the rosemary flavoured popovers, this makes a complete meal in itself. It's the kind of soup where I have to be restrained from having five helpings.

Because of the pumpkin, the beans and the various cheeses, all blended in together, I'm going to choose a Rhine wine from Germany. Deidesheim produces full, soft, slightly smoky wine, but with a grapy perfume and a refreshing acidity – the effect is slightly sweet and goes with the slight sweetness of the pumpkin.

Frances and I are both favouring sturdy red for the lasagne, but I'm choosing wine from the Rhône valley just south of Lyon. The lasagne combines the strong gamy, almost ink-rich flavours of the hare with a milder sweeter creaminess, both of the chestnuts and the white sauce. So I want a burly red wine, but one with sweet fruit too – and the blackberry and raspberry fruit tinged with pepper of a Crozes-Hermitage will be just right.

As for the pudding – the rare but intensely concentrated Pedro Ximenez sherry is one of the great sweet wine experiences. But if I can't find a bottle, I'll enjoy the wonderfully refreshing grapy sweetness of the lightly sparkling Moscato d'Asti – I'll have used one bottle already in making the compote!

A Winter Celebration *for 2*

This is the sort of meal I like to cook for our wedding anniversary which falls in the middle of winter, but you could just as well cook it as a winter birthday present for someone. It also makes a good Christmas meal for two. A turkey would be very out of place so a small tasty game bird such as pheasant is a very practical solution.

Robust red wines are perfect companions to many game dishes. but pheasant is a delicate, pale meat ideally suited to one of the fragrant, crisp and fruity wines from the Rheingau or Rheinpfalz in Germany.

Since it is a celebration, I like to start with Champagne, preferably a rosé Champagne. After pouring out the two glasses I use the rest of the bottle to make a refreshing pink granita for dessert. One of the sweeter Champagnes, such as a *demi-sec*, is an excellent partner to many desserts including iced ones.

MENU

*

MUSSELS BAKED IN POTATOES

POT-ROAST PHEASANT WITH BLACKBERRY SAUCE

BRAISED FENNEL

WILD RICE

*

HAZELNUT CRISPS

PINK CHAMPAGNE GRANITA

*

Rosé Champagne
or Chardonnay de Savoie

Rheingau Riesling Kabinett
or Australian Shiraz

Demi-Sec Champagne
or Rosé Champagne

MUSSELS BAKED IN POTATOES

This is a wonderfully versatile recipe which I first made with snails instead of mussels. You could also use prawns, oysters or mushrooms.

6 fresh or ready-cooked mussels
6 small potatoes, about 50g/2oz each
40g/1½oz butter
2 teaspoons finely chopped fresh parsley
1 small clove garlic, peeled and crushed
Salt
Pepper

If using fresh mussels, scrub them well under running water to remove any sand and knock off any barnacles. Remove the 'beard'. Discard any that do not close. Rinse and put in a lidded saucepan with just the water clinging to them. Cover and steam for 5–7 minutes then discard any that haven't opened. When cool enough to handle remove from the shells, place in a bowl and cover with cool water to stop them drying out.

Scrub the potatoes well and only peel if necessary. With a melon baller scoop out a hole from each potato large enough to hold a mussel and some butter. Take a small slice off the bottom of each potato so it will stand firm. Parboil them for 8 minutes.

Melt a little of the butter and brush the potatoes all over. Mix the rest of the butter with the parsley, garlic and a little salt and freshly ground pepper. Place a drained cooked mussel in each potato case. Spread a little butter on each and level the top. Place the potatoes on a lightly oiled baking sheet and bake in a preheated oven, 180°C, 350°F, Gas Mark 4, for 10–12 minutes until golden brown and tender.

POT-ROAST PHEASANT WITH BLACKBERRY SAUCE

Only the pheasant breasts are needed for this recipe. Use the meat from the legs to make potted pheasant or a pasta sauce on another occasion. Serve this dish with the wild rice and braised fennel and, perhaps, a spoonful of blackberry jelly.

1 oven-ready hen pheasant
1 tablespoon finely chopped fresh herbs such as parsley, coriander, chervil and tarragon
50g/2oz butter
1–2 tablespoons brandy or Calvados
Small glass of port, vermouth or red wine
2 teaspoons blackberry jelly
Salt and pepper

Trim any excess fat from the cavity of the pheasant. Mix the herbs, seasoning and butter together. Smear some over the bird and put the rest in the cavity. In a heavy, non-stick frying pan, fry the bird all over; pour on the brandy and set it alight. Transfer the bird to a small lidded casserole. Pour the port or wine into the frying pan and swill it around to collect up the cooking residues. Pour over the pheasant, cover and cook in the top half of a preheated oven, 180°C, 350°F, Gas Mark 4, for about an hour. Remove from the oven and set aside in a warm place.

To finish the sauce, strain the cooking juices into a small saucepan, add the blackberry jelly and simmer gently, reducing it until you have a good, but not too sticky, consistency.

Remove the breasts from the bird and serve with the sauce.

Opposite **POT-ROAST PHEASANT WITH BLACKBERRY SAUCE, BRAISED FENNEL, WILD RICE**

MUSSELS BAKED IN POTATOES

EXTRAS

For some reason I see this as a late evening meal and I'm not sure that I would serve cheese with it. If I did, it would probably be a slice of goats' milk cheese on toast, popped under the grill until brown and bubbling and served with a small sharp salad of watercress and chicory.

As an alternative to coffee I like to offer my guest a herbal tea or tisane. These are soothing and full of flavour but contain no caffeine. Pleasing combinations can be made by infusing mint and lemon verbena, or mint and lime flowers.

Since it's a special occasion, a few chocolate truffles would be very nice with the tisane, some of bitter dark chocolate and some of white chocolate. If you think you might need a canapé or two to serve before dinner, one of the simplest things you can do is to drain a can of anchovies, mash them with softened butter, a little black pepper and lemon juice and spread this on fingers of hot wholemeal toast.

PLANNING AHEAD

In advance: Make the hazelnut crisps and store in an airtight tin.

The day of the party: If you're using fresh mussels steam them, remove them from their shells, and refrigerate until needed. Trim and season the pheasant.

Start cooking about 1¼ hours before you sit down.

Begin cooking the wild rice as soon as you have the bird in the oven. If it is cooked to your liking in 45 minutes, do not worry. Keep it warm in a bowl set over a pan of hot water.

Put the fennel in oven when pheasant is half-way through cooking. Put potatoes in oven when pheasant is three-quarters cooked.

The granita should freeze while you're eating dinner. When you've poured the first two glasses of Champagne, mix the rest with the sugar and put it to freeze.

PRESENTATION

Although it is for only two people, this is one of my more formal dinner parties. Use it as an excuse to bring out the fine china and glassware and lay the table with a crisp white cloth and matching napkins.

When serving German wine I like to use hock glasses, with a round bowl and long stem, though I do not much care for the ones with a brown stem (or indeed Mosel glasses with a green stem). Long stems keep your hands away from the wine, thus keeping it cool, and the round bowl retains the fragrance of the wine. Serve the Champagne in tall, narrow glasses, or flutes, so that you can see the bubbles coursing up to the surface.

If this is to be a romantic dinner for two, soft gleaming candlelight would be appropriate and flowers on the table. I am not a good flower arranger so I usually choose two or three small flowers to place in low, unobtrusive glass vases that do not get in the way of conversation.

BRAISED FENNEL

With its celery-like crispness and sweet aniseed flavour, this is one of my favourite winter vegetables. Indeed, a fennel salad dressed in walnut oil and lemon juice would follow the pheasant perfectly.

375g/12oz bulb fennel
½ lemon
15g/½oz butter
150ml/¼ pint water, pheasant or chicken stock or white wine
25g/1oz fresh breadcrumbs
25g/1oz freshly grated Parmesan cheese
Sea salt and white pepper

Trim away any discoloured portions of the fennel and cut off the green stalks. Slice the fennel or cut it into small wedges and rub it all over with lemon so that it will not discolour. Butter an ovenproof dish and lay the fennel in it. Sprinkle with salt and pepper and pour the liquid over it. Cover loosely with foil and bake in a preheated oven, 180°C, 350°F, Gas Mark 4, for 30 minutes.

Mix the breadcrumbs and cheese, sprinkle evenly over the fennel and finish off under a hot grill for 5 minutes to brown the topping.

SEE PAGE 98.

WILD RICE

A little wild rice goes a long way and it is not, therefore, as extravagant as it might at first seem. Wild rice takes much longer to cook than white rice, up to one hour if you like it very soft and fluffy.

50g/2oz wild rice
250–300ml/8–10fl oz water

Put the rice in a heavy saucepan and pour on four times its volume of water. Bring to the boil, cover and simmer gently until the water is absorbed. Add a little more water and cook further if necessary. Any left over will be excellent served in a clear pheasant broth made by simmering the pheasant carcass in water. The rice can also be cooked in the bottom of the oven at 180°C, 350°F, Gas Mark 4.

SEE PAGE 98.

HAZELNUT CRISPS

It isn't sensible to make these biscuits in smaller quantities than this, which makes about 18 biscuits, but they keep well, and can be made in advance. Serve them with the pink Champagne granita.

50g/2oz blanched hazelnuts
1 egg white
Pinch of salt
50g/2oz caster sugar
1 tablespoon plain flour, sifted
½ teaspoon grated orange rind

Finely grind the hazelnuts in a blender. Whisk the egg white until foamy. Add a pinch of salt and continue whisking until firm. Gradually add the sugar to the egg white and whisk until stiff. Carefully fold in the ground hazelnuts, flour and rind.

Line baking sheets with greaseproof paper and drop teaspoonfuls of the mixture on to them. Bake in a preheated oven, 140°C, 275°F, Gas Mark 1, for about 25 minutes until set and golden. Cool on a wire rack.

PINK CHAMPAGNE GRANITA

This is a useful recipe for other distinctive wine granitas: Muscat, Gewürztraminer or Beaujolais, for example, with or without added sugar depending on the type of wine you use.

2 tablespoons sifted icing sugar
½ bottle rosé Champagne

Stir the icing sugar into the Champagne and, when it has dissolved, freeze the mixture in a sorbetière or ice cream maker following the manufacturer's directions; or freeze in a suitable container in the ice-making compartment of the refrigerator or in the freezer. This latter method will require you to stir the mixture from time to time with two forks, so that it freezes evenly and with crystals that are not too large. The last stirring is particularly effective if done in a food processor before returning the mixture to the freezer. Do not let the granita freeze too hard. It should be soft and grainy. An hour or so should be enough time to prepare this dish.

PINK CHAMPAGNE GRANITA, HAZELNUT CRISPS

Oz Clarke's
WINE NOTES

Celebrations have to have fizz. It doesn't always even matter what the fizz is, it doesn't always matter when you drink it, or how you drink it, just so long as it's there. There's that moment when you go to the fridge, pull out a nicely chilled bottle, place a couple of tall, thin glasses between you, and ease out the cork with a gentle pop which says – our celebration has begun. Chink the glasses, look at each other for a moment with feelings of more than mere friendship, and you're on your way.

So I'm definitely following Frances' idea of pink Champagne. My only worry is I might need a second bottle, because I'll certainly start drinking it before dinner is ready and if I'm to leave enough for the granita – well, anyway, I'll put a second bottle in the fridge, just in case. It'll go very well with the mussels, or I might like a glass of something white. Savoie in eastern France, makes wonderfully tangy dry whites, with just the kind of lemony zest which complements those mussels. If they're difficult to find, try the new-style Chardonnays from France's *vins de pays* – either the Yonne or the Loire's Jardin de la France would top the list.

German white wines and their cousins from Alsace, just on the French side of the Rhine do go remarkably well with young game, and the fuller styles are a good match with pheasant, partridge and wild boar. However I'm one of those who hangs his pheasant until even the breast is moist and decayed, so I'll go for a hearty red, and with blackberry sauce and the fennel to come, I'll choose a red which is rather rich and jammy – and often does have flavours of blackberry and anis – Australian Shiraz. By which time I might be getting a bit embarrassed about opening *another* bottle of Champagne, so I'll stick with what's left of my rosé.

JOSCELINE DIMBLEBY

BUFFETS

The idea of a buffet party does not conjure up visions of wonderful food. All too often you are faced with bowls of unidentifiable mixtures, which are further mixed into an unattractive pile on the plate. But apart from drinks parties, buffet parties are the only answer when you want to entertain a large number of people, and a party where you are given a meal and time to talk afterwards is much more of a treat than the brief shouting battle of a drinks party.

With a little thought the food you offer need not be an unappetizing muddle. The most vital thing is to avoid having too many different dishes. A spread of many dishes may seem more impressive – but the effect on the stomach is terrible. Choose things which can be eaten together for those unrestricted and hungry eaters who insist on taking a bit of everything all at once. If possible, provide a dish which strict vegetarians can eat, another for those who will only eat fish, and perhaps a treat for the carnivorous too. The food must be manageable – not the kind which will slip or scatter off the plate as it is carried across the room and, ideally, it should be easy to eat using only a fork.

The best thing about buffet parties is that they are very informal and friendly. Numbers can be flexible so you can invite more people at the last moment and sexes, equally, do not have to match each other in numbers. Introductions often look after themselves and spare the host one responsibility. As people move around to get their food they have every opportunity not to get stuck with someone they long to escape from. Standing with others choosing the food also encourages shy guests to talk easily to people they have not met before.

Some people experience a degree of awkwardness and discomfort when they eat standing up, so organize places where they can sit or even just perch, and clear surfaces for them to put down their glasses – it will make all the difference to how your guests enjoy themselves.

As long as you plan carefully and give yourself time, cooking for a large party always seems surprisingly easy. You achieve so much with not a great deal more effort than it takes to prepare a three-course dinner party for eight. And the pleasure you give to so many makes a lasting impression.

Opposite **SUMMER BUFFET** *PAGE 122*

Exotic Buffet for 24

This really is a buffet after my own heart. I like the loose term 'exotic' as it allows me to indulge in my love of spices without having to stick to a specific type of Oriental cuisine. I gained the confidence to use different spices in a wide variety of my own recipes after years of travelling in India, North Africa and all over the Middle East.

For large parties I find that spiced food is particularly appreciated. With the excitement and animated conversation of a party, blander dishes, even when they are delicious, are often consumed but not really noticed by the guests. Spicy food makes an impact; it is remarked upon and people want more because despite other distractions they have really tasted the food. So it is much more rewarding for the cook.

By spicy food I do not mean hot food which burns your mouth, but dishes which are tantalizingly aromatic and subtle so that you can really identify the taste of different spices. The following recipes for fish, chicken and mixtures of vegetables will complement each other even if the guests insist on piling all of them on their plates.

MENU

*

SALMON OF EASTERN PROMISE

SPICED POTATOES AND PARSNIPS WITH LADIES' FINGERS

THE MEMSAHIB'S PARTY CHICKEN

AROMATIC VEGETABLES

*

MANGO UPSIDE-DOWN ALMOND AND CITRUS CAKE WITH COCONUT CREAM

*

Champagne
Côte de Brouilly
Australian Liqueur Muscat

SALMON OF EASTERN PROMISE, SPICED POTATOES AND PARSNIPS WITH LADIES' FINGERS

SALMON OF EASTERN PROMISE

A whole large fish cooked with Oriental spices and aromatics is a splendid dish to present at a large party. The most practical fish to cook for such parties is salmon. We are used to cold salmon with mayonnaise at almost every summer wedding lunch but farmed salmon, which is now plentiful and relatively inexpensive, makes an excellent vehicle for imaginative spicing. Of course salmon is a fish of northern latitudes and is not usually associated with spices, but the two combine surprisingly well.

3·25–3·75kg/6½–7½lb salmon, gutted, tail trimmed, with the head left on
4–5 large cloves garlic
7cm/3in piece fresh root ginger
2 fresh red chillies
8–10 cardamom pods
4 teaspoons coriander seeds
6 cloves
3 teaspoons ground turmeric
1 tablespoon tandoori paste
1 tablespoon tamarind purée or lemon juice
4 tablespoons natural yogurt
Sunflower oil
Salt
1 bunch fresh coriander or flat-leaved parsley
Red chillies, to garnish (optional)
Mayonnaise, to serve

Wash the fish thoroughly inside and out and pat dry with kitchen paper. Using a sharp knife make slightly slanting diagonal slices across the salmon on both sides about 2·5cm/1in apart.

Peel the garlic and ginger and chop roughly. In a little cold water cut the chillies in half and remove the seeds and stem. Put the flesh of the chillies with the garlic and the ginger and chop all together as finely as possible. Remove the seeds from the cardamom pods and put them into a coffee grinder or into the bowl of a pestle and mortar. Add the coriander seed and the cloves and grind together finely. Put the ground spices, including the turmeric, into a bowl and add the chopped garlic, ginger and chilli and the tandoori paste, the tamarind purée and the yogurt. Mix the ingredients together thoroughly and add salt to season.

Lay a very large piece of foil on a flat surface and smear all over with sunflower oil. Put the salmon on to the foil and smear all over with the mixture from the bowl, pressing it well into the cuts. Wrap the fish in foil and then wrap it up very securely in two more layers of foil to stop the juices escaping while cooking. Leave the fish parcel in the fridge or a cool place for several hours if possible before cooking for it to absorb the spices.

To cook the salmon, lay the fish parcel on the centre shelf of a preheated oven, 140°C, 275°F, Gas Mark 1, and cook for 8 minutes per 500g/1lb. This should produce lightly cooked, moist salmon – overcooking ruins its texture.

When cooked, remove the salmon from the oven and leave it wrapped in the foil for about 20 minutes. Open one end of the foil and carefully tip the juices into a bowl. Open the rest of the foil and slit the skin below the head of the fish and at the back of the tail. Then simply peel off the skin. Turn the fish over carefully and remove the skin from the other side. Wrap the fish up again and leave to cool.

When the cooking juices are cold, mix them with the mayonnaise to make an excellent sauce.

To serve *Put the fish on to a large serving dish, roughly chop the coriander leaves and scatter them over the fish – you can add a few chopped coriander leaves to the sauce too. Finish the garnish with thinly sliced red chillies or chilli 'flowers', but don't eat them unless you like your food really hot. Serve the salmon with spiced mayonnaise and raita (see 'Extras').*

EXTRAS

You will need some mayonnaise to mix the fish juices with but as it will be a spicy sauce bought mayonnaise is perfectly acceptable – stir the cold juices gradually into the mayonnaise until the sauce is the thickness you want. If you like, when the fish is cooked, you can boil the juices in a saucepan for a few minutes to reduce the quantity and intensify the taste for spicing the mayonnaise later.

Make a cooling raita to accompany the spicy dishes. Simply peel a whole cucumber and a red onion and chop finely. Also chop finely 2 or 3 handfuls of fresh mint leaves. Halve about 500g/1lb of red or yellow cherry tomatoes. Add the chopped ingredients and the tomatoes to a mixing bowl containing three 600ml/1 pint cartons of natural yogurt and stir in lemon juice and salt to taste.

Your guests will also appreciate some Naan bread which is one of the best Indian breads and can usually be bought ready made. If you can't get Naan buy some sesame-topped white bread or pitta bread.

Simple green salads go well with exotic dishes. Slice chicory, tear up fresh, small spinach leaves or use them whole if they are small enough and add thinly sliced canned water chestnuts. Finely grate the rind of two lemons to sprinkle on the salad and make a vinaigrette with a little finely chopped or crushed garlic to dress it.

It is always a good idea to have bowls of fresh seasonal fruit around for people who won't eat puddings or to eat later in the evening. Lychees are suitably exotic, look pretty and are very refreshing. Seedless or fragrant Italia grapes, or strawberries in summer, are also possibilities.

Unsalted butter to spread on the bread, black pepper from a mill, sea salt and mineral water should also be on your shopping list.

SPICED POTATOES AND PARSNIPS WITH LADIES' FINGERS

PLANNING AHEAD

In advance: You can mix up the spicy paste for the salmon two days in advance if you like – smear it on the fish according to the instructions and keep it in the fridge until you cook it either later the same day or the next day. Once cooked, drained of its juices and skinned, the salmon can be wrapped in foil again and kept in the fridge for at least a day. The memsahib's chicken can be made up completely as much as three days beforehand as long as it is covered with clingfilm and kept in the fridge.

The day before: Make the spiced potatoes and parsnips with ladies' fingers and keep, covered with clingfilm, in a cool place, but not the fridge. Make the mango cakes and keep them in their dishes.

The day of the party: Make the spiced mayonnaise for the fish, and the raita. Prepare the aromatic vegetables. Make the coconut cream and place in the fridge to chill. Shortly before the party re-heat the mango cakes and turn out. Place the salmon on its serving dish and decorate. Wrap the Naan in foil and heat through in the oven just before serving.

PRESENTATION

The colours and tastes are very definite in this buffet so you can afford to be bold in your decoration too. If you have any Indian or Eastern tablecloths, or even just lengths of washable exotic-looking material, now is the time to use them. The flowers you choose should also look exotic and dramatic; orchids are becoming far less expensive to buy and you could decorate the room with a jungly palm or two. Or buy some inexpensive shimmering material from Indian sari shops to drape round picture frames or mirrors and then light the room by candlelight so that everything sparkles.

I always call okra (known as *bhindi* in India) ladies' fingers because that is what I first knew them as when I was seven years old and living in Syria. Tapering to a fine point, their shape certainly did evoke the elegant fingers and painted fingernails of the sophisticated Damascene women whom I glimpsed at my parents' dinner parties. Some people develop a dislike for okra having only eaten it overcooked and over-spiced. Briefly boiled, still bright green and fresh, it is quite a different thing. Cooked in this way it contrasts well with the smoothness and flavour of the potatoes and parsnips which are suffused with mild aromatic spices. These vegetables can be prepared the day before and stored in a cool place, but not the fridge.

1·5kg/3lb small firm potatoes
1·5kg/3lb parsnips
1kg/2lb fresh okra
6 large cloves garlic
7cm/3in piece fresh root ginger
1 large red pepper
350ml/12fl oz groundnut oil
2 tablespoons ground cinnamon
2 tablespoons ground coriander
4 teaspoons ground cumin
1½ teaspoons ground cloves
1½ tablespoons caraway seeds
1½ tablespoons black mustard seeds
1½ teaspoons cayenne pepper
125ml/4fl oz lemon juice
Salt
Olive oil (optional)

You will have to cook the potatoes and parsnips separately as they take different amounts of time to reach the right point. Scrub the potatoes but don't peel them. Cut them into quarters and either steam or boil until soft. Peel the parsnips and cut into roughly 2·5cm/1in pieces. Steam or boil until just tender but not so soft that they are beginning to lose their shape – parsnips overcook easily. Put the cooked potatoes and parsnips into a large mixing bowl. Cut the top ends off the okra. Bring a pan of salted water to the boil, add the okra and cook for 5–8 minutes until just tender and still bright green. Drain the okra immediately and rinse with plenty of cold water so that they cool down quickly and don't cook any longer.

Meanwhile, peel the garlic and ginger and slice across in the thinnest possible slivers. Cut the pepper in half, remove the seeds and stem and then slice across again as thinly as you can.

Put the oil into a deep frying pan over a fairly low heat. Stir in the ground cinnamon, coriander, cumin and cloves, followed by the sliced red pepper, the garlic and the ginger. Cook very gently, stirring often, until the pepper is completely soft. Add the caraway and mustard seeds and the cayenne pepper and stir for another minute or two. Finally add the lemon juice and remove from the heat.

Leave for a few minutes and then add salt to taste. Pour the hot mixture over the potatoes and parsnips and toss gently with two large wooden spoons so that the vegetables absorb the spiced mixture. Then lightly mix in the cooked okra, reserving a handful of them. Transfer the mixture and any unabsorbed juice to a large, fairly shallow serving dish (or several smaller dishes) and arrange the reserved okra decoratively on top.

Cover the dish loosely with clingfilm and leave in a cool place until you are ready to serve it.

To serve *Just before serving dribble some olive oil over the top of the dish if liked.*
SEE PAGE 104.

THE MEMSAHIB'S PARTY CHICKEN

On my first journey to India with two friends I was designated as the tour leader, otherwise known as the memsahib. So many things can go wrong while travelling in India that the responsibility of making daily decisions is a heavy one. My heart used to sink when my friends asked, 'Well then, what are the memsahib's plans for today?' The following recipe is for a memsahib who is too busy to cook elaborately but who wants to please her friends with something more exciting than coronation chicken. Coating pieces of cold chicken with a spicy sauce is easy and effective. It goes well with bread or new potatoes and a green salad and is easily made in large quantities.

AROMATIC VEGETABLES, THE MEMSAHIB'S PARTY CHICKEN

4 × 1·75–2kg/3½–4lb fresh roasting chickens
10–12 tablespoons mayonnaise
1kg/2lb Greek yogurt
4 tablespoons tomato purée
6–8 tablespoons tikka paste
2 large bunches fresh coriander
Large bunch of parsley
Salt
Black pepper

Roast the chickens beforehand in a preheated oven, 200°C, 400°F, Gas Mark 6, for 1–1½ hours and leave until cold. Carve the breast of the chicken in smallish pieces and then pick all the flesh you can get off the rest of the chicken.

Put the mayonnaise, yogurt and tomato purée in a large bowl. Mix together and stir in the tikka paste to taste, adding salt and black pepper if you feel the mixture needs it.

Save some of the best sprigs of big leaves of the coriander for decoration and then pull the rest of the leaves off the stems and chop roughly. Chop the parsley finely. Stir the chopped coriander leaves and parsley into the yogurt mixture. Add the chicken pieces to the mixture and stir with a wooden spoon so the chicken is thoroughly coated.

Cover the bowl loosely with clingfilm and refrigerate until needed.

To serve *Spoon the chicken mixture into a shallow serving dish and decorate it with the whole coriander leaves.*

Oz Clarke's WINE NOTES

A party! Let's break out the Champagne. It is a party, isn't it? Why else would you have 24 people round at your place? And an 'exotic' buffet promises a whole lot more than lukewarm tea and cold sausage rolls.

Josceline has a most original and exciting way with her use of Oriental spices. Since wine is not really a part of most Oriental cultures, any attempt at making exact pairings between the wine and the food is unlikely to work.

So it is a party, and the best possible way to make any group of people buzz is to ply them with fizz. I've chosen Champagne as much because of how it feels – the bubbles breaking on the roof of your mouth, the ice-cold shock of pleasure as you swallow it – as much as for the taste. But if you don't want to spend that much money I'd go for a Prosecco – less fizzy but still full of bright, breezy froth – or Australian sparkling wine, gently creamy and fizzy too – Seppelt makes a good range.

If you feel like a red wine, you want something with lots of easy-going flavour, something enjoyable by itself, yet not likely to react against the food flavours. Beaujolais is the answer – especially one from the top 10 villages in the region, called the *crus* or Growths. Wines like Regnié, Côte de Brouilly and St-Amour, from the most recent vintage possible, will go happily right through the meal.

If you still feel like drinking wine after all that exotic food, the wonderful upside-down cake will tax any wine. I'd choose a heady, tea-leaf, rose-petal, honey-and-raisin-flavoured Australian Liqueur Muscat, preferably from Baileys or Stanton & Killeen. If not, a Spanish Moscatel or a French Muscat de Rivesaltes would do fairly well.

AROMATIC VEGETABLES

Almost all spicy food seems to taste just as good eaten cold, which makes it particularly ideal for large parties. This dish, which is rather like an exotic ratatouille, is especially useful because not only will it please the vegetarians but it also combines well with meat or fish dishes. Don't worry about the quantity of whole garlic cloves – if garlic is cooked long and gently it becomes mild. It is easiest to make this in a very large pan such as you would use for jam-making.

3kg/6lb tomatoes
6 large or medium red peppers
3 heads garlic
6 aubergines
175ml/6fl oz lemon juice
9 tablespoons groundnut oil
4 teaspoons paprika
6 teaspoons ground cinnamon
4 teaspoons ground mace
1½ teaspoons ground cloves
1 tablespoon onion seeds
1·5kg/3lb carrots
2 cauliflowers
3 small bunches spring greens
1½ tablespoons clear honey
750g/1½lb Greek yogurt, to serve
Salt
Cayenne pepper

Working with a few at a time, put the tomatoes into a bowl, pour boiling water over them, wait a minute or two, then drain, skin and chop roughly. Cut the peppers in half lengthways, remove the seeds and stems and slice fairly thinly

Peel all the garlic cloves but keep them whole unless they are very big, in which case cut them in half lengthways. Cut the stalks off the aubergines, cut them into 1cm/½in slices and then cut each slice into quarters – sprinkle lemon juice on the aubergines as you cut them so that they don't discolour.

Put the groundnut oil into a very large saucepan or flameproof casserole over a high heat. When hot add the sliced peppers, aubergines and lemon juice and stir constantly for 3–4 minutes. Add the ground spices and the garlic and stir for another minute. Finally add the chopped tomatoes and the onion seeds. Cover the pan and simmer gently over a very low heat for 20–30 minutes until everything is soft.

While the mixture is cooking prepare the other vegetables. Scrape or peel the carrots as necessary, top and tail and slice as thinly as you can lengthways. Pull the cauliflower apart into very small florets. Wash the spring greens, remove any coarse outer leaves and slice across the bunches as thinly as you possibly can with a sharp knife.

When the pan mixture is mushy add the honey and then season to taste with salt and cayenne pepper. Add the sliced carrots and cauliflower, cover the pan again and cook over a low heat for 10–15 minutes until the carrots and cauliflower are tender. Finally add the sliced greens and bubble in the closed pan just for a minute until bright green.

Cool the mixture quickly by putting the pan in a sink of cold water.

To serve *Spoon the vegetables on to a serving dish. Place the yogurt in a bowl and allow the guests to help themselves, or, if you are sure that all of them like yogurt, spoon it roughly over the platter of vegetables. This dish should be served cold but not refrigerated.*

MANGO UPSIDE-DOWN ALMOND AND CITRUS CAKE WITH COCONUT CREAM

This light, moist cake is most delicious as a hot or warm pudding but is also good cold, though never chilled. The base, which becomes the top when the cake is turned out, consists of shining slices of fresh mango. The coconut cream complements the mango and enhances the exotic character of the cake. Make the cream before you make the cakes as it should be well chilled.

MANGO UPSIDE-DOWN ALMOND AND CITRUS CAKE WITH COCONUT CREAM

Coconut cream:
125g/4oz creamed coconut
125ml/4fl oz milk
1 teaspoon salt
4 tablespoons golden caster sugar
600ml/1 pint double cream

Mango cakes (2):
425g/14oz butter
500g/1lb golden caster sugar
4 ripe mangoes
125ml/4fl oz lemon juice
Grated rind of 2 lemons and 4 oranges
10 eggs
300g/10oz ground almonds
100g/4oz plain flour
4 teaspoons baking powder
1 teaspoon salt

To make the coconut cream, break up the coconut roughly and put into a small saucepan with the milk. Dissolve the coconut in the milk by stirring over a medium heat. Add the salt and caster sugar and stir until the sugar has dissolved. Remove from the heat and stir in the cream. Pour into a serving bowl and chill well before serving.

To make the cakes, smear 25g/1oz of the butter over the bottom and up the sides of each of two 28cm/11in diameter flan dishes. Sprinkle 50g/2oz of the caster sugar evenly over the bottom of each dish. Peel the mangoes and, using a sharp knife, cut across in thin, half moon slices. Arrange the slices in a neatly overlapping circular pattern over the bottom of the dishes, leaving no gaps. Sprinkle the mango slices with lemon juice.

Beat the remaining butter and caster sugar until fluffy and then whisk in the grated lemon and orange rind. Whisk in the eggs and ground almonds alternately. Finally sift the flour, baking powder and salt on to the mixture and fold in with a metal spoon. Spoon the mixture on to the mango slices and spread evenly, dividing it equally between the two dishes. Bake in the centre of a preheated oven, 180°C, 350°F, Gas Mark 4, for 50–60 minutes or until a small knife inserted in the centre comes out clean.

To serve *Loosen the edges of the cakes carefully, using a knife if necessary, and turn on to large flat serving plates.*

SEPARATE TABLES

for 8, 16 or 24

This is a sit-down buffet with separate tables seating eight guests each (it is possible to hire round tables – which are the best for conversation and for fitting into a small space). Each of the dishes serves eight people; the idea is to make one aspic or pie or whatever for as many tables as you are preparing.

Your guests will breathe a sigh of relief when they realize they are going to eat sitting down, and it makes quite a different kind of party; far more time will be spent eating with the result that the food is more likely to be properly appreciated. You need not make so many different dishes but as they will be comfortably seated your guests will be inclined to eat a larger quantity of food.

As the tables will probably be close together an informal atmosphere should still be possible with guests talking across tables to each other. If you are bold enough to be bossy you can even instruct them to change tables for each course but I feel this always separates people who are at the budding of a new friendship or simply enjoying each other's company and they may well resent the next hour or so spent talking to someone else.

MENU

*

SEAFOOD IN WINE AND FRESH ORANGE ASPIC

TURKEY AND FENNEL PIE WITH PARMESAN PASTRY

VELVET SPINACH PURÉE WITH VEGETABLE STARBURST

*

CHOCOLATE AND LEMON MERINGUE TART

*

Fino Sherry

Alsace Pinot Gris

Spanish Moscatel

SEAFOOD IN WINE AND FRESH ORANGE ASPIC

SEAFOOD IN WINE AND FRESH ORANGE ASPIC

Setting things in aspic is a wonderfully simple way of making them look both beautiful and grand. This pretty dish of seafood in a subtly flavoured aspic makes a perfect first course for this type of buffet – the only kind where you can really separate the courses. The aspic is wine with a touch of orange, mildly flavoured with fresh ginger and garlic. When you are feeling more lavish you could substitute salmon fillet for the smoked cod. If you are making many of these aspics borrow cake tins and moulds from friends and neighbours. Borrowed space in a neighbour's fridge would be welcome too.

250g/8oz small squid
500g/1lb smoked cod fillet, skinned
450ml/¾ pint medium-sweet white wine
300ml/½ pint freshly squeezed orange juice
2 teaspoons salt
2–3 large cloves garlic, peeled and roughly chopped
2·5–5cm/1–2in piece fresh root ginger, peeled and roughly chopped
6 teaspoons powdered gelatine
1 small bunch fresh dill or coriander
250g/8oz peeled prawns
Salt
Cayenne pepper
Unpeeled cooked prawns, to garnish (optional)
Dill or coriander sprigs, to garnish

Wash the squid but try not to push off the thin film of speckly skin. Cut the head off the squid pulling out the innards as you do so. Cut off the tentacles and reserve, cutting them in half if they are large. Discard the black eyes and hard bit of the head. Pull the plastic-looking bone out of the body of the squid and squeeze out any soft innards left inside. Then slice the body fairly thinly.

Cut the cod fillet into 1·5cm/¾in chunks. Put about 600ml/1 pint of water into a fairly wide saucepan and bring to the boil. Add the cod and squid, including the tentacles. Cover the pan and bring up to bubbling again for barely a minute, until the fish turns opaque. Remove immediately from the heat and, using a slotted spoon, drain the cod and squid, and set aside.

Put the wine into a saucepan, strain in the orange juice through a fine sieve and pour in 300ml/½ pint of water. Add the salt, garlic and ginger. Cover the pan and bring to the boil. Reduce the heat and simmer gently for 15 minutes. Strain the liquid through a fine sieve into a jug and discard the garlic and ginger.

Taste the liquid in the jug and add more salt and a little cayenne pepper to taste. Pour about a quarter of the liquid back into the saucepan and sprinkle in the gelatine. Put over a very low heat and stir constantly until it has completely dissolved. Remove from the heat and gradually stir in the liquid remaining in the jug.

Pull the leaves off the dill or coriander stems and arrange some on the bottom of a fairly shallow and wide 1·6 litre/2¾ pint mould or cake tin. Arrange a layer of squid and prawns over them, followed by the fish and remaining squid and prawns, scattering the rest of the dill or coriander leaves among them.

Gradually pour in the wine and orange liquid. Leave until cool and then refrigerate for 4 hours or until thoroughly set.

To turn out the aspic, loosen the edges with your fingers and then dip the mould for a second or two into a sink of hot water. Tip the mould upside down on to a serving plate and give a good shake, holding the mould to the plate until you feel the aspic loosen from the sides.

Chill until ready to serve.

To serve *Garnish with unpeeled, cooked prawns and more dill or coriander. Serve with hollandaise sauce or mayonnaise and, if required, crusty bread or thin toast.*

EXTRAS

As there are plenty of vegetables included in the menu you will need only a simple green leaf salad as an accompaniment. Crisp lettuce leaves with some lamb's lettuce leaves and cress among them are ideal.

You could serve a potato salad: use unpeeled new potatoes cut in half and dressed with a garlic vinaigrette while hot.

A white or brown *pain de campagne* or large crusty loaf sliced across beforehand should also be on each table, or alternatively you could put a soft wholemeal roll by each plate.

You will also need hollandaise sauce or mayonnaise to go with the fish aspic and remember to get some unpeeled prawns and extra dill or coriander leaves for garnish.

Serve a small jug of double cream with the chocolate and lemon meringue tart, and, as an alternative to the tart, bunches of fresh grapes.

There should be a mill for black pepper, sea salt in a bowl or mill and a little unsalted butter on each table.

Remember a bottle of mineral water for each table too.

TURKEY AND FENNEL PIE WITH PARMESAN PASTRY

PLANNING AHEAD

In advance: The pastry can be made a few days in advance, wrapped in clingfilm and kept in the fridge. If you want to begin preparation really early you can make the pastry weeks before and freeze it until needed. When you have rolled out the pastry and covered the filled pie dishes you can keep them, with the pastry still uncooked, in your refrigerator, and possibly your neighbour's too, for up to two days.

Two days before: Make the seafood aspic if it helps but a day in advance would be preferable. If you are making several aspics it would be sensible to make them ahead, especially if the party is during hot weather when they will take longer to set. Make the filling for the turkey and fennel pie, allow to cool and refrigerate.

The day before: If fridge space is limited cover the pie dishes with the pastry the day before the party, cook them as instructed and keep the cooked pies in a cool place to reheat before the party.

Make the spinach purée and keep it, covered, in the fridge. Make the chocolate and lemon meringue tart except for the meringue top.

The day of the party: Cook the vegetables in the morning, and assemble them an hour or two in advance but don't dress them until just before you serve the meal. Make the potato salad and dress it while it's still hot. Make the meringue and finish off the tart about an hour before the guests arrive. Make the green salad and dress it just before the guests arrive. If you're serving it, make the toast to accompany the aspic.

Hot pies are always a festive sight. They can also be made in stages, well in advance, so that they are very little trouble just before the party. If you can manage one pie for each table it will look wonderful. If you have only a small oven you may have to re-heat some of the pies in a neighbour's house. If re-heating the pies really is a problem they still taste good eaten at room temperature, but I don't think pastry ever tastes quite right really cold.

Filling:
875g/1¾lb turkey breast fillets
4 large fennel bulbs
Groundnut oil for frying
50g/2oz butter
2–3 large cloves garlic, chopped
½ teaspoon grated nutmeg
50g/2oz plain flour
4 tablespoons natural yogurt
600ml/1 pint milk
500g/1lb small tomatoes
Salt and black pepper

Pastry:
375g/12oz strong plain flour
1 teaspoon salt
½ teaspoon caraway seeds
75g/3oz strong Cheddar cheese, coarsely grated
50g/2oz Parmesan cheese, finely grated
175g/6oz chilled butter
1 large (size 2) egg, separated
3 tablespoons cold water

To make the filling, cut the turkey fillets in half and slice across in 1cm/½in slices. Cut off the stalks and any marked outer parts of the fennel bulbs, but reserve any feathery leaves. Cut the bulbs lengthways into several pieces.

Heat 2 tablespoons of oil in a large frying pan over a high heat, add the turkey slices and toss around just to brown. With a slotted spatula, transfer the turkey to a large bowl on one side and then fry the fennel pieces until tinged with brown, adding more oil if necessary. Put them with the turkey slices.

Melt the butter in a large flameproof casserole, add the chopped garlic and the grated nutmeg and stir around for a moment or two. Remove from the heat and stir in the flour with a wooden spoon. Stir in the yogurt, followed by the milk, a little at a time. Put back on a fairly high heat and bring to the boil, stirring all the time in one direction. The sauce will gradually thicken as you stir. When it comes to the boil, reduce the heat and keep stirring for another 2–3 minutes. Remove from the heat and add salt and pepper to taste. Add the turkey and fennel slices to the sauce.

Put the casserole back on top of the stove over a fairly high heat and bring to bubbling, stirring constantly. Cover the casserole and put in the centre of a preheated oven, 180°C, 350°F, Gas Mark 4, for 45 minutes.

Meanwhile put the tomatoes in a bowl, pour boiling water over them, leave for a minute, then drain. Skin them and leave on one side.

When the turkey and fennel has cooked for 45 minutes add the whole, peeled tomatoes and distribute gently without breaking them. Cover the casserole and put back in the oven for another 15 minutes.

Remove the casserole from the oven, check for seasoning, pour gently into a 2–2·3 litre/3½–4 pint traditional pie dish and leave until cold.

For the pastry, sift the flour and salt into a bowl and mix in the caraway seeds and grated cheeses with a knife. Cut the butter into small pieces, stir into the flour and cheese and then rub in with your fingertips until the mixture is crumbly.

Using a fork, lightly whisk the egg white (reserving the yolk) with the water and pour it gradually into the flour mixture, mixing it in with the fork until it sticks together. Then press the dough into a ball, wrap it in clingfilm and refrigerate.

When the turkey and fennel mix-

ture is quite cool, roll out the pastry on a floured board to 2·5cm/1in bigger than the pie dish. Cut a strip of pastry from around the edge. Dampen the edge of the pie dish and lay the pastry strip on top. Dampen the strip and cover the pie with the remaining pastry. Cut off the excess pastry and then press the edges with the back of a knife to seal.

Roll out the trimmings and cut out decorations for the top of the pie. Cut two holes for the steam to escape.

At this point you can refrigerate the pie for up to two days or you can cook the pies at once and keep them for up to a day in a cool place before re-heating them for the party.

To cook the pies, heat the oven to 200°C, 400°F, Gas Mark 6. Brush the pastry with the reserved egg yolk and bake the pie in the centre of the oven for 30–40 minutes until richly browned.

The pies can be kept warm in a low oven for at least an hour.

TURKEY AND FENNEL PIE WITH PARMESAN PASTRY, VELVET SPINACH PURÉE WITH VEGETABLE STARBURST

PRESENTATION

At a party where people sit down you should pay more attention to the look of both crockery and glasses simply because the guests will have more of a chance to notice them and to appreciate a prettily arranged table.

Separate tables at a party can look really magical if you light each table with two or three candles or a candelabra. It is possible to hire silver-plated candelabra, which look very grand and festive, from catering hire firms.

If you have enough tall candles you will probably find that you need no other lighting in the room. With any party no form of lighting is as pretty or as inviting as candlelight, and it is flattering both to the food and to the guests.

Tablecloths can simply be sheets as there will be plenty of pretty food on the table to disguise them. If possible at this elegant party use real napkins or else very thick, good-quality paper ones.

Make room for a low bowl of pretty, informal flowers in the centre of the table as they, like the food, will really be noticed when people are sitting down close to them.

The seafood aspic looks even more beautiful if you use imaginatively shaped tins: I use a shell-shaped mould or a heart-shaped tin, but any interesting shape will do. Borrow from friends if you haven't any. The aspic would look especially pretty on a green serving plate and the velvet spinach purée with vegetable starburst goes well on a pale green or white plate.

For the pies, traditional earthenware dishes are ideal though a shallower ovenproof dish will give you a larger area of pastry so that everyone gets a proper piece.

Oz Clarke's *WINE NOTES*

This is a slightly more formal affair than the usual 'dive-in and grab what you can' buffet which I normally end up at. In fact, I have a definite feeling Josceline would expect me to wear a tie at this gathering and possibly even a suit and polished shoes as well. So I think I'll be fairly traditional in my wine choices for fear of being thrown out.

I'll start with sherry. Real dry sherry, real *fino* or *manzanilla* or Puerto Fino sherries, from the south-western tip of Spain, are magical wines. They're bone dry with a piercing, unnerving flavour of fresh bread yeast and polished old wooden banisters (honest! The first thing I thought of when I tried my initial glass of *fino* sherry was the burnished mahogany banister at home I used to slide down when my mother's back was turned).

We think of dry sherry as a rather genteel aperitif, but the Spaniards have got the message much better. They chill it right down and quaff it liberally with their local seafood. It's a magic combination.

To be honest it'll go brilliantly with the turkey and the spinach purée as well, but you may want to change to something less demanding. Alsace makes the most delicious, scented, gently flavoured yet robustly structured white wines in France. Wines like Sylvaner and Gewürztraminer are dry, but full of soft ripeness and floral perfume. Alsace Pinot Gris tastes of honey and peaches and spring flowers – you'd swear it isn't dry, but it is.

Spanish Moscatel isn't dry. It's one of the only wines which could cope with a chocolate and lemon meringue tart. The lightest is from Valencia, the brownest, most raisiny is from Málaga, and the freshest is from Chipiona in the sherry region. Take your pick.

VELVET SPINACH PURÉE WITH VEGETABLE STARBURST

This is a simple vegetable dish which looks like a beautiful starburst or a many-petalled flower. The centre is a velvet-smooth purée of spinach and fromage frais from which fans out a border of slivered carrots and broccoli dressed simply with good olive oil and lemon juice. The spinach purée can be made the day before. Cook the vegetables on the morning of the party and assemble the dish an hour or two before the guests arrive.

1kg/2lb spinach
2 teaspoons green peppercorns
500g/1lb 8% fat fromage frais
500g/1lb carrots
750g/1½lb broccoli florets
Small bunch of parsley
4 tablespoons lemon juice
6 tablespoons olive oil
Salt and black pepper

Wash the spinach, then remove any thick, coarse stalks and discard. Plunge the leaves into a large pan of boiling salted water (you may have to do this in two batches unless you have a very large pan), cover and cook for 8–10 minutes until the spinach is quite soft.

Drain the spinach and press out as much water as you can with a large wooden spoon. Leave until cool and then put into a food mill or food processor with the peppercorns (again you may have to do this in batches depending on the size of your processor) and whizz until smooth.

Transfer the purée to a bowl, add the fromage frais and mix together thoroughly. Season to taste with salt and pepper. Cover the bowl and keep in the fridge until you are ready to assemble the dish.

To prepare the vegetables, scrape or peel the carrots as necessary, top and tail and, depending on the size of the carrots, cut in half or in quarters lengthways. Boil in salted water until tender and then drain.

Slice the broccoli florets fairly thinly lengthways, keeping all but the base of the stem – they should still have a flat floret shape. Plunge them into a saucepan of boiling, salted water for 3–5 minutes until just beginning to be tender but still bright green. Drain and rinse with cold water so that they don't go on cooking.

To serve *Spoon the spinach purée into the centre of a large round serving dish. Arrange the carrots and broccoli fanning out in alternate sections so as to make a striped effect.*

Chop the parsley finely and sprinkle into the centre of the purée with some scant scatterings reaching out to the vegetables.

Strain the lemon juice into a bowl, mix in the olive oil with a fork and season with salt and pepper. Just before you put the dish on the table, spoon this dressing over the vegetables and a little on to the spinach purée as well.

SEE PAGE 113.

CHOCOLATE AND LEMON MERINGUE TART

This is a far cry from lemon meringue pie. The tart has a crisp, dark chocolate pastry crust and is filled with a light and sharp fresh lemon mixture topped with soft meringue and sprinkled with grated chocolate. Only the meringue top needs preparing on the day of your party. The rest of the tart can be made the day before so it is perfectly practical to make several tarts in advance. The tarts can be eaten either warm or cold – they will be equally delicious.

Pastry:
175g/6oz strong plain flour
2 tablespoons cocoa powder
4 tablespoons icing sugar
1 teaspoon salt
125g/4oz butter
1 tablespoon water

Filling and meringue:
6 eggs
Finely grated rind of 1 lemon
325g/11oz caster sugar
Juice of 5 lemons
125g/4oz unsalted butter
¼ teaspoon salt
40–50g/1½–2oz plain chocolate, chopped small or grated

Butter a 25cm/10in fluted flan tin with a loose base.

To make the pastry, sift the flour, cocoa powder, icing sugar and salt into a bowl. Gently melt the butter with the water and stir into the flour mixture with a wooden spoon until you have a smooth dough. Press the dough evenly over the base and up the sides of the flan tin and refrigerate while you prepare the filling.

Put 4 egg yolks (reserving the whites) and 2 whole eggs into the top of a double saucepan or a bowl that can be set over a pan of gently simmering water. Add the lemon rind and whisk together thoroughly with a fork. Mix in 150g/5oz of the caster sugar.

Pour the lemon juice into a measuring jug and make up to 300ml/½ pint with water, if necessary. Gradually mix into the egg yolk mixture. Heat over gently simmering water and stir until the mixture thickens enough to lightly coat the back of a spoon. Add the unsalted butter bit by bit and stir until melted. Leave until cool.

Pour the cold filling into the chilled chocolate case. Cook in the centre of a preheated oven, 190°C, 375°F, Gas Mark 5, for 20–25 minutes. Remove from the oven and leave to cool for at least 10 minutes or store in a cool place until next day.

On the day of your party, not too early on, prepare the meringue top. Put the egg whites into a large bowl, add salt and whisk until the whites stand in soft peaks. Whisk in about half the remaining caster sugar and then fold in the rest with a metal spoon. Spoon the meringue on top of the lemon filling and sprinkle with grated chocolate (alternatively sprinkle with chocolate after cooking the meringue). Cook in the centre of a preheated oven, 180°C, 350°F, Gas Mark 4, for 10–15 minutes until the meringue is pale golden.

CHOCOLATE AND LEMON MERINGUE TART

Vegetarian Buffet

for 12

It is unlikely you will have a party at which every guest is a vegetarian but a growing proportion of the population are either vegetarian or semi-vegetarian. Young people often become vegetarians and many others find that they eat meat far less frequently as they get older, so this could be a buffet which would suit a predominantly young party such as a 21st. Many people, my daughter and several of our friends included, eat vegetables with the addition of fish and shellfish which seems to be an almost ideal diet.

But, whether you are vegetarian or not, from time to time it is refreshing to eat a meal which consists almost entirely of vegetables, and to realize just how good vegetables can be. Of course it is all far easier nowadays with such a variety of fresh vegetables available all year round as well as ingredients to complement them, and food processors to transform them into purées, paper-thin slices or the finest shreds or whatever you want.

To devise a vegetarian feast for a large gathering was an especially enjoyable challenge and I hope that it will satisfy even the most carnivorous guest.

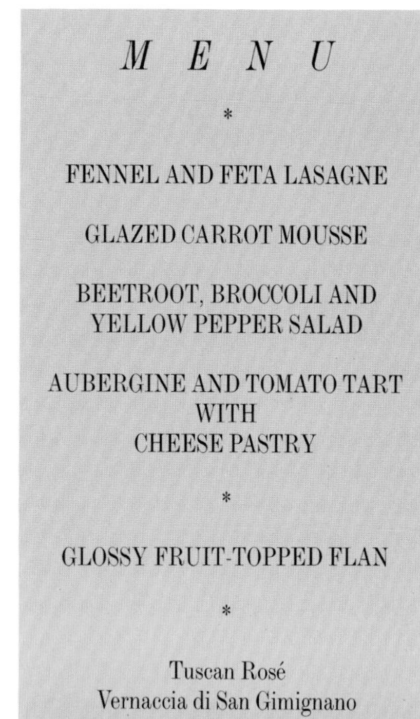

Menu

*

FENNEL AND FETA LASAGNE

GLAZED CARROT MOUSSE

BEETROOT, BROCCOLI AND YELLOW PEPPER SALAD

AUBERGINE AND TOMATO TART WITH CHEESE PASTRY

*

GLOSSY FRUIT-TOPPED FLAN

*

Tuscan Rosé
Vernaccia di San Gimignano
Muscat de Beaumes-de-Venise

GLAZED CARROT MOUSSE, FENNEL AND FETA LASAGNE

FENNEL AND FETA LASAGNE

For a large party, lasagne must be one of the most practical and popular dishes there can be. It is complete, satisfying and easy to manage with only a fork, something you should always think about if people are going to have to eat standing up. Vegetable lasagnes tend to be lighter and moister and I find that a yogurt sauce makes it all far less heavy and cloying than the more usual rich cheese sauce. In this version the filling is predominantly bulb fennel which combines very well with the slight sharpness of feta (a non-rennet cheese) and the aromatics of green peppercorns and coriander seeds. Strict vegetarians who object to renneted cheeses will omit the final sprinkling of Parmesan.

375g/12oz green lasagne sheets (the 'no pre-cooking' type)
8–10 medium to large bulbs fennel
1 tablespoon coriander seeds
4 teaspoons green peppercorns
4 tablespoons olive oil
2 very large onions, chopped roughly
4 large cloves garlic, chopped finely
2 teaspoons caster sugar
500g/1lb feta cheese
2 rounded tablespoons cornflour
4 tablespoons milk
2 × 450ml/¾ pint cartons natural yogurt
4 tablespoons grated Parmesan cheese (optional)
Sea salt
Black pepper

Put the lasagne sheets into a sink full of very hot water for 15–20 minutes until they have softened but are not breaking up. Remove the sheets and lay them on pieces of kitchen paper.

Cut the base and stems off the fennel bulbs and remove any marked outer layers (keep any feathery bits to chop and scatter over the cooked dish before serving). Slice the fennel across fairly thinly. Bring a pan of salted water to the boil, add the sliced fennel and cook for 10 minutes or until soft. Drain the sliced fennel, put it into a large mixing bowl and set aside.

Grind the coriander seeds and green peppercorns in a pestle and mortar until well broken down. Heat 2 tablespoons of the olive oil in a large frying pan and fry the onions over a gentle heat until soft and translucent. Add the garlic and stir for another 2–3 minutes before adding the crushed green peppercorns and coriander seeds. Stir thoroughly and remove from the heat. Add the contents of the pan to the cooked fennel and mix in well. Finally stir in the caster sugar and a little sea salt.

Spread the remaining olive oil on the bottom of two ovenproof dishes measuring approximately 28 × 20cm/11 × 8in. (One very large dish will do if it will fit in your oven.) Cut the feta cheese into thin slices. Place a layer of lasagne in each dish. Then spread one third of the fennel and onion mixture evenly over the lasagne. Arrange a third of the feta cheese slices on top. Add another layer of lasagne and continue as before ending with a final layer of lasagne.

To make the sauce, put the cornflour into a fairly large saucepan, add the milk and stir until smooth. Stir in the yogurt. Put the pan over the heat and bring to the boil, stirring in one direction only. Allow to bubble, still stirring, for 2–3 minutes. Season with black pepper but no salt as the feta cheese should give enough saltiness to the dish. Then spoon the yogurt sauce evenly over each dish of lasagne and sprinkle with the grated Parmesan.

Keep the uncooked lasagnes in a cold place or in the fridge and cook them shortly before the party. Bake them in in the centre of a preheated oven, 200°C, 400°F, Gas Mark 6, alternating the dishes if on different shelves, for about 35 minutes until speckled brown on top.

EXTRAS

These colourful and delicious vegetable dishes need only the simplest of salad accompaniments.

One salad should be of crisp lettuce such as Cos. If you have fennel growing in your garden chop some roughly and throw it in with the salad leaves – it will complement the cooked fennel in the lasagne.

A second salad could be sliced fruity tomatoes dressed with a mustardy vinaigrette and sprinkled with sprigs of fresh basil.

You will also need a well-flavoured vinaigrette dressing for the beetroot and broccoli salad.

About 1·8 litres/3 pints cream, yogurt, or yogurt with whipped cream folded into it (which I love) is needed to go with the fruit flan. And offer fresh seasonal fruit as an alternative dessert.

Don't forget wholemeal rolls, sliced wholemeal French sticks, unsalted butter, sea salt, black peppercorns in a mill and plenty of mineral water.

PLANNING AHEAD

In advance: Make the flan base, wrap in clingfilm and freeze.

Two days before: Prepare the lasagnes and keep them uncooked in the fridge or a really cold place. Make the carrot mousse, cover and refrigerate.

The day before: Make the aubergine and tomato tarts. Cook the beetroot.

The day of the party: Take the fruit flan bases out of the freezer in the morning. Three hours before the party, prepare the fruit topping and glaze. Two hours before, bake the lasagnes and keep them warm in a low oven. Reheat the aubergine and tomato tarts (or bring to room temperature). Blanch the broccoli and grill and skin the peppers. Assemble this and the extra salads shortly before the guests arrive.

GLAZED CARROT MOUSSE

PRESENTATION

The food for this buffet is particularly colourful and decorative in shape so the plates and tablecloth should ideally be white to show it off. There should be plenty of mixed garden flowers on the table, and maybe white or dark green candles too.

Cook the lasagne in rectangular earthenware dishes; dark green ones look good if you can find any. Serve the aubergine and tomato tarts on white or green serving plates if possible. A large, shallow, oval or rectangular dish is right for the arrange[illegible]e beetroot and broccoli salad a[illegible]ther dark green china or glass would really set it off beautifully.

The carrot mousse looks pretty on a white plate, setting off the bright orange top.

For the flan a white porcelain plate with a decorative border looks best but as it is so difficult to find really large, round and flat serving plates you could use a silver cake board a little bigger than the flan, or a large round bread board.

If you are serving yogurt and whipped cream with the flan spoon it into a glass bowl.

GLAZED CARROT MOUSSE

It seems almost magical that something as homely and modest as the carrot can be transformed into this light, dazzling and extremely delicious mousse with its brilliantly coloured glossy top of carrot slivers set in a lemon-tinged aspic. Non-vegetarians can substitute gelatine for agar-agar powder.

Glazed top:
250g/8oz carrots
300ml/½ pint salted water
½ teaspoon agar-agar powder
(or 1 teaspoon gelatine)
4 tablespoons lemon juice
Fresh coriander leaves, flat-leaved parsley or fennel leaves
Salt
Cayenne pepper

Mousse:
500g/1lb carrots
1½ teaspoons agar-agar powder
(or 3 teaspoons gelatine)
25[illegible]/8oz cream cheese
[illegible]poons white wine vinegar
1[illegible]on caraway seeds
3[illegible]/½ pint whipping cream
Oil for greasing
Coriander leaves, to garnish
Salt
Cayenne pepper

Make the glazed top first. Scrape the carrots and slice them in rounds as thinly as possible with a sharp knife or using the slicing blade of a food processor. Put the sliced carrot rounds in a saucepan with the salted water, cover the pan and bring to the boil, then simmer for about 5 minutes or until the carrots are softened. Using a slotted spatula, remove the carrots and put aside. Sprinkle the agar-agar powder into the pan of cooking water and stir over a low heat until dissolved. Remove from the heat and add the lemon juice. Season to taste with salt and cayenne.

Strain a little of the pan juice through a fine sieve into the bottom of a deep cake tin or soufflé dish of 1·4–1·7 litre/2½–3 pint capacity. Make a pattern on the bottom of the tin with the coriander leaves. Then lay a complete layer of carrot rounds in a neatly overlapping pattern and arrange the rest of the carrot rounds evenly on top. Strain in the remaining pan juices. Cool and then transfer to the fridge to set.

Meanwhile prepare the mousse. Scrape the carrots and cut them up roughly. Put them into a saucepan with enough salted water just to cover. Boil until soft then remove from the heat and spoon 6 tablespoons of the hot carrot water into a cup. Sprinkle the agar-agar powder into the water and stir thoroughly until dissolved.

Drain the carrots and purée through a sieve or in a food processor. Add the dissolved agar-agar, the cream cheese and the wine vinegar. Mix well or whizz until completely smooth. Add the caraway seeds and season with salt and cayenne pepper, rather stronger than to taste as you will be diluting the mixture with cream later.

Oil the sides of the cake tin or dish above the aspic. When the carrot mixture is cool (it doesn't have to be completely cold), whip the cream until thick but not stiff. Fold it fairly roughly into the carrot mixture leaving it slightly streaky and then spoon it into the tin on top of the aspic. Chill in the fridge for several hours.

When ready to turn out, loosen the edges of the mousse with a round-bladed knife allowing air under the glaze to release the vacuum, and rub the bottom and sides of the tin with a cloth dipped in very hot water. Put the tin on to a serving plate and, giving a good shake, turn the glazed mousse out. Just before serving garnish the sides of the mousse with whole coriander leaves.

BEETROOT, BROCCOLI AND YELLOW PEPPER SALAD

This is a beautiful, fairly substantial salad for a party. It is arranged in broad stripes of bright green broccoli, ruby-red beetroot and smoky grilled and skinned yellow peppers. I use a very large, shallow oval dish so that the vegetable stripes follow the oval shape, or a rectangular dish, arranging the vegetables in either vertical, horizontal or diagonal stripes.

1kg/2lb uncooked beetroots
5 large yellow peppers
750g–1kg/1½–2lb calabrese broccoli florets
1 good handful fresh fennel leaves or parsley, roughly chopped
Vinaigrette dressing

Boil the whole, unpeeled beetroots in salted water for 40–60 minutes (depending on size) until tender. Drain and leave on one side. While the beetroots are cooking, slice the peppers in half lengthways and remove the seeds and stems. Put the pepper halves, skin side upwards, under a very hot grill until the skin has burnt and blackened in patches all over. Then put them in a sealed paper or plastic bag (to make the skin come off more easily later) and leave to cool.

Cut any long thick stalks from the broccoli florets and then cut the florets in half so that they look like little trees. Steam or boil the broccoli for only 2–4 minutes just until bright green and still crunchy. Then put the broccoli into a sink of cold water to cool quickly. Slice the stalks and ends off the cooled beetroot and slip off the skin before slicing across fairly thinly. Take the peppers out of the bag and pick off all the skin. Slice the peppers lengthways in medium strips.

To assemble the dish, drain the broccoli thoroughly and arrange the pieces in a border round the outside of the dish. Then arrange a stripe of overlapping beetroot pieces and finish with a centre of yellow pepper strips, or arrange the vegetables in stripes across the dish. Scatter the chopped fennel or parsley over the vegetables.

To serve *Before serving drizzle a good vinaigrette dressing all over the dish.*

BEETROOT, BROCCOLI AND YELLOW PEPPER SALAD, AUBERGINE AND TOMATO TART WITH CHEESE PASTRY

Oz Clarke's
WINE NOTES

There used to be a feeling that vegetarians were the kind of people who didn't drink. Well, that's certainly not true any more. Several of the most enthusiastic wine people I know are vegetarians, and whenever I'm trying to make myself feel healthier I go on a vegetables-only diet for a week or two, and keep on drinking my wine. I suppose I could give up the wine as well and feel twice as healthy twice as fast – but there are limits to the sacrifices I can subject myself to!

Josceline has created some delicious flavour combinations here. But they're the kind of dishes which demand good glugging wine, rather than delicate flavours to ponder over. So rosé, nice and cold and full of fruit, is ideal.

Tuscan rosé can be quite superb, especially from a top red-wine estate, since it will be from the run-off juice of the red wine and have that extra bit of flavour. Vinruspo from Capezzana is absolutely delightful. Otherwise choose a young dry pink from Provence or the Rhône valley in France.

The cheese in both the main dishes, and the vinaigrette on the salad, demand a full, but soft-textured white. The new wave of Italian whites is at last beginning to give us this style, and if we want to stay in Tuscany, the greengage and lemon-flavoured Vernaccia di San Gimignano would be ideal. Otherwise go for a Soave Classico Costalunga from near Verona, or a Tocai Friulano from north of Venice.

And since our fruit flan is made from whatever fruits are freshest in the shops, let's choose the freshest, fruitiest – and trendiest – of all the French sweet wines, Muscat de Beaumes-de-Venise.

AUBERGINE AND TOMATO TART WITH CHEESE PASTRY

This is a wonderfully full-flavoured and colourful tart. As with all pastry dishes it tastes better hot than cold – in fact it is most perfect served just warm. However, if you want to make several tarts in advance and haven't a big enough oven to reheat them in they will still be delicious as long as you serve them at room temperature, not chilled. Vegetarian Cheddar can be substituted for the strong Cheddar in the pastry but the flavour will not be so good.

Filling:
4 medium to large aubergines
4 large cloves garlic
1 lemon
6 tablespoons olive oil
4 teaspoons cumin seeds
2 × 425g/14oz cans chopped tomatoes
2 tablespoons tomato purée
½ teaspoon cayenne pepper
4 tablespoons fresh mint leaves
175g/6oz firm white goats' cheese
2 small yellow peppers
Salt

Pastry:
350g/12oz plain flour
2 teaspoons salt
175g/6oz butter
125g/4oz strong Cheddar cheese, grated
Cold water to mix

To make the filling, chop the aubergines into 1·5cm/¾in pieces, discarding the stem. Peel the garlic and chop finely. Remove any pips from the lemon and slice into small pieces. Heat the olive oil in a large, deep frying pan over a medium heat.

Add the aubergine pieces and cook, stirring often, for about 10 minutes until the aubergine has browned and is soft right through. Add the chopped garlic and the cumin seeds and stir for a minute. Pour in the chopped tomatoes and stir in the tomato purée. Add the lemon pieces and cook over a gentle heat for another 8–10 minutes.

Finally, increase the heat and bubble for another minute or two until the mixture has reduced and is fairly thick. Remove from the heat and season with the cayenne pepper and salt to taste. Then turn the mixture into a large bowl and leave until cold.

Meanwhile make the pastry. Sift the flour and salt into a bowl. Cut up the butter into small pieces and rub into the flour with your fingers until it is like breadcrumbs. Then stir in the grated cheese with a knife. Add a very little cold water, stirring it in with the knife until the dough just begins to stick together.

Gather the dough into a ball and, if there is time, wrap and refrigerate for half an hour or more. Butter two 28cm/11in loose-bottomed fluted flan tins. Divide the pastry in half and roll out each piece on a floured surface to a circle big enough to line one flan tin. Turn the overlapping edges over double but leave the edge of the pastry a little above the edge of the tin. Refrigerate until you are ready to cook the tarts.

Chop the mint leaves fairly roughly and mix into the cooled filling. Divide the filling between the pastry cases and spread level. Crumble half the goats' cheese roughly in the centre of each. Cut the yellow peppers lengthways, discard the seeds and stems and slice very thinly lengthways in strips. Arrange the strips in a fan shape on top of the tarts.

Cook in the centre of a pre-heated oven, 200°C, 400°F, Gas Mark 6, for 25–35 minutes until richly browned in patches, swopping shelf positions half-way through.

SEE PAGE 119.

GLOSSY FRUIT-TOPPED FLAN

GLOSSY FRUIT-TOPPED FLAN

The top of this flan can be very much your own work of art. You arrange a mixture of seasonal fruits on top of a very light but crunchy sponge base and glaze it with fruit jelly. Try soft fruit in the summer or halved grapes, banana and tropical fruits in the winter. In the late summer and autumn seedless green grapes with blackberries and slices of peach or nectarine is a delicious combination.

Flan base:
75g/3oz plain fine sponge flour
1½ teaspoons baking powder
¼ teaspoon salt
3 large (size 1) eggs
75g/3oz fine demerara sugar or soft brown sugar
25g/1oz toasted hazelnuts, chopped
25g/1oz pecan nuts or walnuts, finely chopped

Fruit topping and glaze:
1kg/2lb mixed fresh fruits
375g–500g/12oz–1lb fruit jelly
2 tablespoons lemon juice

Butter a 28cm/11in diameter flan dish or tin and line with a disc of buttered baking parchment.

Sift the flour with the baking powder and salt two or three times and put on one side. Put the eggs into a large bowl over a large saucepan of hot water. Whisk with an electric whisk until fairly thick and pale lemon coloured. Then whisk in the sugar and continue whisking until the mixture is greatly increased in volume and thick enough to stand in peaks.

Then, using a metal spoon, lightly fold in the chopped nuts. Sprinkle the sifted flour on top and gently cut and fold into the mixture. Pour into the prepared flan dish and bake in the centre of a preheated oven, 180°C, 350°F, Gas Mark 4, for 15–20 minutes until browned, risen and springy to touch in the centre.

Lay a folded tea towel on a wire rack. Carefully loosen the sides of the flan with a knife and turn out on to the cloth. Peel off the baking parchment. Put a large round serving plate or a cake board on top of the flan and turn it upside down on to the plate with the help of the rack. Allow to cool.

For the topping prepare the fruits, removing pips, peeling and slicing as necessary, and arrange them on top of the flan. Put the fruit jelly and lemon juice into a pan over a medium heat to melt, stirring until smooth. Spoon the jelly over the fruit, spreading it evenly over the sides of the flan too.

To serve *Serve with cream, yogurt or yogurt with whipped cream folded in.*

SUMMER BUFFET
for 16

A summer buffet should be one of the easiest parties to give. If you are lucky the weather may be good enough to use your garden for extra space – have plenty of rugs or straw mats ready to put out on the grass so the scene will be like a large romantic picnic. If it is an evening party on a hot night Chinese lanterns with nightlights look beautiful hung from the trees.

During the summer shops are bursting with every kind of delicious ingredient including many that need no cooking and little preparation. Fresh fish can simply be marinated, varieties of salad leaves abound and soft fruits can be piled high. Flowers from your garden can be scattered among your salads with fresh herbs to make them even prettier; nasturtiums and their leaves, rose and chrysanthemum petals are all edible.

With food and flowers at their peak and your guests relaxed and cheered by warmer, brighter days, much of the success of your party will have been naturally created for you – with the extra effort on your part it should be a triumph.

MENU

*

MARINATED SALMON

MIDSUMMER MACKEREL

RAINBOW CHICKEN ROLLS

*

FRESH ORANGE AND REDCURRANT JELLY

STRAWBERRIES WITH WHOLE ORANGE AND COINTREAU ICE CREAM

*

Côtes du Lubéron Rosé
Australian Chardonnay
Asti Spumante

RAINBOW CHICKEN ROLLS, MIDSUMMER MACKEREL

MARINATED SALMON

This is a variation of *gravad lax* made with coriander rather than dill and served with a simple sauce of lemony, seasoned fromage frais.

2·5cm/1in piece fresh root ginger
1kg/2lb tail piece of salmon, scaled, boned and cut into two fillets
3 teaspoons roughly crushed green or white peppercorns
50g/2oz demerara sugar
2 tablespoons sea salt
Good bunch of fresh coriander

Sauce:
375g/12oz fromage frais
2–4 tablespoons lemon juice
Salt and pepper

Peel the ginger, slice roughly and crush in a garlic press to extract the juice. Smear it over the flesh of the salmon. Mix peppercorns, sugar and salt in a bowl and pat the mixture on to the fillets. Reserve a few coriander leaves for the sauce and chop the rest roughly. Put one fillet in a shallow dish, skin side down, and spread the coriander over it. Place the other fillet on top, skin side up. Cover with clingfilm and put a board on top weighted down heavily. Refrigerate for 3–4 days (turn it after 2 days to marinate evenly). Make the sauce just before serving. Finely chop the reserved coriander and beat into the fromage frais with lemon juice and seasoning to taste.

To serve *Wipe off some of the peppercorns and herbs; slice the fish fairly thinly cutting at an angle towards the skin across the width of the fillet. Arrange on a serving plate. Spoon the sauce into a bowl.*

MARINATED SALMON

MIDSUMMER MACKEREL

Mackerel is an underrated fish. It has plenty of flavour, an excellent smooth texture and is nutritious. In this recipe it is added to a bubbling rich red sauce which cooks the fish gently as it cools.

8–10 medium mackerel, filleted and skinned
300ml/½ pint extra virgin olive oil
5 red peppers, deseeded and sliced
1 tablespoon dill seeds
1·5kg/3lb tomatoes, skinned and chopped
8 large cloves garlic, sliced thinly
3 tablespoons tomato purée
125ml/4fl oz lemon juice
Finely grated rind of 1 lemon
1 tablespoon caster sugar
1 large bunch fresh dill, chopped
50g/2oz pine kernels
Salt and black pepper

Slice the mackerel fillets across in 2·5cm/1in pieces and keep in the fridge. Pour the olive oil into a very wide, heavy saucepan or flameproof casserole. Add the red pepper and stir over a fairly high heat for about 5 minutes. Then add the dill seeds and stir for a minute before adding the tomatoes and garlic. Stir in the tomato purée, lemon juice and rind. Season with salt and pepper, cover the pan tightly and simmer very gently for half an hour, stirring now and then until the tomatoes have become a mushy sauce.

Add the sugar and adjust seasoning to taste. Bring the sauce back to a brisk boil and drop in the mackerel. Cover the pan and remove immediately from the heat. Leave to cool to room temperature. After 15 minutes, stir in the chopped dill.

Spoon the mixture on to shallow serving plates. Heat a dry frying pan over a high heat and toss the pine nuts in it for 1–2 minutes until golden. Scatter over the mackerel mixture. Serve at room temperature.

EXTRAS

This menu needs very little in the way of accompaniments – some good rye bread, both light and dark, thinly sliced to go with the marinated salmon, and chunks of crusty wholemeal to mop up the juices of the mackerel dish.

I would also serve a large bowl of mixed salad leaves dressed with a good fruity vinaigrette. Balsamic vinegar adds lively sweet flavours, and sherry vinegar is also good. There's no set recipe for the salad; choose from whatever is available at the time. I always try to get a variety of colours – red-tinged lollo rosso or feuille de chêne, the dark green of spinach leaves and the very pale and delicate frisée fronds. If I can find them I may add some small bright red or yellow cherry tomatoes.

Also on the table should be sea salt, black peppercorns in a mill, unsalted butter on small plates and, of course, mineral water.

One tip on making salads in large quantities – the last time we had a big party (a summer party for about 150 people) I cut up the salad ingredients and put them into a brand new plastic dustbin, then simply mixed them together with my hands and divided the salad between several large bowls. Just before serving I added the dressing.

You may wish to serve cream with the strawberries as well as the orange and Cointreau ice cream.

RAINBOW CHICKEN ROLLS

PLANNING AHEAD

In advance: Make the ice cream in its serving dish and keep it in the freezer (it must, in any case, be made at least seven hours before the party).

Four days before: Begin marinating the salmon, turning it after two days.

Two days before: Make the jellies and leave in their moulds in the fridge. Prepare the rainbow chicken to the foil stage and refrigerate.

The day before: Make the midsummer mackerel and refrigerate.

The day of the party: Take the mackerel out of the fridge an hour before the party to enable it to reach room temperature. Place it on a serving dish and sprinkle with the toasted pine nuts. Take out the salmon and chicken and slice them while they are still very cold. Place on serving dishes and cover with clingfilm. Prepare the strawberries. Make the salad and dress it just before serving. Take the ice cream out of the freezer about 30 minutes before serving. Take the jelly out of the fridge at the last minute.

PRESENTATION

With fresh herbs and edible flowers available, it is easy to make summer food look pretty. Dishes can be edged with parsley, fennel or lovage, or you can toss nasturtium flowers into salads or rose petals among bowls of soft fruit.

This buffet already has rich strong colours in the food, so present them against a cool background. Plain white china or clear glass dishes on a white tablecloth look wonderful with the reds, orange and green. Use white flowers, too: roses, gypsophila or lilies. If it is an evening party have white candles in elegant holders.

Serve the jelly on a raised cake stand for maximum impact. Shallow dishes are best for the chicken and mackerel.

These are fillets of chicken breast rolled up with bacon, fennel, red peppers, spinach and Mozzarella. They are eaten cold, cut across into thin slices which reveal the pretty layering of colours.

12 skinless chicken breast fillets
Lemon juice
24 thin rindless rashers smoked streaky bacon
3 medium fennel bulbs
3 medium red peppers
375g/12oz fresh spinach
2 × 150g/5oz Mozzarella cheeses
Salt and black pepper
Leaves, to garnish

Using a rolling pin or other heavy implement flatten the fillets between sheets of clingfilm. Sprinkle with lemon juice and pepper. Lay out the bacon rashers in pairs. Place a fillet on each pair and set aside. Slice the fennel across fairly thinly and boil until soft. Cut the peppers in half, remove the seeds and stem, and grill them skin side up until blackened all over. Peel away the skin and slice the peppers thinly. Chop the spinach leaves finely discarding the stalks. Slice the cheeses thinly. Spread the spinach evenly on each fillet, then place on the pepper, cheese and fennel.

Oil 12 largish pieces of foil. Fold the chicken and bacon over roughly, enclosing the stuffing. Don't worry if it falls apart a bit, just press it together between your hands, put on to a piece of the oiled foil and wrap the foil round to enclose the chicken in a compact bundle. Repeat with the remaining fillets and filling and then wrap each bundle in a second piece of foil to retain the juices. Put the bundles in a roasting pan and cook in a preheated oven, 190°C, 375°F, Gas Mark 5, for 45–50 minutes. Leave the bundles to cool and then chill in the fridge, still wrapped in foil.

To serve *Unwrap the bundles and slice across into 1cm/½in slices. Arrange on a large, flat serving plate and garnish with some pretty leaves.*
SEE PAGE 122.

ORANGE AND REDCURRANT JELLY

Now that you can buy bottles of freshly squeezed fruit juice, a jelly made from fresh juice and fruit is one of the quickest and easiest things to make and is always tremendously popular. This jelly is stunning in appearance as well as taste with its glassy orange top and scarlet berried base. It is wonderful with strawberries or raspberries.

550g/18oz redcurrants, destalked
1·3 litres/2¼ pints freshly squeezed orange juice
125g/4oz caster sugar
9 teaspoons gelatine
Fresh orange segments and redcurrants, to decorate (optional)

Divide the redcurrants between two 1 litre/2 pint jelly moulds. Strain the orange juice through a fine sieve. Pour 200ml/7fl oz of the juice into a pan, add the sugar and heat gently, stirring until it dissolves. Allow to cool slightly. Sprinkle in the gelatine and stir over a low heat until dissolved, then stir into the remaining orange juice. Gradually pour juice into the jelly moulds. Refrigerate for several hours until set.

To unmould, loosen the jelly by pulling the edges back with your fingers and then turn out on to a plate, giving the mould a firm shake

To serve *Place on a pretty plate and surround with skinned orange segments and fresh redcurrants. Serve with or without cream or with the orange and Cointreau ice cream.*

STRAWBERRIES WITH WHOLE ORANGE AND COINTREAU ICE CREAM

If you have a party during the strawberry season it seems foolish not to make the most of them. However, it is also exciting to offer an alternative accompaniment to cream. Oranges enhance the flavour of strawberries and this ice cream, made with an intense purée of whole orange, is flavoured with Cointreau, also made from oranges.

2 small oranges
140ml/4½fl oz lemon juice
175g/6oz demerara sugar
4 egg whites
200ml/7fl oz fresh orange juice
300g/10oz granulated sugar
900ml/1½ pints whipping cream
125ml/4fl oz Cointreau
2·7kg/6lb strawberries
Orange rind, to decorate (optional)

Cut the oranges into quarters and remove any pips. Put the quarters into a saucepan with the lemon juice. Cover the saucepan, bring the juice up to bubbling and then simmer gently for about half an hour until the orange skin is very soft. Add the demerara sugar, stir to dissolve and then bubble, uncovered, for 3–4 minutes until the juice is syrupy. Press the orange pieces and the juice through a sieve or put in a food processor and whizz very thoroughly until as smooth as possible. Pour into a bowl and leave until cold.

Whisk the egg whites until frothy. Put the orange juice into a saucepan with the granulated sugar and stir over a low heat to dissolve the sugar. Increase the heat and boil rapidly for 3 minutes. Pour immediately on to the egg whites in a thin stream, whisking all the time at high speed. Continue whisking until very thick. Whisk in the orange purée. Whip the cream into soft peaks and fold into the egg white and orange mixture. Fold in the Cointreau a tablespoon at a time. Spoon the mixture into a serving bowl and freeze for at least 6 hours.

Remove from the freezer about 30 minutes before serving. Decorate with strips of orange rind. Pile the strawberries into a large bowl.

Oz Clarke's
WINE NOTES

If only the weather holds, ah, if only. The number of plans I've made to have lunch parties out on the terrace and the number of times we've all ended up huddled in the kitchen as the heavens opened just when I was about to serve the watercress soup.

But I still persevere. What's the point of being English if you don't approach every new summer with an almost insane optimism that *this* year the skies will be bright and the breezes will send the clouds scurrying like puffballs to the far horizon.

All-purpose wines are best for a summer buffet like this one and, to be honest, if the weather holds I don't think we'll need a red – just a really well-chilled pink and a full-flavoured but less-chilled white. The best pink in France is made in the south of the Rhône valley, and the Côtes du Lubéron, a few miles to the east of Avignon produces gorgeous strawberry-flavoured, dry rosé to drink as young and as cold as possible.

We've got some fairly strong spice flavours here, especially in the salmon dish, so I'm going to choose an oak-aged Chardonnay. Chardonnay is in any case the classic wine to go with salmon and the extra honey and tropical fruit ripeness of one from Australia will be the perfect accompaniment.

But what if you've got a slightly sweet tooth – or if perhaps you just feel frivolous and devil-may-care. The most wonderful frothy, juicy sweet yet meadow-fresh outdoors wine for summer is Asti Spumante served as cold as can be.

If Josceline invites *me* to this party, I might drink this through the entire meal!

FRESH ORANGE AND REDCURRANT JELLY, STRAWBERRIES WITH WHOLE ORANGE AND COINTREAU ICE CREAM

WINTER BUFFET
for 12

Winter and summer are both party seasons but it is winter which really needs parties. One of the best ways to liven up the long grey months is with good food and good company. The bleakest and most socially sparse time is between January and March so this is a particularly good moment to choose. It is also probably the time when you will most enjoy being cosily in the kitchen preparing food for a party.

Winter party food must warm and revive and comfort. It may not look as beautiful or ethereal as summer fantasies can do but it should appear irresistibly appetizing. If at least one dish is served hot the smell of it wafting into your hall when the guests arrive will make an encouraging first impression. The whole house should be at its most welcoming and it is important to get the lighting exactly right so that guests feel attractive despite their wintry pale, centrally heated complexions.

Appetites are keener in winter and cold, damp days also make you long for a little indulgence, so that is why I have included two puddings in this buffet – designed to be eaten either together on the same plate or separately.

MENU

*

SMOKED FISH PIE WITH GOLDEN ROOT TOP

CHICK PEA AND OLIVE SALAD

PORK MARBLED WITH SPINACH, CASHEW NUTS AND ORANGE RIND

*

HONEYED APRICOT ALMOND FLAN

PURE CHOCOLATE PUDDING

*

Amontillado Sherry
Australian Shiraz
Mosel Riesling Spätlese
Greek Samos Muscat

SMOKED FISH PIE WITH GOLDEN ROOT TOP

SMOKED FISH PIE WITH GOLDEN ROOT TOP

At a winter party one hot dish makes all the difference, and a good fish pie always seems to be popular, even with people who aren't generally very keen on fish. This pie can be part-prepared a day in advance and assembled and cooked shortly beforehand. Keep it warm in a low oven until needed. It is extremely easy to eat with a fork. The smoked fish is cooked in a richly cheesy sauce which, combined with the delicious purée of root vegetables on top, transforms it into a dish far removed from the nursery food with which fish pie is usually associated.

Filling:
750g/1½lb smoked cod fillets, skinned
500g/1lb smoked haddock fillets, skinned
3 large cloves garlic
125g/4oz butter
175g/6oz plain flour
1·2 litres/2 pints milk, warmed
150g/5oz Red Leicester cheese, grated coarsely
125g/4oz strong Cheddar cheese, grated coarsely
4 teaspoons wholegrain mustard
3 teaspoons dried oregano
4–6 pinches cayenne pepper
Salt

Topping:
750g/1½lb parsnips
500g/1lb sweet potatoes
250g/8oz carrots
75–125g/3–4oz butter
½ whole nutmeg, grated
Salt
Black pepper

To make the pie filling, cut the smoked fish fillets into roughly 2·5cm/1in pieces. Peel the garlic and chop finely. Melt the butter in a very large saucepan over a gentle heat. Add the chopped garlic and stir for a minute or so. Remove the pan from the heat and, using a wooden spoon, stir in the flour until smooth. Return to a moderate heat and bubble gently for 2–3 minutes, stirring continuously. Stir in the warmed milk a little at a time. When the mixture is smooth bring it to the boil stirring continuously and continue to stir while it bubbles for 2 minutes. Put 2 rounded tablespoons of the grated Red Leicester cheese on one side and stir the rest into the white sauce with the grated Cheddar cheese. Stir until the cheese has melted. Add the mustard and oregano then remove from the heat. Season to taste with the cayenne pepper and a little salt if necessary – remember that the fish will also add a certain amount of saltiness. The pie can be prepared a day ahead to this point, and the sauce cooled and refrigerated until needed. When ready to cook, stir the smoked fish into the sauce and transfer the mixture to a large, fairly shallow ovenproof dish which is big enough to take a fairly thick layer of topping as well.

To make the topping, peel the parsnips, sweet potatoes and carrots and cut them up roughly. Steam or boil them all together until they are all very soft. Press through a sieve or whizz in a food processor in relays with the butter and nutmeg until you have a smooth purée. Put all the purée into a bowl and season to taste with salt and plenty of black pepper. Spoon the purée topping evenly over the fish filling, spreading it out and roughly flicking it up. Sprinkle the remaining grated Red Leicester cheese on top.

Cook the pie in a preheated oven, 190°C, 375°F, Gas Mark 5, for 35–40 minutes or until golden brown on top. Reduce the oven heat to as low as possible to keep the pie warm until you are ready to eat.

EXTRAS

For the other buffets in this chapter I haven't felt that cheese was needed but, if you wish, a half Stilton would look and taste in keeping for this party. As Stiltons vary enormously try to taste it before you buy, if possible, to make sure that it is creamy and mild. You could of course serve a smaller piece of Stilton and a generous piece of mature farmhouse Cheddar on the rind. Little bits of these cheeses sliced off the wedge are easy to eat in your fingers and so are good to nibble at later in the evening when people begin to feel a little hungry again.

If you decide to serve cheese offer good crisp biscuits such as Bath Olivers to go with it. On the table you will also need sliced wholemeal bread or seeded soft bread rolls to accompany the savoury dishes.

The simplest green salad is all that is needed with this buffet. I usually choose little gem lettuces which keep well in the fridge and can therefore be bought with your advance shopping. They are a good cross between a crisp and a soft lettuce and can either be cut across, sliced downwards in sixths or served as whole separated leaves. Dress the salad with a plain vinaigrette or one made with wholegrain mustard.

You will also need a jug of pouring cream to go with the apricot flan.

A bowl of little clementines is always welcome at a winter party and they look very pretty too, especially if you buy the ones which still have some of their glossy green leaves attached.

Also on the table of course should be sea salt and black peppercorns in a mill, unsalted butter for the bread and mineral water.

CHICK PEA AND OLIVE SALAD

Dried pulses are so useful for more filling winter salads, and chick peas are among the best of them. They have two great advantages – an excellent nutty flavour and a capacity not to disintegrate – so there is no worry of overcooking them. This salad is absolutely delicious and quite substantial enough to satisfy any strict vegetarian you might have at your party.

500g/1lb dried chick peas
175g/6oz pitted black olives
3 large cloves garlic
7cm/3in piece fresh root ginger
2 oranges
2 lemons
1 bunch spring onions
150ml/$\frac{1}{4}$ pint groundnut oil
150ml/$\frac{1}{4}$ pint olive oil
3 teaspoons paprika
1 tablespoon caster sugar
2 large bunches fresh parsley
Salt and black pepper

Soak the chick peas in cold water for 8 hours or overnight. Drain and cook in plenty of boiling salted water for 45 minutes–1 hour or until soft.

Meanwhile make the dressing. Roughly chop the olives. Peel the garlic and ginger and chop finely. Coarsely grate the rind of the oranges and lemons and squeeze the orange and lemon juices through a fine sieve into a saucepan. Trim the spring onions and chop across finely using as much of the green stalk as possible. Add the oils to the juices and stir in the grated rinds, the ginger and garlic, the paprika and the olives. Sprinkle with a little salt, cover the saucepan and bubble the mixture over the heat very gently for 15–20 minutes, stirring occasionally. Stir in the spring onions and the caster sugar and remove from the heat. When the dressing has cooled, stir gently and add salt and black pepper to taste.

When the chick peas are cooked, drain and put them into a large bowl. Pour the dressing on to them while they are still hot and mix well. When cold, cover and leave in a cool place until the party.

To serve *Shortly before the party pull the leaves from the parsley stalks and chop finely. Mix the chopped parsley into the chick peas and spoon the salad into one large or several small serving dishes.*

PLANNING AHEAD

In advance: Cook the pork at least six hours ahead so it has time to chill well for easy slicing, but up to three days ahead if you choose. The apricot flan can be made up to three days in advance. Turn it out on to the serving plate and keep in a cool place inside a puffed-up bin liner which won't spoil the top.

The day before: Make the dressing for the meat and keep it in a screw-top jar. Prepare the fish pie sauce and keep in the fridge overnight. The chick pea salad can be made and dressed at least a day before the party. Put it into a large bowl, cover and keep in the refrigerator. Make the chocolate pudding.

The day of the party: Bring the flan to room temperature. Take the chick pea salad from the refrigerator several hours before the party and add the chopped parsley. Finish the fish pie. It can be kept warm in a low oven for at least an hour until needed. An hour or two before take the chocolate pudding out of the fridge, add the *crème fraîche* and sprinkle cocoa powder on top. Just before people arrive slice the pork, arrange it on a serving plate and spoon over the dressing.

PRESENTATION

The look of a winter table should be as cheering and comforting as the food. There should certainly be candles – dark green ones go well with the golden colours of this buffet. The food is homely so the dishes, plates and glasses should not be too delicate. You could use a coarse-weave or patterned tablecloth, though not too bold.

Serve the sliced wholemeal bread on a wooden platter or in a basket – put a cloth over the top until the meal starts. It's difficult to find flat serving plates large enough for very big flans so if you can't find one use a large round bread board, or failing that a cake board.

PORK MARBLED WITH SPINACH, CASHEW NUTS AND ORANGE RIND

Many people prefer to eat pork cold, and cold meat goes much further than hot as it can be sliced very thinly. In this recipe the spinach adds both moisture and flavour to the meat and there is an interesting and attractive marbled appearance to the joint when the slices are cut. The hard skin of the meat should be removed, leaving the soft fat underneath.

PORK MARBLED WITH SPINACH, CASHEW NUTS AND ORANGE RIND, CHICK PEA AND OLIVE SALAD

375g/12oz spinach
2–3 cloves garlic
Finely grated rind of 1 large orange
2 tablespoons olive oil
1·5kg/3lb boned and skinned shoulder joint of pork
40–50g/1½–2oz unsalted cashew nuts
Honey
Black pepper
Salt

Wash the spinach, cut off the stalks and roughly chop the leaves. Bring a pan of salted water to the boil, put in the spinach leaves and boil for 2–3 minutes until the leaves are limp. Drain the spinach very well, pressing out any excess liquid, and put into a bowl. Peel the garlic and chop finely. Add the garlic, grated orange rind and olive oil to the spinach and mix them all together very thoroughly. Season with plenty of pepper and a little salt.

Cut any string from the boned pork and lay the meat out flat, fat side down. Press the spinach mixture over the meat, then roll up the meat fairly loosely and tie the joint together with string, and skewers too if it helps.

Make incisions in the meat with a small sharp knife and press the nuts in as far as you can. Sprinkle the joint with salt and black pepper, smear liberally with honey and place in a greased roasting tin.

Cook in the centre of a preheated oven, 190°C, 375°F, Gas Mark 5, for 2 hours, basting now and then with the honey juices – the outside of the meat should turn a dark brownish black.

When it is thoroughly cooked transfer the joint to a large plate and leave to cool, then wrap in clingfilm and chill in the refrigerator until you are ready to serve it.

To serve *Slice the meat thinly and lay the slices neatly overlapping on a serving plate. Cover with clingfilm so that the meat doesn't dry out. Just before serving I like to spoon a dressing of seasoned olive oil mixed with a little cider vinegar and some fresh orange juice over the meat.*

Oz Clarke's
WINE NOTES

I can see people arriving at the front door, champing to be let in from the cold. One week they'll be stamping the snow from their boots, another week they'll be trying to shake the rain from their coats so as not to flood the hallway, another week they'll be chilled to the bone by a fierce north-westerly.

So let them in, slam the door shut and deposit them in front of a roaring fire. And before you feed them, a glass of deep, nutty old Amontillado sherry might bring a glow back to their cheeks.

We're going to need some good white wine with that delicious fish pie, but I always have a sweeter tooth in winter than summer, so I've gone for some late-picked, slightly sweet German wines, whose fresh acidity will cut through rich, cheesy sauce and whose perfume will remind us that summer is not too far away.

If you like more zing to your wine, choose a late-picked (Spätlese) wine from Germany's Mosel valley from the villages of Brauneberg, Zelting or Wehlen. If you like a spicier, softer wine, choose a Rhine Spätlese, from Nierstein, Bingen, Johannisberg or Forst.

You could happily drink the German wine with the pork, too, but if you like red – with all that orange rind and garlic and those cashews and honey, it's going to have to be a rich, soft red. Australia's the place for them, and I'll go for one of those soft, succulent Cabernet Sauvignons or Shirazes.

Two puddings! Yummy! Apricots, honey and almonds in one, oodles of chocolate in the other – a big sweet juicy Muscat is the only answer. Muscat from the island of Samos is just about Greece's best wine, and is thick with the flavour of rich raisins and marmalade orange rind. A southern French Muscat would do if you can't find the Greek one.

HONEYED APRICOT ALMOND FLAN

Dried apricots are a wonderful ingredient at any time but during the winter, when there is not so much good fresh fruit around, they are unbeatable. They have a more intense flavour than fresh apricots ever have and a beautiful deep colour. This is a light upside-down almond flan and the top of honey-glazed apricots looks dazzling when it is turned out. If your guests choose not to combine a piece of this flan with some of the chocolate pudding, which is a perfectly delicious combination, offer them some pouring cream instead. If you decide to make several of these flans you can start two or three days in advance and keep them in a cool place. For fewer people, this flan is delicious served warm – any left over can then be eaten cold the next day.

500g/1lb dried apricots
5 generous tablespoons clear honey
2 tablespoons lemon juice
175g/6oz butter
200g/7oz fine demerara or golden caster sugar
5 eggs
125g/4oz ground almonds
Finely grated rind of 1 lemon
150g/5oz unblanched almonds (the unpeeled kind), chopped roughly
65g/2½oz plain flour
1½ teaspoons baking powder
½ teaspoon salt
Flaked blanched almonds, to decorate (optional)

Soak the apricots in a bowl of cold water for 2 hours or more. Drain and cut them neatly in half through the middle, so as not to destroy their round shape. Put the honey in a bowl and stir in the lemon juice. Spread this mixture over the bottom of a lightly buttered 28–30cm/11–12in flan dish. Arrange the halved apricots skin side downwards on top of the honey mixture, close together in neat circles, filling in with a second layer of any remaining apricots.

Put the butter and sugar into a mixing bowl and whisk together until light and fluffy. Lightly whisk the eggs in a bowl and then whisk thoroughly into the butter and sugar mixture alternately with the ground almonds. Stir in the grated lemon rind and the chopped almonds. Sift the flour, baking powder and salt together on to the mixture and lightly fold in with a metal spoon. Spoon the mixture on top of the arranged apricots and smooth level.

Bake in the centre of a preheated oven, 180°C, 350°F, Gas Mark 4, for 50–60 minutes until firm and springy to a light touch in the centre. Remove from the oven and leave in the dish for about 10 minutes. Loosening the edges of the flan if necessary, turn out carefully on to a large, flat serving plate or board. Leave to cool.

To serve *Sprinkle blanched, flaked almonds (optional) on top of the cake and serve with the pure chocolate pudding or with pouring cream.*

PURE CHOCOLATE PUDDING, HONEYED APRICOT ALMOND FLAN

PURE CHOCOLATE PUDDING

There are certain things which are almost bound to be winners at a party and one of them is definitely a chocolate pudding or cake. It has to be deeply chocolaty and with a good texture too. This pudding is wonderful because it is intense and rich as chocolate should be but not at all sickly.

250g/8oz plain chocolate
250g/8oz unsalted butter
450ml/¾ pint warm water
175g/6oz soft light brown sugar
6 large eggs (size 1)
25g/1oz self-raising flour
1 tablespoon cocoa powder
1 teaspoon cream of tartar
½ teaspoon salt
600ml/1 pint *crème fraîche*
Cocoa powder, to decorate (optional)

Lightly butter a 2·4–3 litre/4–5 pint fairly deep ovenproof dish (or 12 individual dishes). Put a roasting tin half full of hot water on the centre shelf of a preheated oven, 200°C, 400°F, Gas Mark 6.

Break the chocolate into smallish pieces and cut up the butter. Put both into a bowl set over a pan of very hot water. Stir until the chocolate and butter have melted then remove from the heat. Gradually add the warm water to the mixture, stirring constantly. Stir in the sugar.

Separate the eggs. Add the yolks to the chocolate mixture and put the whites into another bowl. Whisk the yolks thoroughly into the chocolate mixture then sift the flour and cocoa powder on to the mixture and whisk until smooth.

Add the cream of tartar and the salt to the egg whites and, using clean beaters, whisk to soft peaks. With a large metal spoon, lightly fold the whisked egg whites into the chocolate mixture.

Pour into the prepared dish (or dishes), and place in the roasting tin of water. Cook at 200°C, 400°F, Gas Mark 6, for 10 minutes (or 6 minutes for individual dishes) then reduce the oven temperature to 160°C, 325°F, Gas Mark 3, and cook for a further 30 minutes (or 20 minutes for individual dishes).

Remove from the oven and leave to cool.

To serve *Spoon the* crème fraîche *in a thick layer all over the top of the pudding.*

Alternatively, I sometimes like to use whipped cream with some natural yogurt folded in to it. Using a very fine sieve, sprinkle a whisper of cocoa powder on to the centre of the crème fraîche.

SOPHIE GRIGSON

Picnics & Barbecues

It's one of those inexplicable, delightful facts of life: food tastes twice as good eaten in the open air as it does indoors. Who knows why? Is it merely that a breath of fresh air makes our bodies function more vigorously, kicking our taste-buds into top gear? Or perhaps it is the escape from formality that gives us time to relax and enjoy what we are eating at a leisurely pace. Outdoor meals fall neatly into two camps, 'home' and 'abroad'. Firstly there are the back-garden feasts, where food and paraphernalia have to travel only a little way from the kitchen to the table. Secondly there are picnics, running the range from the single sandwich to the grandest five-course affair, all bound together by the plain fact that the chosen setting lies well away from base.

A back-garden meal may be no more than a matter of transferring location from the dining room to the patio, terrace, lawn, or whatever else you have out there, but barbecues need special planning. The very thought of meat, fish or vegetables grilled over open charcoal or coals is enough to make me hungry – those glorious smells, wafting up and around the garden, precursors to the smoky flavour of the food itself. With proper organization a barbecue party is one of the most enjoyable ways to entertain, and with luck there'll be some keen volunteer willing to slave over the hot coals (strange, isn't it, that people who normally show no interest in cooking can suddenly become wildly enthusiastic at the prospect of donning the chef's hat for a barbecue).

Picnics can be as basic or grand as the occasion warrants. Quality makes all the difference between a memorable picnic and a total non-event. Even if you decide that you want no more than a few sandwiches, make them with the freshest, most delicious bread, and pack them with generous quantities of filling with appropriate relishes and lively salad stuffs. And please take a bag with you for rubbish. Finding a spot in the countryside, or the park, that isn't ruined by discarded wrappers, is hard enough these days. Don't add to the problem.

Opposite **JAPANESE BARBECUE** *PAGE 148*

COUNTRY PICNIC
for 8

A long ramble in the countryside, breathing in great lungfuls of fresh air, is a sure-fire way to build up a hearty appetite for substantial food saturated with full, robust tastes. There's nothing half-hearted or namby-pamby about this picnic. From the first mouthful of soup, to the last crumb of chocolate chip cookie, it is a riot of satisfying, true flavours, as pleasing as the colours of the food itself.

To get the meal off to a swinging start, there's a vibrant orange-hued soup, partnered by sunshine-yellow muffins with a spirited kick of fresh chilli.

And there's plenty more to tuck in to: a big sandwich, filled to overflowing and impossible to eat in a refined manner; squares of kuku – a chunky baked omelette – and a heap of chocolate and orange chocolate chip cookies.

Finally, offer some juicy peaches for everyone to tackle as the mood takes them, merely suggesting that the adults in the group try slicing them into a glass of red wine to create the laziest of fruit desserts.

MENU

*

TOMATO, CARROT AND APRICOT SOUP

SWEETCORN AND CHILLI MUFFINS

THE BIG SANDWICH

COURGETTE AND RED PEPPER KUKU WITH FETA CHEESE

*

CHOCOLATE AND ORANGE CHOCOLATE CHIP COOKIES

*

Rheingau Riesling Kabinett

Sweet Red Lambrusco

TOMATO, CARROT AND APRICOT SOUP

A handful of dried apricots gives this vegetable soup a subtle fruity flavour. It tastes as good hot as cold, so check the weather before you decide how to serve it.

2 onions, chopped
500g/1lb carrots, diced
125g/4oz dried apricots
2 sprigs fresh rosemary
4 sprigs parsley
1 sprig thyme
3 tablespoons olive oil
500g/1lb tomatoes, skinned and roughly chopped
1·8 litres/3 pints light chicken or vegetable stock
2 tablespoons lemon juice
Salt and pepper
2 tablespoons chopped fresh chives and 250g/8oz natural yogurt, to serve

Sweat the onion, carrots and apricots and the herbs, tied together in a bundle, in the oil in a covered pan for 10 minutes. Add the tomatoes, stock, salt and pepper. Bring up to the boil and simmer for 20 minutes or until the carrots are tender. Discard the bundle of herbs, then liquidize or sieve until smooth. Stir in the lemon juice. Taste and adjust seasonings. Cool, cover and store in the fridge until needed.

Before you set out for the picnic, assess the weather situation. If it promises to be a fine warm day, rinse out the vacuum flask(s) with iced water. Stir a little extra water or stock into the soup if it is too thick to pour, and pour into the chilled flask, adding a few cubes of ice. If there is an ominous chill in the air, reheat the soup and pour into vacuum flasks rinsed out with hot water. Knot the chopped chives in a small plastic bag.

To serve *Pour the soup into bowls or mugs, sprinkle with chopped fresh chives and float a dollop of natural yogurt on top.*

SWEETCORN AND CHILLI MUFFINS

American-style muffins are at their best on the day they're baked, although they will happily survive overnight in an airtight container. They are quick to throw together, so if you're not going to be too caught up in other things, make them on the morning of the picnic.

175g/6oz fresh or defrosted frozen sweetcorn
1 green chilli, very finely chopped
125g/4oz self-raising flour
1 tablespoon baking powder
1 teaspoon salt
275g/9oz polenta or fine cornmeal
125g/4oz butter, melted
2 eggs, beaten
300ml/½ pint milk

SWEETCORN AND CHILLI MUFFINS, TOMATO, CARROT AND APRICOT SOUP, THE BIG SANDWICH, COURGETTE AND RED PEPPER KUKU WITH FETA CHEESE

Mix sweetcorn and chilli and toss in 2 tablespoons of the flour. Set aside. Sift the rest of the flour with the baking powder and salt. Stir in the cornmeal. Make a well in the centre and add butter, eggs and milk. Mix briefly to a slightly lumpy batter.

Stir the sweetcorn and chilli into the mixture and pour into greased bun tins, filling two-thirds full. Bake in a preheated oven, 200°C, 400°F, Gas Mark 6, for 15–20 minutes until golden brown. Cool for a few minutes in the tins, then turn out on to a wire rack to finish cooling.

EXTRAS

Take along some whole tomatoes, radishes and sticks of celery to nibble at, and some mayonnaise.

Have an adults-only, optional, DIY pudding. Take a pannier containing at least eight ripe peaches or nectarines with you to the picnic, and a small tub or bag of sugar. Keep at least one bottle of red wine in reserve.

Each person slices their own peach or nectarine into their wine glass or cup, adds a light sprinkle of sugar, and then pours in enough wine just to cover the fruit. Then they eat the wine-scented slices of fruit and drink the wine left at the bottom of the glass.

Children, or grown-ups who have had quite enough to drink, can, of course, eat the peaches as they are.

PLANNING AHEAD

In advance: Make the olive dressing for the big sandwich.

The day before: Make the chocolate and orange chocolate chip cookies. Make the big sandwich. Make the soup. Make the muffins if you will not have time on the day and the kuku.

The day of the party: Reheat the soup or chill in flasks. Assemble the crockery and pack up the picnic.

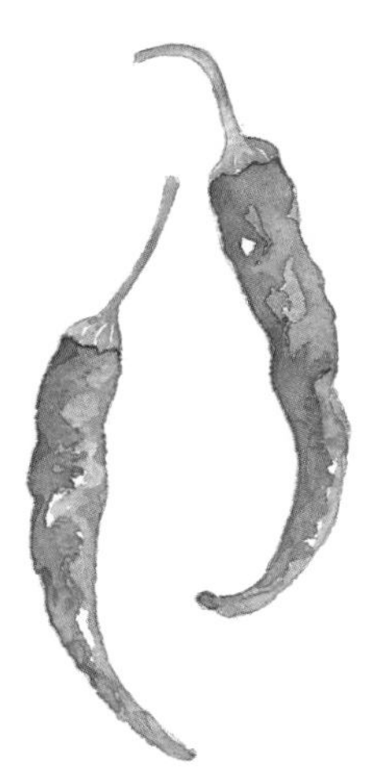

ORGANIZING A PICNIC

By definition, a picnic is a meal eaten away from home base, and quite possibly at some distance from any shops. If you've forgotten to pack the corkscrew, or a packet of paper hankies for wiping sticky fingers, that's tough, and you will have to cope without as best you can.

The more ambitious your picnic, the more important it becomes to plan efficiently. Draw up lists of all the bits and pieces you need to take, including the food, and double check that everything is present and correct before you set off. Cool bags, while not essential, are extremely useful, particularly on a hot day. Pretty basketwork hampers are aesthetically pleasing, and if well designed can make packing easier. On the other hand a sturdy cardboard box will do the job just as well.

The food for this picnic is all easy to pack and transport, and most of it can be prepared in advance, so you can set off in good time. You'll need little in the way of cutlery. Serve the soup in mugs or paper cups, and all you will need are a sharp knife for cutting the sandwich, a few smaller knives for slicing up the peaches, and forks to eat them with when they have soaked up the wine, 3 teaspoons (for yogurt, mayonnaise and sugar), salt cellar or mill, pepper mill, paper napkins or kitchen paper, corkscrew and bin liners for rubbish.

THE BIG SANDWICH

Forget the tiresome task of buttering endless slices of bread for sandwiches. It's much simpler to make one huge, lusty sandwich which can be cut into wedges when everyone is ready to tuck in.

Dressing:
50g/2oz pitted green olives, very finely chopped
50g/2oz pitted black olives, very finely chopped
2 cloves garlic, very finely chopped
1 anchovy fillet, very finely chopped
2 teaspoons capers, finely chopped
3 tablespoons finely chopped parsley
1 teaspoon dried oregano
150ml/¼ pint olive oil
Freshly ground black pepper

Sandwich:
1 large round flat loaf (such as pain de campagne), split in half horizontally
4 large thick slices cooked ham (approximately 500g/1lb)
6 slices Gruyère cheese (approximately 375g/12oz)
4 tomatoes, sliced
½ cucumber, thinly sliced
4 large lettuce leaves, shredded

Make the dressing at least 24 hours and up to 1 week in advance. Simply mix all the dressing ingredients together, cover and refrigerate.

To make the sandwich, brush the cut sides of the loaf generously with some of the dressing. Lay the ham, then the cheese on the base, trimming to fit (put the trimmings into the sandwich as well). Top with tomatoes, cucumber and lettuce. Spoon 4 tablespoons of the dressing over the top; clamp the lid firmly on the sandwich. Wrap tightly in foil. Place it in the fridge and weight down heavily. Leave for 4–24 hours. *SEE PAGE 134.*

COURGETTE AND RED PEPPER KUKU WITH FETA CHEESE

A kuku is a Persian baked 'omelette', thick with vegetables. It is cut into chunks to be eaten hot, warm or cold.

500g/1lb courgettes, grated
1 tablespoon salt
3 red peppers, quartered and deseeded
4 spring onions, finely chopped
3 tablespoons finely chopped parsley
9 eggs, beaten
175g/6oz feta cheese, crumbled
Butter, for greasing
Salt and pepper

Spread the courgettes out in a colander. Sprinkle with the salt, mix lightly and set aside for an hour to drain. Rinse under a cold tap and squeeze dry, first with your hands and then in a clean tea towel.

Grill the peppers, skin side up, as close as possible to a very hot grill, until blackened and blistered all over. Drop into a plastic bag, knot and leave until cool enough to handle. Strip off the skin, and shred.

Stir the courgettes, peppers, spring onions, parsley, a little salt and plenty of pepper into the beaten eggs.

Generously butter an ovenproof dish (a gratin dish 7cm/3in deep, 30cm/12in long is ideal) and spoon half the mixture into it. Sprinkle the feta evenly over, and cover with remaining egg mixture. Cover with foil and bake in a preheated oven, 180°C, 350°F, Gas Mark 4, for 40 minutes. Remove the foil and bake a further 15–20 minutes, until the eggs have set and the top is golden. *SEE PAGE 134.*

CHOCOLATE AND ORANGE CHOCOLATE CHIP COOKIES

These giant, melting, densely chocolaty biscuits are quite irresistible, and sure to be a hit with both children and adults.

250g/8oz slightly salted butter, softened
175g/6oz light muscovado sugar
125g/4oz caster sugar
2 eggs
½ teaspoon vanilla essence
2 tablespoons orange juice
250g/8oz plain flour
1 teaspoon bicarbonate of soda
50g/2oz cocoa
250g/8oz plain chocolate chips, or roughly chopped plain chocolate
Finely grated rind of 1 orange

Grease 4 baking sheets.

Cream the butter with the sugars until light and fluffy. Beat the eggs with the vanilla and orange juice. Sift the flour with the bicarbonate of soda and cocoa. Beat alternate spoonfuls of the egg and flour mixtures into the creamed butter. Fold in the chocolate chips and the orange rind.

Drop tablespoons of the mixture on to the baking sheets leaving a generous 12cm/5in between dollops. Flatten down to a thickness of about 1cm/½in. Bake in a preheated oven, 160°C, 325°F, Gas Mark 3, for 16 minutes.

Let the cookies cool for 5–10 minutes until they firm up, then transfer to a wire rack to finish cooling. Store in an airtight container.

Top **CHOCOLATE AND ORANGE CHOCOLATE CHIP COOKIES, PEACHES IN RED WINE**

Oz Clarke's
WINE NOTES

The weather's going to make a major difference to the kind of hike through the countryside we're going to have. If the weather is poor, there's a positive purpose in tramping up hill and down dale – either in the hope that the longer you trudge on, the more likely it is the sun will break through, or in the desire to build up a formidable appetite so that when you finally stop you'll fall on the food like a vulture regardless of swirling mists and unseasonal showers. But in hot weather the ramble becomes an amble, and the general objective is to find the first half-decent spot, decide on it, spread out all the food, guzzle it down and then snooze it all off till sunset.

I shall certainly guzzle this picnic. It's so appetizing – the wonderful golden orange soup for a start, and chilli muffins are one of the best ideas ever to come out of America. As for the big sandwich – Cecil B. de Mille presents *The Big Sandwich* starring Humphrey Bogart and Sophie Grigson. I *love* it. So it's lots of highly gluggable easy-flavoured wine, not too high in alcohol.

Low alcohol needn't mean low taste and low pleasure. Germany produces a range of wines called Kabinett which will have less than 10 per cent alcohol and can be as low as 7·5 per cent. Lambrusco from Italy is usually about 7·5 per cent but can be even less. So I'd go to the Rhine in Germany, to one of the top villages – Winkel, Giesenheim or Rauenthal – where the Kabinetts are gently grapy, flowery too, not quite dry and deliciously refreshing. Lambrusco is usually drunk on the sweet side, but there's a snappy sharp acidity in good Lambrusco to go with the cherryish fruit, which makes it into a carefree sweet-sour, fizzy, happy juice just as good with the big sandwich as for dunking peaches.

Birthday Picnic for 10

Curling ham sandwiches, soggy sausage rolls and a packet of crisps? Forget it. That's a mean little specimen of a picnic at any time, but a celebratory birthday picnic should be a memorable affair.

Once you've decided to go to town on this picnic, think about the organization. First of all, are you going to do all the work yourself? I'd prefer to share it around, either hiving off the making of the first course, or the salads or the marinated strawberries to fellow picnickers, or better still luring them into my kitchen for a few hours before setting off to provide a helping hand.

Next, consider the transportation and presentation of the food. In fact, start with the presentation, and work backwards from there to the kitchen, making lists as you go. It will make life much easier if you pack the serving dishes and bowls in reverse order to the one in which they are to be used, and jot down which dish is to be used for what. When you arrive at your picnic site, rope in a couple of helpers to set things out, and within ten minutes you can be ready to dine.

MENU

*

FRESH ASPARAGUS WITH PISTACHIO AND LEMON DRESSING

PAPER-THIN CUCUMBER SALAD

TOMATO AND ORANGE SALAD

ROAST FILLET OF BEEF WITH APPLE AND BASIL STUFFING

*

GOATS' MILK CHEESES WITH WATERCRESS AND BATH OLIVERS

*

STRAWBERRY CARAMEL BAVAROIS

STRAWBERRIES IN MOSCATEL

LACE BISCUITS

*

New Zealand Sauvignon Blanc

Australian Cabernet Sauvignon/Shiraz

Champagne

FRESH ASPARAGUS WITH PISTACHIO AND LEMON DRESSING

Long spears of tender asparagus, with their vivid green speckled dressing, are best eaten with the fingers, so take plenty of napkins with you. You can substitute extra virgin olive oil for the sunflower and hazelnut oils in the dressing if you prefer.

50g/2oz shelled pistachio nuts
Finely grated rind and juice of 1 lemon
150ml/¼ pint sunflower oil and 3 tablespoons hazelnut oil
1·5kg/3lb asparagus
Salt and pepper

To make the dressing, put the nuts into a bowl and cover with boiling water. Stand for a minute, then drain and remove the brown skins. Spread out on a baking sheet and dry in a preheated oven, 150°C, 300°F, Gas Mark 2, for 10 minutes. Chop very finely. Place in a large screw-top jar with the lemon rind, lemon juice, oils, salt and pepper. Screw on the lid and shake well. Taste and adjust seasonings. Store in the fridge. Shake the jar before using.

Trim off the woody ends of the asparagus. Divide into two bundles and tie firmly with string. Find a tall pan which will take the bundles standing up, with not too much room to spare around them. Place the asparagus, tips upward, in the pan. Pour in enough water to fill the pan to a depth of 10cm/4in. Add a little salt. Bring up to a gentle simmer and then cover the pan with a lid, or a dome of foil, so that tips are cooked in the steam. Keep simmering for 5–30 minutes, depending on the thickness and quality of the asparagus. Test by inserting a small sharp blade into one or two of the stems – as soon as it slips in easily, take the asparagus out of the water, and rinse under the cold tap. Leave to drain and cool. Place in a rigid plastic box, and cover tightly. Keep cool.

To serve *Arrange the asparagus on one large plate or individual plates. Shake the dressing and spoon about a third over the tips. Pour the rest into a bowl, for guests to dip their asparagus into.*

FRESH ASPARAGUS WITH PISTACHIO AND LEMON DRESSING

EXTRAS

Take brown and white bread rolls with you: a selection of small wholemeal rolls, maybe, and light as air French *petits pains*. If you allow two per person and a few extra for those with capacious appetites, it should see you through the meal.

Don't forget to provide some lightly salted or unsalted butter to go with the rolls. Pack a peppermill filled with black peppercorns (ready ground pepper is a poor substitute), and a salt mill filled with sea salt crystals.

If you have five minutes to spare, make a creamy horseradish sauce to go with the beef: fold together equal quantities of whipped cream and thick Greek yogurt, and add creamed horseradish, salt, pepper and lemon juice to taste.

Apart from the wines you'll need to take about three large bottles of mineral water, and the same number of flasks of hot, real coffee to finish the meal. Serve it with single cream, brown sugar crystals and, perhaps, some wonderful chocolates as a final birthday indulgence.

PAPER-THIN CUCUMBER SALAD

This is one of my favourite summer salads, cool and refreshing. Salting the cucumber draws out the water that would otherwise set the slices afloat and dilute the dressing into non-existence.

3 large cucumbers, peeled and thinly sliced
1½ tablespoons salt
9 tablespoons sherry vinegar or white wine vinegar
3 tablespoons finely chopped fresh chives
Black pepper

PAPER-THIN CUCUMBER SALAD, TOMATO AND ORANGE SALAD, ROAST FILLET OF BEEF WITH APPLE AND BASIL STUFFING

Put the cucumber into a colander and sprinkle with salt. Mix lightly, then leave to drain for an hour. Squeeze out the excess moisture with your hands. Sprinkle over the sherry vinegar or white wine vinegar, mix it in and chill. Pack the salad into a plastic box for carrying.

When you arrive at your picnic place, transfer the cucumber from the box to a serving dish, grind plenty of black pepper over the top, and sprinkle with chopped chives.

PRESENTATION

This is a smart number, so old yogurt pots and plastic boxes, fine for getting things from A to B, have no place on the linen tablecloth (or rug if it has to be) spread out on the grass. Naturally, I'm not suggesting that you jauntily take your priceless cut-glass bowls inherited from your great-grandmother, but pick out serving dishes, bowls and baskets that will display the food in the most appetizing way.

Given this is a special picnic which you'll want to go off without a hitch, here's a complete list of the equipment you'll need to take with you.

General: Large tablecloth or rug, ten napkins (preferably cloth), each one already wrapped around two knives, a fork and a spoon, wine glasses (or the more sophisticated clear plastic wine 'glasses'), salt mill, pepper mill, corkscrew, basket for bread rolls, dish for butter, butter knife, bin liners for rubbish, paper towels for spillages.

First course: One large serving dish for asparagus, one small bowl for extra dressing, small ladle or spoon for dressing, two serving spoons, ten plates.

Main course: One large serving dish for beef, two large shallow dishes for salads, carving board for cutting beef, carving knife, six serving spoons, ten plates, preferably china.

Cheese course: Plate or tray for watercress and cheese, cheese knife, ten plates (optional – you could get away with using main course plates), basket for Bath Olivers.

Pudding: Bowl for strawberries, three serving spoons, basket lined with a napkin for lace biscuits (not the same one again – some people may still be lingering on the cheese), ten bowls.

Coffee: Ten cups and saucers, ten teaspoons, small jug for cream, jar of sugar, bowl for chocolates

TOMATO AND ORANGE SALAD

The sharp-sweet juices of the sliced oranges bring out the full flavour of the tomatoes in this salad.

1kg/2lb tomatoes, sliced
5 oranges, peeled and sliced
2 tablespoons chopped fresh marjoram or oregano

Vinaigrette dressing:
2 tablespoons white wine vinegar
8 tablespoons olive oil
Salt and black pepper

To make the vinaigrette, put all ingredients in a screw-top jar, and shake. Assemble the salad when you arrive at your picnic place. Arrange tomato and orange slices on a large plate. Scatter with majoram. Shake the dressing again, then drizzle over the salad.
SEE PAGE 138.

ROAST FILLET OF BEEF WITH APPLE AND BASIL STUFFING

Tender fillet of beef is quick to cook, easy to transport, and the knife slides through it like butter, to give juicy pink slices of meat with a wedge of basil-scented stuffing.

Stuffing:
1 small onion, finely chopped
2 tablespoons olive oil
1 dessert apple, grated
1 teaspoon creamed horseradish
14 large fresh basil leaves, finely chopped
50g/2oz soft white breadcrumbs
1 egg, beaten
Salt and black pepper

2 × 1–1·25kg/2–2½lb pieces of fillet of beef, trimmed
2 tablespoons creamed horseradish
5 tablespoons olive oil
Black pepper
½ frisée lettuce, to serve

First make the stuffing. Cook the onion in the olive oil until tender, without browning. Tip into a bowl, and mix in the apple, horseradish, basil, breadcrumbs, salt and pepper and enough beaten egg to bind.

Halve the fillets horizontally, cutting from one long side almost but not quite through to the other, as if you were cutting a loaf of French bread. Season with black pepper. Fill with the stuffing, and close. Secure the meat around the stuffing by tying firmly with four lengths of string. Smear the outside with the horseradish. Pour the oil into a roasting tin and turn the fillets carefully in the oil to coat. Place in a preheated oven, 230°C, 450°F, Gas Mark 8, and cook for 5 minutes. Reduce the temperature to 180°C, 350°F, Gas Mark 4, and cook for a further 25 minutes. Remove from oven, and leave to cool. Wrap in foil and store in the fridge. Carve into 1cm/½in slices at home and wrap in one piece, or slice it when you arrive at your picnic place.

At home, wash and dry the frisée thoroughly. Store in a plastic bag in the fridge. Transport in its plastic bag.

To serve *Make a bed of frisée leaves on a large plate and arrange the sliced beef on top of it.*
SEE PAGE 138.

PLANNING AHEAD

Two days before: Make the pistachio and lemon dressing for the asparagus and store in the fridge. Make the lace biscuits to accompany the pudding and keep in an airtight tin.

The day before: Make the strawberry caramel bavarois and leave in the fridge overnight. Stuff and roast the fillet of beef, wrap it well and keep in the fridge overnight.

The day of the picnic: Cook the asparagus. Allow it to cool before packing it in its plastic box. Make the cucumber salad. Wash and dry the frisée lettuce and the watercress. Marinate the strawberries. Slice the tomatoes and oranges for the salad and make the dressing. Make horseradish sauce if there's time. Pack the plates, glasses, cutlery and serving bowls and other equipment.

Just before leaving: Make the coffee and pour it into vacuum flasks rinsed out with hot water. Assemble and pack up the food for the picnic.

GOATS' MILK CHEESES WITH WATERCRESS AND BATH OLIVERS

Just as cows' milk cheeses can be soft, hard or buttery, mild, piquant, or mellow, so goats' milk cheeses vary considerably in texture and taste. Choose a variety of cheeses, some fresh and soft, some mature, some with white rinds, some black, some with a herby coat. Have one or two pyramid shapes and perhaps a classic log and a Camembert-type cheese. You'll need at least four small cheeses, more if they are very small, for this number of people.

Goats' milk cheese is excellent with the fresh pepperiness of watercress so buy a large bunch, pick it over, removing any brownish or damaged leaves, wash and dry well. Store in a plastic bag in the fridge until you are ready to leave.

At your picnic place, once the main course is drawing to a close, arrange the watercress in a bed on a large plate or wicker tray. Arrange the cheeses on the watercress and serve with the most sophisticated of cheese biscuits, plain Bath Olivers.

Top **GOATS' MILK CHEESES WITH WATERCRESS AND BATH OLIVERS**

STRAWBERRY CARAMEL BAVAROIS

This is a heavenly creamy pudding laden with the fragrance of fresh strawberries. Serve it with a tumble of marinated strawberries, and crisp lace biscuits (see page 143).

250g/8oz caster sugar
200ml/7fl oz water
2 sachets powdered gelatine
750g/1½lb strawberries, hulled
2 tablespoons lemon juice
Icing sugar (optional)
450ml/¾ pint whipping cream

STRAWBERRY CARAMEL BAVAROIS, STRAWBERRIES MARINATED IN MOSCATEL, LACE BISCUITS

Put the caster sugar into a heavy-based pan with 4 tablespoons of the water. Stir over a low to moderate heat until the sugar has dissolved completely to give a clear syrup. Brush down the crystals stuck to the side of the pan with a brush dipped in cold water. Boil without stirring until the syrup turns a deep caramel brown. Draw off the heat and immediately add another 4 tablespoons of water. Swirl and then stir to mix evenly. Cool until tepid.

Warm the remaining water in a small pan until hot but not boiling. Sprinkle the gelatine evenly over the surface and leave to become spongy for 3 minutes. Stir over a very low heat until the gelatine has completely dissolved. Mix in the caramel. Cool until tepid.

Liquidize or mash the strawberries with the lemon juice. Beat 3 tablespoons into the tepid gelatine and caramel mixture – if it becomes lumpy, warm again gently to dissolve the gelatine. Tip it all back into the remaining strawberries and mix well. Sieve. Taste and add icing sugar to sweeten if needed. Leave in the fridge until the mixture is beginning to set.

Whip the cream until it just holds its shape. Fold it into the strawberry mixture, and spoon it into a 1·5 litre/2½ pint serving bowl. Cover the bowl, and leave it in the fridge for at least 4 hours to set.

To transport the dessert, wrap the bowl first in clingfilm, then in dampened newspaper. Stand it upright in an insulated bag if you have one, or in a double carrier bag. Keep it well away from heat and direct sunlight and take it out of its wrappings only when you are ready to serve it.

LACE BISCUITS

The use of rolled oats may suggest a rather homely lumpen biscuit, but these lace biscuits are as delicate, crisp and light as you could possibly hope and delicious with desserts such as the strawberry caramel bavarois. The quantities make about 40 biscuits, so with luck you'll have some left over for another day, but don't bank on it.

125g/4oz rolled oats
1 tablespoon plain flour
250g/8oz caster sugar
$\frac{1}{4}$ teaspoon salt
125g/4oz butter
1 egg, beaten
$\frac{1}{2}$ teaspoon vanilla essence

Line 3 baking sheets with non-stick baking parchment. Mix the oats, flour, sugar and salt. Melt the butter and, while still hot, pour over the dry ingredients. Stir until evenly mixed. Make a well in the centre and add the beaten egg and vanilla flavouring. Mix it all together thoroughly.

Drop teaspoons of the mixture on to the baking sheets at 5cm/2in intervals. Bake in a preheated oven, 170°C, 325°F, Gas Mark 3, for 10–12 minutes until golden brown. Cool on wire racks until completely cold.

Store and transport to the picnic in an airtight tin.

STRAWBERRIES MARINATED IN MOSCATEL

Sweet Moscatel wines have a delicious raisiny fragrance that is sensational with strawberries, but if you prefer to do without any more alcohol, or if there are strawberry-hungry children in the party, replace the wine with the juice of two or three oranges and a dash of sugar. Perhaps the best solution to keep everybody happy is to prepare half the strawberries with wine, and half with orange juice.

1kg/2lb strawberries, hulled and halved or quartered if large
150ml/$\frac{1}{4}$ pint Moscatel wine, or other sweet fragrant dessert wine

Mix the prepared strawberries with the wine in a large bowl. Cover the bowl and keep the mixture cool in the fridge, stirring it gently from time to time. Eat the marinated strawberries within 24 hours, either as they are or with the strawberry caramel bavarois (see page 142) and the lace biscuits.

Oz Clarke's WINE NOTES

Sophie assures me this is a summer birthday and the sun always shines on her picnics, so we've got to have plenty of Champagne – and it's got to be kept cool. Will five bottles be enough? Take along a few more just in case.

Buy the Champagne at least the day before so that you can give the bottles a long time in the fridge – five or six hours, overnight even. If you've got one of those big insulated cooler bags, put the bottles straight in there, ice cold from the fridge, and, if you have them, pack 'chill blocks' from the ice compartment round the bottles. They'll keep cool for most of the day.

If you don't have either of those, wrap damp dishcloths round the bottles, because the evaporation of water chills things down. And if Sophie's having her picnic by a stream – as surely she will – the stream will also be a great chiller – just remember to secure the bottles or they'll drift away with the current and make someone very happy about 5 miles downstream!

Just in case you get tired of drinking fizz – perish the thought – a nice juicy Australian Cabernet Sauvignon/ Shiraz red wine would go awfully well with that wonderful roast fillet of beef.

The snappy green fruit flavours of New Zealand Sauvignon Blanc will be perfect with the goats' cheese, and you may as well carry on drinking the Moscatel with that scrumptious strawberry pudding – better than a birthday cake any day!

Vegetarian Barbecue for 15

If a vegetarian barbecue sounds to you like a contradiction in terms, then you've obviously not been getting the most out of your barbecue. There's no rule that a barbecue is only for cooking hunks of meat.

All manner of vegetables can be barbecued, onions, leeks (par-boil them first), mushrooms, courgettes, thickly sliced aubergines (salt them first to extract bitter juices), wedges of fennel, sweet peppers. If there's time, marinate the vegetables for a few hours first. Then just brush with oil, season and grill.

Tofu – bean curd – is high in protein, but often dismissed as being simply too bland to bother with. In fact its blandness is a positive attribute, since it readily absorbs other flavours, and its creamy texture is the perfect foil to grilled vegetables. Given a bath in a spicy marinade, then barbecued until patched with brown, it takes on a whole new and delicious character.

Add some interesting salads, crusty bread and a freshly baked fruit tart, and you have a feast that is sure to satisfy vegetarians and meat-eaters alike.

Menu

*

BARBECUED CORN ON THE COB WITH OLIVE AND LEMON BUTTER

TOFU, MUSHROOM AND COURGETTE KEBABS

GRILLED PEPPERS AND ONIONS WITH PESTO

TABBOULEH

CARROT AND SESAME SALAD

*

APPLE AND HONEY TART

*

Lugana *or* Single-Vineyard Soave Classico

Friuli Cabernet Sauvignon

Sauternes

BARBECUED CORN ON THE COB WITH OLIVE AND LEMON BUTTER

Barbecued corn on the cob, juicy and tender, has a superb sweet smoky taste, emphasized by the saltiness of olives in the flavoured butter as it melts over the hot kernels. Soaking the corn plumps up the kernels, ensuring that they don't dry out over the hot charcoal.

15 heads corn on the cob
Salt
Oil

Olive and lemon butter:
125g/4oz pitted black olives
250g/8oz lightly salted butter, softened
Finely grated rind of 1 lemon
2–3 tablespoons lemon juice
1 clove garlic, crushed

Place all the ingredients for the butter in a food processor, and whizz until smooth. If you don't have a processor, chop the olives very, very finely, and mash with the butter and remaining ingredients. Add extra lemon juice to taste. Pile into a bowl, cover loosely and chill.

Strip the husks and silky threads off the corn. Immerse in a bucket of lightly salted water, and leave to soak for at least half an hour, and up to 3 hours. Just before grilling, pat dry. Grill the corn over high heat, turning, until patched with brown. Serve with the flavoured butter.

TOFU, MUSHROOM AND COURGETTE KEBABS

Don't skip the initial draining of the tofu clamped between baking sheets. Fully drained tofu will absorb more of the marinade.

1kg/2lb firm tofu, plain or smoked
750g/1½lb small courgettes, sliced 1cm/½in thick
750g/1½lb small button mushrooms

Marinade:
Rind and juice of 2 lemons
2 onions, chopped
3 cloves garlic, chopped
125ml/4fl oz olive oil
2 teaspoons coriander seeds, lightly crushed
2–3 green chillies, finely chopped
2 bay leaves, broken in half
2 sprigs thyme
4 large sprigs parsley, roughly chopped
1 sprig rosemary
2 teaspoons light brown sugar
150ml/¼ pint water

TOFU, MUSHROOM AND COURGETTE KEBABS, GRILLED PEPPERS AND ONIONS WITH PESTO, CARROT AND SESAME SALAD, TABBOULEH, GREEN SALAD WITH TOASTED WALNUTS

To drain the tofu, place it in a single layer on a baking sheet. Set a second sheet on top, and weight down with cans. On the draining board, prop one end of this 'sandwich' up on a small can, so that the liquid can drain out thoroughly. Leave for at least half an hour.

Meanwhile, prepare the marinade. Put all the ingredients in a pan, and bring up to the boil, stirring occasionally. Simmer for 3 minutes then cool. Cut the drained tofu into 2·5cm/1in cubes and place in a shallow dish. Place the courgettes in a second dish. Pour the marinade over the tofu and courgettes. Cover and leave for at least 8 hours, preferably 24 hours, turning occasionally.

Thread the tofu, courgettes and mushrooms on to skewers. Strain the marinade into a bowl. Brush the kebabs with the marinade, and grill for 6–7 minutes, turning and basting frequently with the marinade, until they are tender and lightly brown.

BARBECUED CORN ON THE COB WITH OLIVE AND LEMON BUTTER

EXTRAS

To accompany the barbecue, serve thick slices of crusty bread. You'll need about four large round loaves. Have some slightly salted butter to go with it and maybe a single large wedge of vegetarian Cheddar, weighing about 750 g/1½lb. You might also offer a simple green salad of Cos or crisp lettuces dressed with a sunflower oil and walnut oil vinaigrette and scattered with chopped toasted walnuts.

To serve with the tart you'll need about 1·2litres/2 pints cream or yogurt.

PLANNING AHEAD

The day before: Marinate tofu and courgettes. Make olive and lemon butter. Make tabbouleh. Bake pastry cases, but do not fill.

The day of the party: Strip corn and soak. Fill and bake apple and honey tart. Wash lettuce, store in the fridge in a large, knotted plastic bag. Mix *pesto* with oil. Make vinaigrette. An hour before guests arrive prepare onions and peppers, cover and keep cool. Make carrot salad. Thread up kebabs, strain marinade. Half an hour before guests arrive light the barbecue. When guests arrive assemble the salad. Start grilling corn.

ORGANIZING A BARBECUE

There's no point in attempting a barbecue party unless you do it properly. Buy, or build, the barbecue itself and give it a couple of test runs before the party.

Finding the best possible position for the barbecue is a priority. If it is a free-standing one, find a spot of smooth even ground, where it will not wobble dangerously. Keep it away from over-hanging branches, shrubs, and plants that might suffer in the heat. Make sure there is plenty of room around it so that the 'chef' is not cramped and crowded as he or she works. There should also be enough space to set up a table for ingredients, equipment and first aid kit.

Get used to the individual properties of the type of fuel you are using. One of the trickiest things about barbecuing is timing the lighting so that the flames have died down, and the coals are at their hottest, precisely when you want to get going on the food, not half an hour before or after. As a rough guide, charcoal takes 30–60 minutes and wood takes around two hours.

Do not start cooking until the flames have completely died down. The heat will be most intense in the centre, gentler towards the edges. The art of barbecuing lies in getting the food cooked properly, and avoiding the all too familiar charred black crust and raw interior. Thicker pieces of food are best cooked over a moderate heat, allowing plenty of time for the heat to make its way right through, before the outside becomes inedible.

Safety is of paramount importance, particularly if there are children running around the garden. There should be one adult, two at most if the barbecue is a large one, in charge of cooking and tending the barbecue. To avoid congestion around the barbecue, set out salads, bread, and other bits and bobs that are not essential to the cooking process, on a table a fair distance away.

GRILLED PEPPERS AND ONIONS WITH PESTO

Grilling peppers and onions over a barbecue, or under the kitchen grill, works a complete transformation on their flavours, intensifying their natural sweetness and dampening the raw hiss of the onion.

5 tablespoons ready-made pesto sauce
4 tablespoons olive oil or sunflower oil
10 large onions, red or white
5 assorted large peppers, deseeded and cut into eighths

Beat the *pesto* with the oil, and spoon into a bowl. Peel the onions, and cut into 15mm/¾in slices. Push a wooden cocktail stick through each slice, from one side through the centre, like a lollipop, to keep rings together.

Brush the pieces of pepper and onion generously on both sides with the *pesto* mixture. Grill the peppers skin side to the heat first, turning when mottled with black. When the inside is lightly spotted with black, they are done enough. Grill the onion slices, turning occasionally, until the cut sides are a deep dark brown, and just beginning to burn. Don't worry if the ends of some of the cocktail sticks burn off, but do remember to warn guests that there is three-quarters of a stick running through the centre, before they take a big bite! Serve with any remaining *pesto* and oil as a relish.

SEE PAGE 144.

TABBOULEH

Bulgar is cracked wheat, already cooked and dried so that it merely needs to be moistened before use. It forms the basis of this minty salad.

500g/1lb bulgar
4 tomatoes, deseeded and very finely diced
1 cucumber, very finely diced
10 spring onions, or 1 onion, very finely chopped
125ml/4fl oz olive oil
4 tablespoons lemon juice
1 large bunch fresh mint, finely chopped
1 bunch parsley, finely chopped
Salt and pepper

Pour boiling water over the bulgar; soak for 15 minutes. Drain, then squeeze out as much water as you can. Mix with the remaining ingredients. Refrigerate for 4–24 hours. Adjust seasoning before serving.

SEE PAGE 144.

CARROT AND SESAME SALAD

Grating carrots is not the most entertaining job, but it is worth it for this salad, with its thick yogurt dressing, spiked with mustard.

12 tablespoons Greek yogurt
2 tablespoons sunflower oil
1 tablespoon French mustard
3 tablespoons sesame seeds
2kg/4lb carrots, scraped or peeled, coarsely grated
Salt

Mix the yogurt with the oil, mustard and salt to taste. Toast the sesame seeds. Cool. Set aside 1 teaspoon of seeds, and mix the rest with the carrots and yogurt. Scatter over the reserved seeds before serving.

SEE PAGE 144.

APPLE AND HONEY TART

Open, French-style fruit tarts are always popular. This apple tart, with the subtle scent of honey, is particularly good. The base can be baked in advance, but leave the final baking until the day it is to be eaten, so that the pastry doesn't become soggy.

500g/1lb shortcrust pastry

Filling:
2kg/4lb cooking apples, roughly chopped
5 cloves
1 teaspoon ground cinnamon
5 tablespoons water
Clear honey, to sweeten and glaze
6 dessert apples, quartered, cored and thinly sliced
2 tablespoons caster sugar

Divide the pastry in two, and roll each piece out to a thin circle on a floured board. Line two 25cm/10in tart tins. Rest for half an hour in the fridge. Place a baking sheet in the oven, and preheat to 200°C, 400°F, Gas Mark 6.

Prick the pastry all over with a fork, then line with greaseproof paper or foil, and weight down with baking beans. Stand the tins on the baking sheet and bake for 10 minutes. Remove the paper and beans and return to the oven for 5–10 minutes to dry out, without browning.

Put the cooking apples, core and all, into a pan with the cloves, cinnamon and the water. Cover and cook over a very gentle heat, stirring occasionally, until the apple collapses to a purée. If necessary, add a little extra water to prevent catching. Sieve, pressing through as much of the apple pulp as possible. Add honey to taste, but keep the purée slightly on the sharp side. Cool.

Spread the purée thinly on the base of the two pastry cases. Arrange half the dessert apple slices in concentric circles on each tart. They will shrink a little as they cook, so pack quite tightly. Sprinkle evenly with sugar. Bake for 25–30 minutes until the edges of the apples catch and brown.

Heat about 4 tablespoons of honey gently in a small pan until very runny. Brush over the apples. Serve cold with Greek yogurt or cream.

Oz Clarke's
WINE NOTES

I couldn't agree more, Sophie. The bane of the barbecue is the totally inedible leather tough pork chop which looked so plump and appetizing as it lay ready for the flames yet now could do several weeks' sterling service as the sole of your sandal. And the drumstick. I suppose, looking at the chubby round shape of a chicken drumstick, it is going to be virtually impossible for all but the most inspired genius of the griddle to penetrate the core before the skin is as black and frazzled as a Spanish *doña's* shawl. I'm not a vegetarian, but the average carnivore's barbecue is as good an incentive as any to give it a try!

And I can't think of a better way to start than with that corn on the cob, all sweet and the butter made salty and bitter-edged by the black olives, oozing over your chin and fingers. Mmm! I think I'll have a soft, dry slightly creamy or nutty Italian white for this – one that won't mind getting mixed up in the glass with blobs of melted butter – a Lugana, or a single-vineyard Soave Classico.

This might be the wine for the tofu as well, because the spicy marinade may actually enhance the slightly neutral fruit. But you could do with a red, lightly chilled perhaps, and the one for this, as well as for the irresistible combination of sweet onion and pepper with *pesto*, and for the minty tabbouleh is a light, sharply blackcurranty Cabernet Sauvignon from Italy's Friuli (north-east of Venice).

With that apple and honey tart I'm going to treat myself to a really good Sauternes. Most dessert flavours overwhelm Sauternes, but the apple and the honey will complement the honey and butterscotch sweetness of the wine quite beautifully.

APPLE AND HONEY TART

Japanese Barbecue *for 10*

This menu draws its inspiration from Japanese *yakimono*, grilled foods. As you might guess, this is no slap-dash affair. The seasonings and methods used are simple and straightforward, skilfully chosen to bring out the true, pure flavours of superb fresh ingredients. Meat, fish and vegetables are beautifully trimmed and cut into bite-sized pieces that will cook quickly in the fierce heat of the grill. Smaller fish are often left whole, skewers threaded through them so that they curve and undulate elegantly as if they were swimming through the sea. The art of the chef is to grill the food until the exact moment when the outside is crisp but not charred, while the inside is still moist and succulent, cooked to the appropriate degree.

For this barbecue I've chosen a selection of poultry, seafood, and vegetables, all threaded on to small skewers so that they can be easily eaten with no call for knives and forks. Even the mixed vegetable pickles can be speared a sliver at a time with the end of the skewer, just enough to contrast with the softer flavours of the grilled foods. The final course, a beautifully arranged tray of fresh cool pieces of fruit, with contrasting colours and textures, is appropriately elegant and simple.

Menu

*

SALT-GRILLED MACKEREL

PINWHEEL PRAWNS

VEGETABLE KEBABS

CHICKEN YAKITORI

CHICKEN LIVERS WITH TERIYAKI SAUCE

*

PLATE OF PREPARED FRUIT

*

Manzanilla Sherry

Pilsener Lager *or* Chinese Beer

Green Tea

CHICKEN LIVERS WITH TERIYAKI SAUCE, SALT-GRILLED MACKEREL, VEGETABLE KEBABS, PINWHEEL PRAWNS, CHICKEN YAKITORI

SALT-GRILLED MACKEREL

The rich oily flesh of mackerel takes well to barbecuing. The skin becomes deliciously crisp and salty. When you turn the fish be careful that it doesn't get pulled off and lost among the charcoal.

5 mackerel, filleted but not skinned
5 tablespoons mirin or sweet sherry
Oil
Salt

Cut each of the fish fillets in half from head to tail, and trim any bones. Halve each strip across the body.

Take a piece at a time, and sprinkle the skin and cut sides lightly with salt and *mirin* or sherry. Lay it skin side down and thread a skewer down the length, as if you were stitching a piece of cloth, without piercing the skin. Arrange on a tray, cover and keep cool until needed.

If you have one, use a double-sided hinged grill for cooking the mackerel. To prevent sticking, oil the bars of the grill rack well, whatever kind you use, before you begin cooking. Grill the mackerel, skin side to the heat, for about 3 minutes until the skin is crisp and brown. Turn and cook for a further 1–2 minutes, until just cooked through.

PINWHEEL PRAWNS

The flavour won't be as good but if you can't get raw prawns, use cooked ones. Prepare in the same way, and grill until piping hot.

20 raw king prawns
2·5cm/1in fresh root ginger, peeled and halved
1 clove garlic, chopped
4 tablespoons dark soy sauce
4 tablespoons sake

Cut the heads off the prawns and peel, leaving just the ends of the tails in place. Put in a shallow dish. Crush the ginger in a garlic press, squeezing the juice over the prawns. Spoon over the garlic, soy sauce and *sake*, and turn to coat evenly. Leave, covered, in the refrigerator for up to 6 hours.

Curl each prawn into a tight spiral, and thread a skewer through, inserting it near the base of the tail end. Thread 2 prawns on to each skewer. Grill for 3–4 minutes, turning once, until pink.

VEGETABLE KEBABS

These are the simplest of kebabs, tiny vegetables threaded on to skewers and barbecued just long enough to heat through.

1·25 kg/2½lb tiny new potatoes
Mint leaves
500g/1lb cherry tomatoes
Large sage leaves, halved
500g/1lb small button mushrooms
Oil
Salt and seven-spice seasoning or pepper

Steam or boil the potatoes in their skins until almost cooked. Drain and cool. Thread skewers with 5 potatoes interspersed with mint leaves or 5 tomatoes with pieces of sage, or 5 button mushrooms, until the ingredients are used up. Cover and set aside. Just before grilling, brush vegetables with oil; season with salt and seven-spice seasoning (see 'Extras') or pepper. Grill tomatoes briefly – 1–2 minutes. Grill potatoes and mushrooms for a little longer.

EXTRAS

Have some bowls of rice crackers around for people to nibble with their drinks while they are waiting for the skewers to be cooked. For convenience serve miniature pitta breads (allow 4–5 per person) instead of rice or noodles.

Serve a variety of accompaniments. Put lemon wedges, bowls of soy sauce, and bowls of Japanese seven-spice seasoning (for salt-grilled mackerel and pinwheel prawns) out on the table or tables, for people to help themselves.

It might be worth warning the unwary that the seven-spice seasoning is powerfully hot and peppery. It is an aromatic blend of spices, sprinkled over food as we might use black or cayenne pepper. If it is unavailable you can substitute more familiar spices to create an equally fragrant anglicized seasoning. Bake strips of peel from 2 tangerines in a low oven until crisp. Cool, and break into small pieces. Dry-fry 3 tablespoons of sesame seeds in a small heavy frying pan, over a high heat, until they begin to jump and give off a delicious nutty aroma. Cool. Mix the tangerine peel and sesame seeds with ½ tablespoon of poppy seeds, 3 tablespoons of black peppercorns, 1 tablespoon each of mustard seeds and dried green peppercorns and 4 tablespoons of chilli powder and grind to a powder in a coffee grinder. Store in an air-tight jar.

Make simple vegetable pickles 24–48 hours in advance. Prepare about 2 large carrots, 2 turnips, an unpeeled cucumber, 20 radishes or a large piece of mooli and a red pepper. Cut them into matchsticks or thin slices or strips. Sprinkle with salt and set aside for 15 minutes then squeeze out as much liquid as you can. Transfer them to a deep bowl and add 2 tablespoons of toasted sesame seeds and about 175ml/6fl oz rice vinegar or white wine vinegar. Mix well, cover and leave in the fridge until needed, stirring occasionally.

PLANNING AHEAD

One or two days before: Make the vegetable pickles.

The day before: Prepare yakitori and teriyaki sauces.

The day of the party: Put the wooden skewers to soak. Prepare the vegetables, meat and seafood, keep covered in the fridge, until needed. Marinate prawns.

Two hours before the guests arrive, prepare the fruit platter.

Ninety minutes before the guests arrive, gather all available helpers and thread up the skewers. Keep them covered in the fridge. Thirty minutes before guests arrive, light the barbecue.

PRESENTATION

Guests may be happy to eat their food in semi-darkness at an evening barbecue, but the barbecue area itself must be well lit. Use the proper implements – long wooden-handled tongs, brushes, forks, and spoons. Hinged, double-sided grills, preferably with long handles, make turning all kinds of food much easier. Oven gloves are essential.

Make sure that you have dipping sauces for basting (labelled so that you know which is which), a bowl of oil for oiling the rack, long-handled tongs, and any other necessary equipment arranged on a table beside the barbecue.

You can't dispense entirely with the usual paraphernalia of dining. Plates and plenty of napkins for sticky fingers are essential. If you are using disposable paper plates, pick out ones that will fit in with the Japanese theme – just plain clear colours, and at most an uncluttered, geometric design.

You'll need 200–250 thin wooden skewers (they're usually made of bamboo). Soak them thoroughly in water before using to prevent them burning on the barbecue. Immerse them in water for at least 2 hours then take them out and thread them up.

CHICKEN YAKITORI

The dark meat of chicken thighs has more flavour, and retains more moisture when barbecued, than chicken breast. When threading the skewers, make sure the skin is exposed, so that it browns crisply.

10 boned, unskinned chicken thighs
12 young leeks or fat spring onions

Yakitori sauce:
300ml/$\frac{1}{2}$ pint dark soy sauce
150ml/$\frac{1}{4}$ pint chicken stock
3 tablespoons caster sugar
150ml/$\frac{1}{4}$ pint sake or dry white wine
75ml/3fl oz mirin or sweet sherry
1 clove garlic, finely chopped

Remove as many tendons as you can from the chicken thighs. Cut into pieces approximately 2·5cm/1in square. Trim the leeks or spring onions, removing tough outer layers. Cut into 2·5cm/1in lengths. Thread the chicken, skin side out, and leeks alternately on to 25–30 skewers. Cover and keep cool until needed.

Place all the sauce ingredients in a pan and stir over a moderate heat until the sugar is completely dissolved. Bring up to the boil and simmer for 1 minute. Remove from the heat and cool. Strain.

Put about a quarter of the sauce into a small bowl to serve as a dipping sauce with the kebabs. Pour the rest into a tall jar for basting the kebabs. Grill the chicken for about a minute, turning once, until the juices begin to run. Then dip the skewers, one by one, into the sauce (or brush the sauce over them). Shake off excess and return to the grill for a further 1–2 minutes, turning once. Repeat the dipping and grilling two or three times until cooked through.

SEE PAGE 148.

CHICKEN LIVERS WITH TERIYAKI SAUCE

The ingredients for teriyaki sauce are similar to those for yakitori sauce but the different balance gives a sweet instead of salty flavour. Mirin is a sweet golden wine much used in Japanese cooking but sweet sherry can be used instead.

500g/1lb chicken livers
3 green peppers, deseeded and cut into 2·5cm/1in squares

Teriyaki sauce:
225ml/7$\frac{1}{2}$fl oz sake or dry white wine
225ml/7$\frac{1}{2}$fl oz mirin or sweet sherry
225ml/7$\frac{1}{2}$fl oz dark soy sauce
4 tablespoons caster sugar

Place all the sauce ingredients in a pan and stir over a moderate heat until the sugar has dissolved. Bring to the boil and simmer for 1 minute. Draw off the heat and cool.

Pick over the chicken livers and remove any greenish-yellow bits. Quarter large livers. Thread pieces of liver and pepper alternately on to 25–30 skewers. Cover and set aside. Put a quarter of the sauce into a small bowl to serve as a dipping sauce with the kebabs. Pour the rest into a tall jar for basting the kebabs.

Oil the grill rack. Grill the kebabs for about a minute on each side. Then dip one at a time into the jar of sauce (or brush over kebabs), shake off excess, and return to the grill for a minute or so, turning once. Repeat until the livers are just cooked through. This is a bit like painting the Forth Bridge: no sooner have you worked through to the last skewer than it is time to start again.

SEE PAGE 148.

PLATE OF PREPARED FRUIT

Prepare the fruit an hour or two in advance, but leave the final arrangement until the last possible moment. Choose a selection of at least five of the ripest and most perfect fruits available, taking care to include contrasting colours, flavours and textures.

A selection of the freshest fruit of the season – allow about 175g/6oz of prepared fruit per person: watermelon, melons, apples, pears, oranges, kumquats, grapes, peaches, nectarines, apricots, greengages and plums, strawberries, raspberries, tayberries or loganberries, mangoes, pawpaws
Lemon juice
Edible flowers and leaves for decoration – such as nasturtium flowers and leaves, twigs of bay leaves, fresh sweet herbs such as rosemary, basil or chervil, roses, pansies, etc
Caster sugar

Cut larger fruits such as melons or mangoes into bite-sized pieces, or thin wedges that can easily be eaten with the hands. Core apples and pears and cut into eighths; turn them in lemon juice as you work to prevent browning. Prepare peaches and nectarines last – halve and discard the stone, then cut into eighths. Leave smaller fruit – apricots, greengages, soft fruits and grapes – whole. Store all the fruit separately, tightly covered, in the fridge.

Arrange larger pieces of fruit and decorative leaves and flowers prettily on one or two large plates or trays before serving. Scatter smaller fruits, such as raspberries, over the arrangement.

Serve with a bowl of caster sugar for people to dip the pieces of prepared fruit into.

Top **PLATE OF PREPARED FRUIT**

Oz Clarke's *WINE NOTES*

I'm not a terribly organized person. I tend always to be in a dreadful rush, forgetting where I've put things, not remembering where I'm supposed to be and with whom, or why. So my general level of entertaining and cooking veers from the scattily well-intentioned, to the hopelessly over-ambitious but under-planned, shovelled on to china plates (not, I fear, of matching patterns) about three minutes after my guests are supposed to arrive. Which must be why I love Japanese food. It is so coolly correct in execution. Every piece of food is part of a pattern of taste, of shape and of colour, and the entire experience has an air of delicacy, of tranquillity, and control. But thank goodness there's a chink in the armour. You get marvellously sticky fingers!

The Japanese are rapidly becoming extremely enthusiastic wine drinkers, but there are few Japanese dishes which go well with ordinary red and white table wines. The dark, pervasive flavour of soy, the sourness of vinegar and the palate-tingling spices all call for either ice-cold beer, or else something with its own stark, assertive flavour. Manzanilla sherry, kept ice-cold and doled out frequently from the ice bucket, has a splendid salty austerity which will match these flavours brilliantly.

And a totally dry, freezer-cold beer, ideally from the original Pilsener breweries of Czechoslovakia, but otherwise in the lean hoppy style several Chinese breweries like Tsingtao adopt, will also do very well.

EASTERN MEDITERRANEAN BARBECUE

for 8

High summer in the Eastern Mediterranean . . . at noon the air shimmers with the unremitting heat, and later, as the shadows lengthen, the oncoming night promises only mild relief from the intense heat of the day. Little wonder that outdoor barbecuing, away from the steamy atmosphere of a small kitchen, is a favourite way of cooking meat and fish, while other dishes, that can be served cold or reheated when called for, are prepared in the cooler early morning.

Recreating such food at home, you will, in fact, find yourself eating a rather better meal than you might abroad. In Mediterranean countries, meat can be dry and stringy unless it is slowly stewed. Here, the lamb is tender and juicy, ideal for barbecuing. A whole leg of lamb, opened out flat, makes the perfect centre piece for a small party. It will take at least 35 minutes to cook, so make sure the barbecue is ready for the meat as soon as guests arrive.

After the fresh, simple flavours of the main course, the moist, syrup-soaked walnut cake, filled with raspberries and whipped cream, makes a glorious finale.

MENU

*

GRILLED BUTTERFLIED LEG OF LAMB WITH YOGURT AND CUCUMBER SAUCE

TWO-BEAN AND POTATO RATATOUILLE

GREEK SALAD

*

WALNUT CAKE WITH ORANGE SYRUP AND RASPBERRIES

*

Retsina

North-East Italian Tocai

Greek Sweet Red Wine

GRILLED BUTTERFLIED LEG OF LAMB WITH YOGURT AND CUCUMBER SAUCE, GREEK SALAD, TWO-BEAN AND POTATO RATATOUILLE

GRILLED BUTTERFLIED LEG OF LAMB WITH CUCUMBER AND YOGURT SAUCE

A butterflied leg of lamb is one that has been boned and opened out flat, like a butterfly. If you have the choice buy a large leg of lamb that has been 'tunnel-boned'. Cut the lamb open along the line of the 'tunnel' at the point where the meat is thinnest. Trim off as much fat, sinew and thin grey fell skin as you can without cutting into the meat.

1 large boned leg of lamb weighing about 2kg/4lb after boning

Marinade:
8 tablespoons lemon juice
1 onion, chopped
3 cloves garlic, sliced
150ml/¼ pint olive oil
2 bay leaves, crumbled
2 teaspoons dried mint
1 teaspoon dried rigani, or oregano
2 tablespoons chopped fresh parsley
8 peppercorns, lightly crushed

Sauce:
1 cucumber, peeled and very finely diced
Salt
375g/12oz Greek yogurt
2 cloves garlic, very finely chopped
2 tablespoons finely chopped fresh mint

Trim the leg of lamb and open it out flat. Mix the marinade ingredients together. Pour a third into a shallow dish large enough to take the lamb. Lay the lamb on the marinade and pour the remaining marinade over the top. Cover, and leave in the fridge or a cool place for 24 hours, turning occasionally.

To make the sauce, spread the cucumber out in a colander and sprinkle with salt. Leave to drain for an hour. Rinse under the cold tap, and pat dry on kitchen paper or a clean tea towel. Mix with the remaining ingredients, cover and keep chilled until needed (up to 5 hours). Taste and adjust seasonings before serving.

If you have a barbecue with an adjustable metal rack, arrange it as close to the charcoal as you can get it. If the rack is fixed firmly in one position then you will have to be flexible when cooking the lamb. With a fixed rack very close to the charcoal, rig up an adjustable rack by using the grill rack from the indoor grill, and a couple of bricks, or stones to be used to raise it when needed. With a fixed rack 10–12cm/4–5in away from the charcoal, you will simply need to cook the lamb for a few minutes longer, and the outside of the meat won't develop such a delicious dark crust.

Brush bits of onion and herbs off the meat, and slash at 3cm/1½in intervals at its thickest parts, so it cooks evenly. Strain the marinade, reserving the liquid for basting. Grill the lamb, cut side to the charcoal first, very close to the heat, for 5–7 minutes on each side to give a deep brown crust. Rearrange the rack so that the lamb is 10–12cm/4–5in from the heat, and give it a further 12–19 minutes on each side, depending on how well done you like it. Baste the lamb with the marinade every time you turn it.

Keep an eye on it, and test by plunging a knife into the centre – I take it off the heat the moment the scarlet translucence of raw meat disappears, to give the most perfect succulent pink lamb.

Lift on to a serving dish, and let it relax, sitting in a warm spot at the edge of the barbecue, for 5 minutes before carving.

To serve *Slice the lamb thickly and serve with the yogurt and cucumber sauce.*

EXTRAS

Pitta bread is traditional with Eastern Mediterranean food. Allow two to three per person. They can be warmed through on the barbecue – around the edges where the heat is less intense. Alternatively, wrap them in foil, in batches of four, and heat through in a moderate oven for about 15 minutes.

Since the lamb takes some time to cook a simple dip with raw vegetables will stave off the pangs of hunger. There are many possibilities – hummus, perhaps, or one made from tahini, sesame seed paste, which can be thinned down to a light cream with water and lemon juice and olive oil to taste, then dusted with ground cumin and cayenne.

To accompany the dip prepare about 1·5kg/3lb mixed raw vegetables, such as radishes, spring onions, sweet peppers, fennel, chicory, Chinese leaf, cucumber, cauliflower and mangetout. Wash and trim them if necessary and cut into convenient pieces.

PLANNING AHEAD

In advance: Make the walnut cake.

The day before: Make the two bean and potato ratatouille. Marinate the lamb.

The day of the party: Make a dip and prepare raw vegetables for dipping. Prepare the ingredients for the Greek salad. Make the sauce to accompany the lamb no more than 5 hours before eating.

Thirty minutes before the guests arrive light the barbecue. Prepare the pitta bread for warming. Whip the cream. Arrange the dip and raw vegetables on a serving plate. Transfer the ratatouille to a serving dish. Assemble the Greek salad, but do not toss.

When the guests arrive start cooking the lamb. Warm the first batch of pitta bread. Serve the dip.

Just before serving fill the cake with cream and raspberries.

Oz Clarke's
WINE NOTES

I know that heat. That insistent sultry heat, which blankets the parched land so that even the most avid sun-worshipper begins to seek the solace of a taverna courtyard, with the dappled shade of trees or the slatted shade of a flimsy reed roof. That heat which seems to smother sound, which stifles energy, and layers your mouth with the tacky discomfort of dust and dehydration.

Is it paradise, or is it purgatory? There's only one way to decide. Raise your arm slowly in the air. Snap your fingers together in the best colloquial Greek you can muster – and as if by magic an ice-cold bottle of Retsina will appear, the beads of condensation coursing down the bottle as brazen temptation to your thirst. This is a magic moment because it is the only time in the world when Retsina will taste like nectar.

But Retsina will only work if the day is a real scorcher. A more typical summer day might be better suited by the full but dry nutty flavour of a Tocai from north-east Italy. The walnut cake deserves a real sticky wine – either Muscat, or Mavrodaphane, which many Greeks describe as their finest wine.

PRESENTATION

The mood of this barbecue is light-hearted, lazily generous and relaxed, so keep the presentation simple. Use glazed earthenware bowls or bishes, and wicker or straw baskets for bread, or cutlery, to emphasize the Mediterranean tempo.

Throw a few twigs of rosemary or thyme on the dying embers of the barbecue as the night wears on. As they smoulder the exotic aromatic scent will meander across the garden, bringing a breath of sun-parched southern hills strewn with wild herbs.

TWO-BEAN AND POTATO RATATOUILLE

Green beans, broad beans and new potatoes are stewed together in a thick tomato sauce scented with dill and parsley to make a more easterly version of ratatouille. Like ratatouille, it tastes best when served at room temperature, although it can be served hot (heat up thoroughly indoors) if you prefer, perhaps when there is a slight chill in the air.

2 onions, chopped
2 cloves garlic, chopped
125ml/4 fl oz olive oil
500g/1lb new potatoes, or waxy salad potatoes, scrubbed, and halved or quartered if large
3 × 425g/14oz cans chopped tomatoes, or 1½kg/3lb fresh tomatoes, skinned and chopped
1 tablespoon tomato purée
1 tablespoon sugar
500g/1lb green beans, topped and tailed and cut in half
500g/1lb shelled fresh or thawed frozen broad beans
Small bunch parsley, chopped
3 tablespoons chopped fresh dill
Salt and pepper

In a wide pan, cook the onions and garlic gently in 75ml/3 fl oz of the olive oil until tender, without browning. Add the potatoes, and cook for a further 5 minutes. Stir in the tomatoes, tomato purée, sugar, salt and pepper. Simmer until the potatoes are half-cooked. Now add the green and broad beans. Set aside 1 tablespoon of the parsley and add the remainder to the pan with the dill.

Simmer for a further 10–15 minutes, stirring occasionally, until the vegetables are tender, and the sauce is thick. If the sauce looks a little watery, increase the heat and boil hard until reduced. Taste and adjust seasonings. Cool and keep covered in the fridge. Allow to return to room temperature before serving.

To serve *Stir and spoon into a dish. Drizzle the remaining oil over the top and scatter with parsley.*
SEE PAGE 152.

GREEK SALAD

To make the essential, refreshing Greek salad, you must begin with good lettuce. Use a crisp, sweet, firm one such as a Cos to balance the saltiness of the Feta cheese.

1 large Cos lettuce
4 tablespoons olive oil
1½ tablespoons lemon juice or 1 tablespoon white wine vinegar
500g/1lb firm tomatoes, cut into chunks
1 cucumber, peeled, halved lengthwise, and cut into 5mm/¼in thick semicircles
1 green pepper, cut into thin rings
250g/8oz Feta cheese, diced
1 tablespoon chopped fresh oregano, or ½ teaspoon dried oregano
1 tablespoon chopped fresh parsley
24 black olives
Salt and pepper

Wash and dry lettuce thoroughly. Piling up half a dozen leaves at a time, cut them into 1cm/½in ribbons.

Place the oil, lemon juice or vinegar, and seasoning to taste (go lightly on the salt, since Feta is very salty) in a screw-top jar, and shake to mix. Just before serving, pour the dressing into a large salad bowl. Cross the salad servers in the bowl. Arrange the lettuce on top, and add the prepared tomatoes, cucumber, pepper and Feta cheese. Scatter with the oregano, parsley and olives. Toss only when you are ready to eat.
SEE PAGE 152.

WALNUT CAKE WITH ORANGE SYRUP AND RASPBERRIES

WALNUT CAKE WITH ORANGE SYRUP AND RASPBERRIES

This moist, sticky cake can be made up to three days in advance, but must be kept covered, once cool, to prevent it drying out.

175g/6oz shelled walnuts
150g/5oz self-raising flour
1 teaspoon baking powder
Pinch of salt
150g/5oz lightly salted butter, softened
375g/12oz caster sugar
3 eggs, beaten
Grated rind and juice of 1 orange
150ml/¼ pint water
4 tablespoons lemon juice
3 cloves
300ml/½ pint whipping cream
550g/1lb raspberries

Butter a 23cm/9in ring mould. Spread the nuts on a baking sheet, and roast for 10 minutes in a preheated oven, 190°C, 375°F, Gas Mark 5. Tip into a metal sieve and shake over newspaper to get rid of flaky bits of skin. Chop finely. Increase the oven temperature to 220°C, 425°F, Gas Mark 7.

Sift the flour with baking powder and salt. Cream the butter with 125g/4oz of the sugar until light and fluffy. Beat in eggs and flour in alternate spoonfuls. Fold in the walnuts and orange rind. Pour the mixture into the tin. Bake for 10 minutes, then reduce the temperature to 180°C, 350°F, Gas Mark 4, and cook a further 25–30 minutes.

Cool for 5 minutes in the tin, then run a knife around the edge, and turn out on to a dish. Pierce the cake in 12 places with a skewer.

Once the cake is in the oven, put the water, remaining sugar, orange and lemon juices and cloves into a pan, and stir over a moderate heat until the sugar has dissolved. Bring to the boil and simmer for 5 minutes. Let it cool. Strain the syrup evenly over the hot cake as soon as it has been turned out. Let it stand for at least 12 hours, loosely covered, occasionally spooning the syrup over the cake until all is absorbed.

To serve *Fill the centre with whipped cream and raspberries. Surround with remaining cream and raspberries.*

PATRICIA LOUSADA

CHILDREN'S PARTIES

Careful planning is the key to giving a successful children's party. No matter what age group you are inviting, if you organize the space, food and activities well in advance the party will have a far better chance of success – otherwise there will be gaps when the children may feel bored and restless and things can get out of hand. Have a list of suitable games to play and lots of prizes ready wrapped. Remove fragile furniture and breakable objects from the rooms you are using. Be sure that anything dangerous, such as trailing electrical wire, harmful cleaners and medicines, is put away. Send invitations that state the time the party starts and when it ends, and directions for getting there.

It is better not to mix age groups and if the party is for the very young keep the numbers small. Young children will be quite happy playing with toys and each other for most of the time. When their attention begins to wander simple games such as 'oranges and lemons' or 'pass the parcel' can be played. If you have a large number of children, five years of age or older, a professional entertainer or magician would be worth considering. Eight to ten year olds will suggest games they have played at other parties and be ready to help run them. Be sure you have enough adult helpers – at least one for every three or four young children.

Some children are suspicious of unfamiliar food and will eat very little away from home and with the excitement of a party. Simple food served in bite-sized pieces and attractively arranged is more likely to be tempting. The food for older children can be more adventurous but some of it should be straightforward for any finicky appetites. Going-home presents and perhaps a slice of cake or some biscuits to take home for another member of the family will ensure a happy end to the event.

Teenage parties still need to be organized but the children themselves will have their own ideas of what they want. Discos are always popular if space allows. Ask a few fathers or older brothers to be on hand – useful if any gate-crashers arrive.

Opposite **TEDDY BEARS' PICNIC** *PAGE 158*

Teddy Bears' 'Picnic'
for 6

This is a party for 5-year-olds and under and all such parties should be kept small so the children will not feel overwhelmed. They will love it if you send invitations to the 'picnic' that invite not only the child but also their favourite teddy.

Young children may not eat very much but if the food is served in small quantities and in attractive shapes it is more likely to tempt them. Serve small meatballs on their own or in a nest of noodles and little crêpes rolled up with ham and cheese. For dessert, fairy cakes decorated with bear sweets and bear-shaped biscuits can be offered as well as honey sandwiches for the bears. If the cakes and biscuits are not eaten they can be wrapped up for the children to take home. If the party is a birthday make a bear mountain cake and deck it out with candles and chocolate bears.

If the weather is fine, you might have the picnic outdoors like a real picnic. As well as the menu food, open ham or chicken sandwiches cut into pretty shapes are a possibility. Ice cream cones can be handed out when the children get fidgety and want to wander about.

If you like you can dip the cones in hundreds and thousands to make them special.

MENU

*

PARTY MEATBALLS

CHEESE CRÊPES WITH HAM

*

TEDDY BEAR BISCUITS

FAIRY CAKES

BEAR MOUNTAIN

*

Fruit Juice

PARTY MEATBALLS

Children will eat these with more relish if they are served in the middle of some plain noodles so they are like eggs in a nest. Alternatively, arrange them on a plate with some lettuce leaves. The quantities make about 22 meatballs.

500g/1lb lean minced beef
50g/2oz soft breadcrumbs
4 tablespoons very finely chopped Spanish onion (or other mild variety)
2 tablespoons single cream
1 egg
3 tablespoons sunflower oil
25g/1oz butter
Salt and pepper

Mix the beef, breadcrumbs, onion, cream and egg together. Season well with quite a bit of salt but only a little pepper. When the mixture is well blended form into balls the size of walnuts using wet hands. Heat the oil and butter together in a big heavy frying pan. Add just enough balls so they fit easily into one layer. Fry gently over a medium-low heat, shaking the pan and turning the balls with a spatula so they cook evenly, for about 15 minutes or until they are cooked through.

They can be refrigerated when cold and reheated immediately before serving.

CHEESE CRÊPES WITH HAM

These crêpes are flavoured with cheese and rolled up with a slice of ham. They are ideal finger food for picnics. The quantities make about 24 crêpes. As an alternative you could make plain crêpes and fill them with slices of chicken or cooked sausage. Plain crêpes can be made three days ahead if refrigerated in an airtight bag.

Crêpes:
125g/4oz plain flour
250ml/8fl oz milk
3 eggs
25g/1oz butter, melted
Extra butter for cooking
Salt

Filling:
175g/6oz Cheddar cheese, grated
12 thin slices of cooked ham, cut into halves

Sift the flour and a pinch of salt together into a bowl. Make a well in the centre and add the milk. Whisk in the milk gradually to make a smooth batter, then whisk in the eggs and melted butter. Let the batter stand in a cool place for about an hour before making the crêpes.

Grease an 18cm/7in crêpe or heavy frying pan with butter and heat until it is very hot. Add a small ladle of batter to the pan, swirling it quickly so the bottom is evenly coated. Cook over medium heat until browned then turn the crêpe over and cook the second side until it begins to brown. Turn the crêpe over again and sprinkle with 2–3 teaspoons of the grated cheese. Cook for a few seconds to melt the cheese. Place a half slice of ham in the centre of the crêpe and roll up like a cigar.

If the first crêpe is too thick add water to the remaining batter before making more. Grease the pan when necessary and continue until the batter is used up. Serve at room temperature. The rolled crêpes can also be wrapped individually when cool to take on a picnic.

PARTY MEATBALLS, FRUIT JUICE, CHEESE CRÊPES WITH HAM

EXTRAS

The most important 'extra' in this menu is the honey sandwiches for the bears. Make them with a mixture of thinly sliced white and brown bread. Remove the crusts and cut the sandwiches into tiny squares or triangles.

To make a more colourful and perhaps more balanced meal for the children, serve plates of raw vegetables to accompany the savoury dishes. Small carrot sticks, celery sticks and tiny tomatoes are always popular, or try baby sweetcorn or, perhaps, lightly cooked french beans. You won't need more than 500g/1lb of any of these vegetables.

As an alternative dessert you might offer fruit jellies made in teddy bear or other animal moulds. You can make these from flavoured jelly cubes, or from fresh fruit juices if you prefer.

Fruit juices in individual containers will provide the most suitable drinks.

Above all, don't worry if the children don't eat much. That's not really the point of such parties. Provide carry-home bags for each child to take leftover cakes and biscuits, as well as small gifts, which seem to be expected at children's parties these days.

TEDDY BEAR BISCUITS

You can either make your own teddy bear pattern out of stiff card to use as a guide or buy a biscuit cutter in a teddy bear shape. These biscuits keep well for at least two weeks in an airtight tin.

175g/6oz lightly salted butter, plus extra for greasing
100g/3½oz caster sugar
Grated rind of ½ lemon
1 egg yolk
275g/9oz plain flour, plus extra for dusting
1 egg, lightly beaten
A few currants, chopped into tiny pieces
Granulated sugar

Cream the butter, either in a processor or by hand. Add the sugar and lemon rind and mix until fluffy, then mix in the egg yolk a little at a time. Sift the flour, then mix with the butter mixture until a dough is formed. Wrap in clingfilm and refrigerate for 30 minutes.

Roll out the biscuit dough to 5mm/¼in in thickness and cut out teddy bear shapes. Place the bears on buttered, floured baking sheets. Brush lightly with beaten egg and set 2 tiny pieces of currants for eyes on every bear. Sprinkle with granulated sugar. Bake in a preheated oven, 190°C, 375°F, Gas Mark 5, for about 10 minutes, or until golden.

When they are cooked remove the biscuits with a spatula to a wire rack to cool. Place carefully in a tin when they are completely cold.

PLANNING AHEAD

In advance: Make the teddy bear biscuits up to two weeks ahead and keep in an airtight tin.

Two days before: Prepare the party meatballs, cover with clingfilm and refrigerate.

The day before: Begin preparing the bear mountain. Pack the ice cream in a bowl and freeze it. Make the fairy cakes.

The day of the party: Make honey sandwiches for the bears. Make the cheese crêpes with ham. Prepare the raw vegetables. Make the meringue for the bear mountain.

Just before serving: Heat the party meatballs through thoroughly. Finish the bear mountain. Pour the fruit juice into individual containers.

FAIRY CAKES

Small children may not get around to eating any cake at a party but they will be pleased to take home a small cake for the next day. The cakes may be decorated by setting a small sugar or chocolate teddy in the icing or piping the child's initial on the top. This recipe will make about 12 fairy cakes.

125g/4oz butter
100g/3½oz caster sugar
Grated rind of ½ orange
2 eggs, lightly beaten
125g/4oz self-raising flour
Pinch of salt
7 tablespoons strained orange juice
250g/8oz icing sugar
12 sugar or chocolate bears, to decorate (optional)

Cream the butter, then add the sugar and beat until the mixture is light and fluffy. Stir in the orange rind. Beat in the eggs a little at a time. Sift the flour and salt together 3 times and carefully fold into the egg mixture. Lightly stir in 4 tablespoons of the orange juice to make a soft dropping consistency. Set paper cases in the wells of bun tins or place one paper case inside another and set the cases on a baking sheet. Spoon the mixture into the paper cases. Bake in a preheated oven, 190°C, 375°F, Gas Mark 5, for 15 minutes or until the cakes are cooked through. Allow to cool before icing.

For the icing, sift the icing sugar into a bowl. Make a well in the centre and pour in most of the remaining orange juice. Stir until the icing becomes smooth, adding more juice if necessary. It should be thick enough to coat the back of a spoon. Cover the tops of the cakes with a smooth layer of icing using a spatula. Set a sugar or chocolate bear in the centre of the icing, or when the icing cools add a drop of food colouring to the remaining icing and pipe the children's initials over the top.

TEDDY BEAR BISCUITS, FAIRY CAKES, BEAR MOUNTAIN

BEAR MOUNTAIN

This dessert which is really a baked alaska can be made in place of a birthday cake. Candles and little chocolate bears can be set in the meringue just before serving.

750ml/1¼ pints flavoured ice cream (not soft scoop)
20cm/8in round sponge cake, single layer
3 egg whites
Pinch of salt
125g/4oz caster sugar
Icing sugar for dusting
Butter for greasing
Chocolate bears, to decorate (optional)

Pack the ice cream in a round mixing bowl with a diameter of about 18cm/7in. Place in the freezer until solid. Grease the removable disc from the bottom of a 23–30cm/9–12in loose-bottomed round cake tin or flan tin. Set the sponge cake in the middle. Run a spatula around the inside edge of the bowl to loosen the ice cream and turn out on to the centre of the cake. Cover with plastic wrap and return to the freezer.

Whisk the egg whites with a tiny pinch of salt until stiff then add the sugar in two goes, whisking in the first amount until the meringue is shiny and stiff before repeating with the rest of the sugar. Spread the meringue over the ice cream and cake in an even layer using a spatula. Cover evenly because the meringue insulates the ice cream when it is baked. Return the meringue-covered ice cream to the freezer until ready to brown and serve. The meringue will keep in the freezer for a few hours but is best if made just before baking.

Preheat the oven to 230°C, 450°F, Gas Mark 8. When ready to serve dust the meringue with icing sugar and place the tin on a baking sheet. Bake for 5–6 minutes or until the meringue is delicately browned.

To serve *Decorate with candles and chocolate bears. Serve immediately.*

PRESENTATION

Places can be set for the teddies at the children's own table or picnic spot or the teddies can have their own special place – perhaps a rug on the floor.

There are lots of ways the party can be arranged. For a winter party you could create an outdoor scene inside by making some cardboard trees (from boxes) and hanging clementines or small red apples on them for the children to pick. You could also hang paper birds or butterflies from the ceiling on threads. Bright coloured tissue paper is very effective and easy to cut into shapes.

The guests will appreciate paper hats for the bears as well as for themselves (make a variety of sizes)! And don't forget balloons – no party for small children is complete without them.

Hallowe'en Party
for 12

I have lots of happy memories of Hallowe'en from my childhood in America where almost every child goes out trick-or-treating. Homemade spooky costumes are worn and there are lots of warm welcomes and bowls of sweets waiting when the neighbours' doorbells are rung. I have no recollection of ever playing or seeing a trick. I expect everyone was too busy collecting goodies for their carry-home bags. Children, especially those from about six years old to nine or ten, love parties with a Hallowe'en theme and if you can organize a little visit to the neighbours at the end of the party it will be a memorable occasion. If you do want to take your party of children out trick-or-treating after dark it is better to alert a few friendly neighbours and even provide the treats for them to give because this particular game is not really the custom in Britain.

You can give prizes to the scariest or funniest costume. It is a good idea to have a few old sheets handy in case any children have come without a costume. Cut a few holes for eyes and you have a ghost. If you are going to go out ringing doorbells you should also have a supply of bags for the children to carry and a few parents to help with the younger children. If you have a party of 12 it is best to split the trick-or-treating into two groups. Also remember some umbrellas. Hallowe'en is a famous night for the rain.

Despite the names of the various dishes the food in this menu is fairly basic – turkey, potatoes and corn. Cherry tomatoes, carrot and celery sticks as well as bowls of apples or clementines can be arranged on the table for the children to help themselves through the meal.

To drink there is a delicious 'witches' brew' – a concoction of mixed fruit juices.

MENU

*

GHOSTS

GOBLINS' PURSES

GRILLED TOADS AND SNAKES ON WITCHES' BROOMSTICKS

*

PUMPKIN SURPRISE

*

Witches' Brew

Ice Cream Sodas

GHOSTS

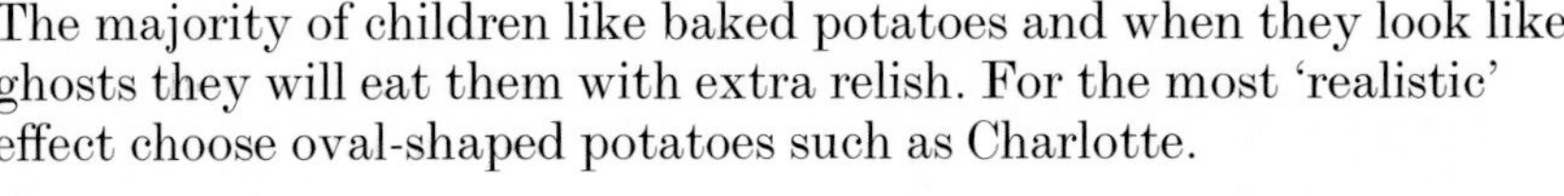

The majority of children like baked potatoes and when they look like ghosts they will eat them with extra relish. For the most 'realistic' effect choose oval-shaped potatoes such as Charlotte.

12–18 small potatoes
50g/2oz butter
150ml/$\frac{1}{4}$ pint milk
150ml/$\frac{1}{4}$ pint single cream
Currants, to garnish
Salt

Scrub the potatoes, pierce with a fork and bake in the usual way. Cut the potatoes in half lengthwise. Scoop out the insides into a bowl, leaving the skins intact. Pass the potato through a food mill. Stir in the butter. Heat the milk and cream together and whisk slowly into the potatoes. You need a soft but not sloppy mixture so adjust accordingly. Season with salt. Spoon the mixture back into the empty shells smoothing the top with the back of a spoon. Cut the currants into tiny pieces and place 2 pieces at the top of each potato to make eyes. Bake in a preheated oven, 180°C, 350°F, Gas Mark 4, for about 25 minutes or until heated through. Hot potatoes retain their heat so be sure they are not burning hot when you serve them.

GOBLINS' PURSES

These take only minutes to make and they will add an exciting touch to the menu. Most children love sweetcorn and it cooks quite perfectly inside the little pastry purses.

75g/3oz butter
12 sheets filo pastry
500g/1lb frozen sweetcorn, thawed

Melt the butter in a bowl set over a pan of simmering water. Unroll the filo and carefully lift off one sheet. Keep the others covered with a sheet of plastic or a damp cloth to prevent them drying out. Using a pastry brush and working quickly, brush one side of the pastry with the melted butter. Cut the sheet in half and place one half over the other. Cut this piece into 2 rectangles. Place one rectangle, butter side down, on a flat surface. Lay the other rectangle, butter side down over this to form a cross. Brush with butter and pile about 1 tablespoon of sweetcorn in the centre. Carefully gather up the pastry ends and pinch the pastry above the corn to make a purse.

Place the purses on a greased baking sheet and bake in the top of a preheated oven, 200°C, 400°F, Gas Mark 6, for 15 minutes. Allow to cool slightly before serving.

EXTRAS

Very little in the way of extras is needed for this menu. I usually serve some raw vegetables, such as celery and carrot sticks, and small fresh cherry tomatoes if available. You may also need apples for 'bobbing' and 'ducking' and little bags of sweets for trick-or-treating. A ghostly alternative to the witches' brew could be ice cream sodas made by adding scoops of vanilla ice cream to tall glasses of American cream soda.

GHOSTS, GOBLINS' PURSES, GRILLED TOADS AND SNAKES ON WITCHES' BROOMSTICKS

PLANNING AHEAD

The day before: Bake the potatoes for the 'ghosts', prepare the filling and refrigerate both separately.

The morning of the party: Make the pumpkin pudding. Prepare the carrot and celery sticks. Remove the filo pastry from the freezer and place in the fridge.

1–2 hours before serving: Marinate the turkey. Fill the potatoes and have them ready for baking. Whip cream for the pudding. Prepare goblins' purses. Arrange turkey and bacon on skewers and grill the brochettes. Make the witches' brew. Finish the ghosts and bake the goblins' purses. Tie fringed paper on to the skewers to make brooms.

PRESENTATION

You can really go to town over the decorations for a Hallowe'en party. Hobgoblins, black cats, owls, spiders, bats and all the other beings that are associated with superstitions and dark nights can be incorporated in the decorations. Silhouettes of black cats and bats can be stuck on the windows and orange and black witches can hang from thread tacked to the ceiling.

Clementines can be transformed into miniature pumpkins by sticking faces on them. A pumpkin lantern is a must: hollow out a pumpkin and cut out a face with a toothy smile.

There are traditional games that you can play as well as trick-and-treating: Bob Apple – apples are suspended from strings and the competitors have to eat the apple without using their hands. Duck Apple – apples are placed in a large tub, half filled with water. The contestants are timed and have to remove the apples as fast as possible without using their hands.

Fortune-telling and ghost stories are also suitable if you don't think they will give the children bad dreams!

GRILLED TOADS AND SNAKES ON WITCHES' BROOMSTICKS

Turkey and bacon brochettes can be magically transformed into toads and snakes on a witch's broomstick. Children can conveniently pick up the wooden sticks in their fingers to nibble at the meat.

4 tablespoons lemon juice
4 tablespoons olive oil
1·25kg/2½lb turkey breast steaks, cut into 2·5cm/1in cubes
175g/6oz unsmoked streaky bacon rashers
2 tablespoons brown sugar
5 tablespoons soy sauce
1 tablespoon cooking oil
Salt
Pepper

Mix the lemon juice and olive oil together and pour over the turkey cubes. Turn the meat in the mixture so it is well covered on all sides. Season with salt and pepper and leave for 1 hour. Cut the bacon into 5cm/2in lengths and set aside.

Meanwhile, fold up a piece of brown wrapping paper and cut 24 rectangles 5 × 15cm/2 × 6in. Cut along the 15cm/6in side of the paper, keeping it attached at the top, to make a fine fringe for the broom. Cut 24 20cm/8in lengths of thick thread.

Using 20cm/8in wooden kebab sticks, thread cubes of turkey meat on to each skewer, alternating with pieces of folded bacon. Once you have threaded on the meat you can snip off the pointed tips with garden cutters if you are worried that they might be dangerous.

Place the brown sugar, soy sauce and oil in a small bowl, stir to dissolve the sugar and set aside until needed for basting. Cook the brochettes under a hot grill for approximately 10 minutes. Turn the skewers over a few times during this cooking time and baste frequently with the soy mixture. Do not overcook the turkey or it will become rubbery. Test a piece of meat after 8 minutes: if it is just white throughout it is done.

When the skewers are cool enough to handle, tie on the paper brooms, securing them with the thread.

SEE PAGE 163.

WITCHES' BREW

There are so many different fruit juices available that any number of combinations will make a delicious brew, so you can vary what I've suggested here according to taste. Alternatively, place the juices on the table and allow the children to make up ther own mixture.

2 x 1 litre/2 pint cartons apple juice
1 litre/2 pint carton cranberry juice
1 litre/2 pint carton peach juice
3 oranges, sliced (optional)

Mix all the juices together in a large jug and chill in the refrigerator for about 30 minutes.

To serve *Pour into tall glasses and, if desired, place a slice of orange on the rim of each glass.*

PUMPKIN SURPRISE

A spicy bread and butter pudding baked in a pumpkin will provide a delicious and festive dessert. Buy a squat, broad pumpkin rather than a tall one if possible to make it easier for the custard to cook and for the pumpkin to be served in neat slices.

1 pumpkin, weighing about 1·75kg/4lb
250ml/8fl oz single cream
250ml/8fl oz milk
3 eggs
150g/5oz granulated sugar
1 teaspoon cinnamon
Several gratings of fresh nutmeg
Handful of raisins
3 thick slices day-old white bread
40g/1½oz butter
300ml/½ pint whipping cream

Wash and dry the pumpkin. Cut a good-sized round lid from the top of the pumpkin and set aside. Scrape out all the seeds. If the interior wall of the pumpkin is very thick and doesn't leave much room for the pudding scrape out a bit of the flesh also. Pop the lid back on and bake the pumpkin in a preheated oven, 180°C, 350°F, Gas Mark 4, for 20 minutes.

Meanwhile put the cream and milk into a pan and bring it to just under boiling point. Whisk the eggs, sugar and spices together in a bowl, then whisk in the hot cream and milk. Add the raisins.

Remove the crusts from the bread, butter it and cut into small squares. Remove the pumpkin lid and discard it. Line the inside of the pumpkin with the bread and pour over the egg mixture. Set the pumpkin in a shallow cake tin and bake at the same temperature as before for 1½–1¾ hours, or until set. It really takes about that length of time for the custard to set so don't be tempted to give it much less.

To serve *Serve the pumpkin pudding at room temperature. Cut it into 12 thick wedges as you would a cake. Whip the cream, pile it into a bowl and pass it around separately for the children to spoon over the pudding.*

ICE CREAM SODAS, WITCHES' BREW, PUMPKIN SURPRISE

Italian Vegetarian Buffet for 24

So many young people today are vegetarians that you may well find yourself having to organize a party that takes this into account. An Italian theme works beautifully as there are many delicious vegetable dishes in Italian cooking that can be used to make up a really exciting spread.

The starter in this menu is a selection of *antipasti* served with Italian-style bread. The pepper salad and marinated mushrooms can be made in advance and the other *antipasti* are easy to assemble or can be bought in. There are dozens of possible variations and you can add any other seasonal vegetables lightly cooked and dressed with a vinaigrette.

The main course is a baked pasta. The components of the dish can be prepared ahead so you will only need to cook the pasta and assemble the dish on the day of the party.

There are lots of options for dessert. A fruit salad served with a plate piled high with Amaretti biscuits would be an appropriate finale but considering the guests are young I have chosen ice cream accompanied by brownies (which are not Italian but are too good to leave out).

MENU

*

Antipasti:

GRILLED PEPPER SALAD

CHICK PEA AND CUCUMBER SALAD

MARINATED MUSHROOMS

PASTICCIO

*

PYRAMID OF ICE CREAM AND BLOOD ORANGE SORBET

BROWNIES

*

Sparkling Water with Lime

MARINATED MUSHROOMS, GRILLED PEPPER SALAD, BEETROOT SALAD, OLIVES, CHICK PEA AND CUCUMBER SALAD, TOMATO SALAD

GRILLED PEPPER SALAD

Grilled peppers have a particularly delicious flavour. They partially cook under the intense heat and the charred skins are peeled off making the peppers far more digestible.

5 red peppers
5 yellow peppers
3 tablespoons capers
Olive oil
Lemon juice
Salt and black pepper

Place the peppers under a hot grill, turning them from time to time, until they are well charred on all sides. Put them in a large paper or plastic bag and close it tightly so the steam will loosen the skins. When the peppers are cool enough to handle (after about 10 minutes) peel off the skin, remove the core and seeds and slice the flesh into long thin strips. Place in a flat serving dish and add the capers. Pour over olive oil, a few squeezes of lemon juice, and salt and pepper. Turn the peppers in the oil. Cover with clingfilm and refrigerate if making ahead.

To serve *Bring the peppers to room temperature so that the oil, which will have solidified in the fridge, will melt again.*

CHICK PEA AND CUCUMBER SALAD

This salad can be made in a matter of minutes and will add variety and some substance to the *antipasti*.

2 × 400g/13oz cans chick peas
4 shallots
1 cucumber
175ml/6fl oz natural set yogurt
4 tablespoons chopped mint
2 tablespoons olive oil
Lemon juice
Salt and black pepper

Drain the chick peas, chop the shallots finely and peel and cube the cucumber. Place the chick peas, shallots and cucumber in a bowl. Mix together the yogurt, mint, olive oil, a squeeze of lemon juice, salt and pepper. Stir the dressing into the chick peas just before serving.

MARINATED MUSHROOMS

This dish can be prepared up to two days in advance. Keep refrigerated but bring to room temperature before serving.

Rind and juice of 1 large lemon
2 small onions, thinly sliced
100ml/3½fl oz olive oil
½ teaspoon dried thyme
2 tablespoons coriander seeds, crushed
600ml/1 pint water
1kg/2lb button mushrooms
Pinch of sugar
Fresh coriander leaves
Salt and pepper

Shred lemon rind and place with the onions and oil in a stainless-steel saucepan. Simmer, covered, until the onions have softened. Add the thyme, coriander seeds, water, lemon juice and salt; simmer for 5 minutes. Add the mushrooms, cover, and boil for 3 minutes. Remove mushrooms. Boil the marinade until syrupy; stir in sugar. Pour over the mushrooms. Sprinkle with fresh coriander.

EXTRAS

The *antipasti* consist of a mixture of cooked and bought-in items. To the marinated mushrooms, chick pea and cucumber salad and grilled pepper salad, add bowls of good black olives (about 250g/8oz), and a simple tomato salad made with approximately 2·25kg/5lb fruity tomatoes, peeled, sliced, dressed with olive oil, a sprinkling of salt and a handful of shredded fresh basil leaves.

Also appropriate – and economical – would be a beetroot salad. Wrap about 1·75kg/4lb fresh raw beetroot in foil and bake in the oven until tender. Rub off the skins, then dice the beets and dress with an olive oil vinaigrette.

Serve the *antipasti* with breadsticks and some good crusty bread, preferably an Italian bread such as Ciabatta or Focaccia. These are made with olive oil and will prove irresistible – a big help in satisfying young healthy appetites.

With the pasticcio you will need only a simple green salad of mixed leaves with a dressing of olive oil and lemon juice.

For drinks I suggest a selection of soft drinks, fruit juices and mineral water. Italians drink lots of mineral water with their meals so large jugs of sparkling mineral water with slices of fresh lime or lemon would be ideal here.

PASTICCIO

PLANNING AHEAD

In advance: The grilled pepper salad can be made several days in advance. Cover it with clingfilm and refrigerate.

Two days before: Prepare the marinated mushrooms; make the beetroot salad; make the tomato sauce for the pasticcio.

The day before: Make the chocolate brownies; make the blood orange sorbet; make the béchamel for the pasticcio.

The day of the party: Finish the pasticcio; make the tomato and green salads; make the chick pea and cucumber salad; shape the ice cream pyramid and refreeze; bring the prepared salads to room temperature.

PRESENTATION

Make everything very bright and fresh looking. The colours of the Italian flag, green, red and white, make the perfect colour scheme and can be used in the dishes and decorations. Paper cups, plates and napkins will make washing up easier.

The dessert will look particularly festive if you present the red and white ice cream balls in a large pyramid, scattered with a few mint leaves and topped with a small Italian flag.

Serve the brownies in coloured paper cases to complete the effect.

PASTICCIO

This baked pasta dish contains both a tomato and béchamel sauce – a little more trouble to make, perhaps, but well worth it for the flavour and texture. Be sure to undercook the pasta when it is first boiled as it has a second cooking when baked.

Tomato sauce:
2 onions, chopped
2 carrots, chopped
2 sticks celery, chopped
2 cloves garlic, chopped finely
Bunch of parsley, chopped very finely
6 tablespoons olive oil
175ml/6fl oz dry white wine (optional)
2 bay leaves
4 × 425g/14oz cans chopped tomatoes
Pinch of sugar
Salt and black pepper

Béchamel sauce:
150g/5oz butter
150g/5oz plain flour
1·75 litres/3 pints milk
1½ bay leaves
Several gratings of nutmeg
Salt and black pepper

Pasticcio:
1·5kg/3lb firm, shiny aubergines
Groundnut oil for frying
1·5kg/3lb pasta shells or quills
50g/2oz butter
250g/8oz shelled walnuts or pine nuts, chopped roughly
375g/12oz Parmesan, Farmhouse Cheddar cheese or vegetarian Cheddar, freshly grated
Salt and black pepper

For the tomato sauce, place the first six ingredients in a heavy-bottomed saucepan and simmer gently, stirring occasionally, until the vegetables soften. Add the wine, if used, and boil until it evaporates; add the bay leaves, tomatoes and sugar, and simmer over a very low heat, covered, for at least 1 hour. Season and set aside.

For the béchamel, melt the butter over gentle heat in a large heavy-bottomed saucepan. Stir in the flour and cook for a few minutes, stirring, without allowing the mixture to colour. Pour in the cold milk and whisk continually until the milk comes to a simmer and starts to thicken. Add the bay leaves and some salt and pepper, and continue to cook, uncovered, for another 15 minutes. The sauce should not be too thick. Remove the bay leaves and add the nutmeg. Taste for seasoning. Float a piece of clingfilm over the surface of the sauce to prevent a skin forming and set aside.

Cut the aubergines into 5mm/¼in slices. Sprinkle the slices with salt and set along the inside of a large colander. Turn them over occasionally and leave to drain for at least 1 hour. Rinse and pat dry with kitchen paper. Pour 1cm/½in of oil into a pan and heat until very hot. Fry the aubergine slices in batches until they are golden on both sides. Do not turn them over more than is necessary and heat any additional oil before adding more aubergine. Blot off the excess oil with kitchen paper.

Cook the pasta in three batches of 500g/1lb each in a large pot of boiling salted water – about 6 litres/10 pints and 2–3 tablespoons of salt per batch. Undercook the pasta – to about 3–5 minutes before the *al dente* stage. Lightly drain the pasta and place in a large bowl. Toss with a knob of butter. Mix in the tomato sauce, removing bay, and half the béchamel.

Butter 3 or 4 shallow oven dishes. Reheat the béchamel sauce enough to make it easy to spread. Cover the bottom of the dishes with a layer of pasta, then a layer of aubergine, a sprinkling of walnuts, a few grindings of pepper and a layer of cheese. Repeat the layers ending with pasta. Spoon the béchamel over the top, dot with butter and cover with cheese. Before serving bake in a preheated oven, 180°C, 350°F, Gas Mark 4, for 35–45 minutes.

PYRAMID OF ICE CREAM AND BLOOD ORANGE SORBET

An attractive pyramid of coloured ice cream balls will give a touch of glamour. Blood oranges have a more intense flavour than ordinary oranges which makes them ideal for sorbets.

PYRAMID OF ICE CREAM AND BLOOD ORANGE SORBET, BROWNIES

300g/10oz granulated sugar
300ml/½ pint water
Juice of 1 lemon
36 blood oranges or enough to make 1·5 litres/2¾ pints juice (or use ready-made juice if available)
Icing sugar if needed
1·75 litres/3 pints good vanilla ice cream
Sprigs of mint, to decorate (optional)

Place the sugar, water and half the lemon juice in a heavy-bottomed saucepan; bring to the boil without stirring, then simmer for 5 minutes. Set aside to cool. Mix with the orange juice and adjust the taste. You are after a sharp yet sweet taste: add more lemon juice or whisk in some sifted icing sugar depending on what is needed.

Pour the mixture into an ice cream maker or metal container. Follow the directions given with your ice cream maker. Otherwise set the container in the fast-freeze section of the freezer or freezer compartment of the refrigerator for about 3 hours, then chop the sorbet into several chunks, put them into a chilled processor and process until smooth, or mash well. Return the sorbet to the freezer for at least another 3 hours.

Remove the ice cream and sorbet from the freezer and keep at room temperature to soften just enough to form balls. Place a small ice cream scoop in a bowl of very hot water. Shake the scoop to get rid of the water before forming the balls. Reheat the scoop as often as you need to make neat scoops.

Place the balls back in several large containers and return to the freezer.

To serve *Arrange a pyramid of mixed red and white balls on a platter. Decorate with small sprigs of mint.*

BROWNIES

Brownies are always a great success and can be made in minutes. Some people will want more than one, so these quantities make 32.

250g/8oz butter
75g/3oz cocoa powder
4 eggs
500g/1lb granulated sugar
125g/4oz self-raising flour
1½ tablespoons vanilla essence
175g/6oz chopped walnuts

Grease two 20cm/8in square shallow cake tins and line the bottoms with baking parchment. Gently melt the butter in a small saucepan. Remove from the heat and stir in the cocoa. In a large bowl, beat the eggs and sugar together until light and then incorporate the cocoa mixture. Sift the flour over the top of the bowl and gently fold it in. Stir in the vanilla and nuts. Spoon the mixture into the tins and spread level.

Bake in the centre of a preheated oven, 180°C, 350°F, Gas Mark 4, for 25–30 minutes. The brownies will firm up as they cool so don't worry if they look undercooked. It is very important not to overcook them because their charm is their soft and moist texture. Leave in the tin until cool before cutting them into 5cm/2in squares.

TEX-MEX PARTY for 30

The influence of Indian and South American cuisines has given us a taste for spicy hot food and older teenagers particularly seem to relish dishes well heated with chillies. They are bound to enjoy a Tex-Mex buffet. The menu is also inexpensive with refried beans, rice and corn as important ingredients.

None of the dishes is difficult to make and most can be made well in advance. It does take an hour or two to make the wheat flour tortillas but if there isn't time you might be able to buy chapattis – a similar Indian flat bread – ready-made.

Cornmeal taco shells can also be bought ready-made. Guests can fill the taco shells with some beans or Texan chilli and top this with shredded lettuce, grated cheese, soured cream and salsa. The tortillas can be filled in the same way or used to accompany the different dishes.

A cooling fruit salad is the best dessert, or offer a favourite ice cream or cake.

MENU

*

TEXAN CHILLI CON CARNE

MEXICAN CORN

ARIZONA REFRIED BEANS

GUACAMOLE

WHEAT FLOUR TORTILLAS

SALSA

*

Tropical Fruit Cocktail

TEXAN CHILLI CON CARNE, MEXICAN CORN, TACOS WITH FILLINGS, SHREDDED LETTUCE, SOUR CREAM, GRATED CHEESE

TEXAN CHILLI CON CARNE

This hot meat chilli should be eaten in small quantities with rice and refried beans. Prepare fresh chillies carefully. Wash your hands afterwards, and keep chillies or their juice well away from your eyes.

6–8 tablespoons oil
3kg/6lb stewing beef, cut into 1cm/½in cubes
1·2 litres/2 pints boiling beef or chicken stock
4 bay leaves, crumbled
10 dried chillies, crumbled
3 tablespoons cumin seeds
3 fresh chillies, deseeded and finely chopped
6 cloves garlic
2 tablespoons dried oregano
4 tablespoons paprika
1 tablespoon sugar
2 tablespoons salt
6 tablespoons cornmeal

Using a large heavy flameproof casserole, heat half the oil until very hot. Pat the meat dry with kitchen paper. Add half the meat to the casserole and stir until the meat loses its raw colour. Spoon the meat out of the casserole into a bowl.

Heat the remaining oil in the casserole and brown the rest of the meat. Return the first batch of meat to the casserole and add the boiling stock. Add the bay leaves and dried chillies. Bring the stock to the boil, cover the casserole, and simmer over very low heat (or in a low oven) for about 1 hour.

Meanwhile, place the cumin seeds in a hot dry frying pan and shake them over moderate heat until they are toasted. Either use a pestle and mortar or blender to make a paste with the cumin, fresh chillies, garlic, oregano, paprika, sugar, and salt. Add the paste to the casserole and simmer, partially covered, for another 30 minutes. Stir the cornmeal into the casserole in a slow steady stream. Continue to cook until the mixture thickens slightly. Taste for seasoning, adding more salt, paprika or chillies if desired.

The chilli can be kept refrigerated for 3–4 days or it can be frozen several weeks in advance.

To serve *Reheat, covered, in a moderate oven for about 35 minutes.*

MEXICAN CORN

A steaming bowl of spicy yellow corn dotted with chopped red chillies and green parsley will add colour and variety to the menu.

4 tablespoons olive or groundnut oil
2 onions, finely chopped
Parsley, very finely chopped
6 celery sticks, diced
2 red chillies, deseeded and finely chopped
400ml/14oz can chopped tomatoes
1·25kg/2½lb frozen sweetcorn
Salt and pepper

Heat the oil in a large saucepan, add the onion, parsley and celery and stir over low heat until the vegetables are soft. Add the chillies, tomatoes and some salt and simmer for another few minutes. The recipe can be prepared up to this point 2 days ahead and kept refrigerated.

Before serving bring to a simmer, stir in the corn, cover, and cook for 5 minutes. Uncover and cook for a few more minutes. Season with more salt if necessary and lots of freshly ground black pepper.

EXTRAS

Rice is often served with refried beans, and both will provide a good base for the hot chilli and salsa, or you can pile it into taco shells with the other fillings. For this number of people about 1·5kg/3½lb long grain rice should be enough. Boil the rice as usual and stir in finely chopped parsley or toasted almond slivers.

You will also need to buy about 40 ready-made taco shells (some people will want more than one), and chapattis if you decide not to make the tortillas. For extra fillings to accompany the beans and chilli, allow 1kg/2lb grated Cheddar cheese, 5 large lettuces, shredded (crisp iceberg lettuces are especially good for this), and about 1·2 litres/2 pints sour cream. Fill bowls with the accompaniments and let people help themselves. Have a few packets of tortilla chips for them to dip into the guacamole.

For dessert make a simple fresh fruit salad using a variety of seasonal fruits, but add a couple of exotic ingredients to give a tropical flavour. About 3kg/6lb of fruit will be plenty. Make it a couple of hours before serving and chill well.

Tropical fruit juice cocktails can be bought ready-made, but you can also make up your own mixing pineapple juice and orange juice with something fizzy, such as lemonade, soda water or sparkling mineral water. Allow approximately 300ml/½ pint drink per head. Slice in some fresh fruit for decoration.

PLANNING AHEAD

In advance: The chilli con carne and the tortillas can be made several weeks in advance and frozen.

Two days before: Make the refried beans and refrigerate. Cook flavouring vegetables for the Mexican corn and refrigerate.

The morning of the party: Prepare the flavouring vegetables for the guacamole. Thaw the chilli con carne. Make the salsa. Grate the cheese.

1 or 2 hours before serving: Prepare the fruit salad, cover and refrigerate. Thaw the tortillas. Make the guacamole. Prepare the rice. Shred the lettuce. Cook the Mexican corn. Reheat the chilli con carne, tortillas and refried beans.

PRESENTATION

A typical dark red patterned Indian tablecloth or bedcover would make a perfect covering for the table. Earthenware bowls for the food and baskets for the tacos and tortillas will help create an earthy Mexican look. Alternate the red salsa, green guacamole and yellow corn with the rice, beans and meat to give the table more colour.

Dried corn on the cob or gourds make attractive centrepieces or you could transform a straw hat with some ribbon into a sombrero and use that for decoration.

Empty cans with lots of holes punched around the sides make perfect Mexican-style candle holders and will help create a party atmosphere.

ARIZONA REFRIED BEANS

In Mexico beans are served up at almost every meal and leftovers are refried for the next meal. The flavour of the beans gets better and better with each cooking.

1·5kg/3lb dried pinto or red kidney beans
4 cloves garlic, finely chopped
2 celery sticks, chopped
2 bay leaves, crumbled
2 tablespoons dried thyme
6 tablespoons chopped parsley
2 leeks, chopped
1 teaspoon ground cumin (optional)
Vegetable oil
3 onions, finely chopped
Salt and pepper

Wash the beans under cold running water until the draining water runs clear, discarding any small stones or shrivelled beans. Place them in large bowls, cover with at least 20cm/8in of water and soak them overnight.

The next day, divide the beans between 2 large heavy-bottomed saucepans. Add enough water to cover the beans and bring to a rolling boil. Boil for 15 minutes, then drain, rinse and bring to the boil again in fresh water. Divide the garlic, celery, bay leaves, thyme, parsley, and leek between the two pans. Continue boiling, stirring the pans occasionally to prevent the beans sticking. Boil for at least 2–2½ hours, partially covered. Top up with boiling water when necessary and stir occasionally. When the beans are well cooked, add 1 tablespoon of salt, lots of freshly ground black pepper and ½ teaspoon of cumin to each pan and cook for a further few minutes.

Meanwhile, heat several tablespoons of oil in a large heavy pan and cook the onions until they are soft and lightly coloured. Stir them into the beans. Heat a few more tablespoons of oil in the pan, place several ladles of beans in the pan and mash them with a potato masher while they fry. When they have absorbed the fat and lost some moisture, turn them into a large casserole. Add more oil to the pan and continue frying and mashing more beans until all the beans are fried in this manner. Cool and refrigerate until needed.

Reheat the beans, covered, in a preheated oven, 180°C, 350°F, Gas Mark 4, for about 45 minutes before serving. If the beans are very dry, stir in a little water before heating.

GUACAMOLE

Use guacamole as a dip with tortilla chips or to garnish the beans and meat chilli. The avocados must be added no more than an hour before serving or the dip will discolour.

1 large Spanish onion, very finely chopped
5 tablespoons chopped fresh coriander leaves
2 chillies, deseeded and very finely chopped
5 large tomatoes, peeled, deseeded and diced
8 small ripe avocados
Juice of 2 limes
Salt
Paprika (optional)

The morning of your party prepare the onion, coriander, chillies and tomatoes and cover with clingfilm.

An hour before serving halve, stone, peel and roughly mash the flesh of the avocados with a fork. Mix with the other prepared ingredients in a serving bowl. Stir in the lime juice and season with salt. Cover immediately with clingfilm. Sprinkle paprika over the top before serving (optional).

WHEAT FLOUR TORTILLAS

Unlike corn tortillas these can be made without a press. They can be frozen and reheated successfully so can be made well in advance. This recipe will make about 40 tortillas.

FRUIT SALAD, WHEAT FLOUR TORTILLAS, ARIZONA REFRIED BEANS, GUACAMOLE, TORTILLA CHIPS, SALSA

1kg/2lb plain flour
2 teaspoons baking powder
1 teaspoon salt
175g/6oz lard or butter, cut into small pieces
About 600ml/1 pint warm water

Mix together the flour, baking powder and salt. Rub in the lard or butter as you would for pastry, then add enough water to form a soft dough. Turn out on to a board and knead with floured hands until the dough is smooth and no longer sticky. Divide the dough into 40g/1 ½oz balls, cover with clingfilm and leave to rest for about 15 minutes.

Heat a heavy frying pan until it is very hot. Working with one ball at a time and keeping the others covered, flatten and roll out with a floured rolling pin until you have a very thin round of dough about 23cm/9in in diameter. Turn the round over once or twice as you roll it out and flour as needed. The rounds may be a bit uneven to start with but they soon improve as you gain more experience.

Place on the dry hot pan until tiny blisters appear. Turn the tortilla over with a spatula and press gently all over the top until more blisters appear. Turn it over again and press with the spatula until the blisters turn a golden brown. Stack the cooked tortillas together in a folded cloth. Continue until all the dough is used. You can cook one tortilla while you make the next if you work near the stove. When the tortillas are cold, place greaseproof paper between them, place in an airtight package and store in the refrigerator for up to 3 days or freeze.

To serve *Defrost if frozen. Make foil packages containing about 12 tortillas each and reheat in a preheated oven, 180°C, 350°F, Gas Mark 4, for 15 minutes*

SALSA

The amount of chillies given in the recipe should make a fairly hot salsa. So even if you like your salsa really hot, don't add more chillies until you have tasted it.

6 tablespoons olive oil
4 celery sticks, very finely chopped
2 large Spanish onions, very finely chopped
3–4 fresh green chillies, deseeded and finely chopped
4 × 425g/14oz cans chopped tomatoes
Fresh parsley or coriander leaves, chopped
Salt

Heat the oil in a large heavy pan. Stir in the celery and onions and cook, stirring, for a few minutes before adding the chillies and tomatoes. Simmer over brisk heat for 10 minutes, uncovered.

Remove from the heat, pour into a bowl and season with salt. Stir the parsley or coriander into the salsa. Refrigerate until needed but serve at room temperature.

CLARE FERGUSON

CELEBRATIONS

Large-scale celebrations differ from everyday entertaining because they involve happy ritual, glamour and long-term planning. They often mark a milestone of some kind: a coming of age, a wedding, a christening, a retirement or a new job. Awards, exhibition openings, and seasonal rites such as Christmas all signal a splurge.

So, is it family, friends, colleagues or a mix? What are the optimum numbers we can cope with comfortably? Is it indoors, outdoors or a moveable feast? Should it be a stand-up buffet, a seated dinner or, better, a little of both? As people arrive finger foods allow guests a chance to meet others, or to chat with old friends. Family gatherings can be more relaxed but big weddings need near military precision!

Big parties mean conviviality – not just excellent food and drink. Good organization and a few well-chosen dishes make for confident hosts and glad guests, but factors which certainly aid enjoyment are appropriate (especially live) music, dramatic lighting, a pleasantly decorated table, candles, flowers, the clink of ice in summer and the roar of a fire in winter. Sparkling cutlery, plates and glasses and crisp table linen create a cheerful atmosphere.

Many jobs can be shared out among family members and friends and for large parties it is essential to have your neighbours as allies since one domestic refrigerator, freezer, microwave or cooker is unlikely to be adequate. Co-operative cooking can make the most boring jobs seem less tiresome, even fun. Commonplace objects such as peelers, graters, beaters, rolling pins, forcing bags and extra-large saucepans can often be borrowed. Hired equipment (Champagne buckets, marquees, etc) must be booked in advance.

Failproof feasting needs a strategy. Make lists and keep to them. Young people can make good chauffeurs, dishwashers, shoppers, waiters and bar attendants if well instructed and imaginatively bribed. They can also be good 'meeters and greeters' – nothing is lonelier than an ungreeted guest. And finally, know your strengths, accept your weaknesses, enjoy yourself: it's a party after all! Peculiarities will be tolerated so long as there is gaiety and good will. Wit and imagination always count for more than culinary perfection.

Opposite **WEDDING FEAST** *PAGE 188*

Champagne Christening Tea Party for 30

*R*ituals associated with naming and blessing a young child and welcoming it into society go back to time immemorial. Since it is a very special occasion it certainly seems worth the effort of a party. This one is designed to take place in the afternoon – at a weekend, perhaps – and though it may seem odd to mix Champagne with afternoon tea, it perfectly combines frivolity with common sense.

Ideally a christening party should be a fairly simple occasion with little to cook on the day, though some preparation, last minute garnishing and decoration will always be necessary.

Since toddlers and other young children are bound to be present there should be some very simple foods and others with which young 'helpers' can assist. The food should be mainly finger food, and self-service, buffet style.

Ice-cold Champagne is ever the suitable tipple and the archbishop's punch is another choice for christening cake toasts. Serve iced-tea fizz for the children and finish up with traditional tea made and served fresh and hot: particularly relevant for those who must be driving home to distant places.

Menu

*

OAT PANCAKES LAYERED WITH HAM, HERBS AND OLIVES

BLUE CHEESE AND CRAB FILO PASTRIES

CLUB SANDWICHES

SPICED CHICKEN POCKET PITTAS

*

BANANA AND NUT LOAF

MERINGUES À LA JAPONAISE

LITTLE ANGEL CAKE WITH HONEY AND RUM SABAYON SAUCE

*

Dry Champagne

Peppermint Tea Fizz

Archbishop's Punch

Earl Grey Tea with Lemon

OAT PANCAKES LAYERED WITH HAM, HERBS AND OLIVES

These dark nutty pancakes taste a little like buckwheat but contain dry-toasted porridge oats: much more readily available. Since the pancake texture is rather tender, it's best not to flip them but to slide them out and turn them gently each time. Once the pancakes are cooked and cooled they are assembled into two towers each with several strong tasty fillings. At serving time cut them into neat segments like a cake. The unfilled pancakes can be made ahead and refrigerated (no more than 2 days), or frozen, thawed and then filled.

Pancakes:
175g/6oz porridge oats
175g/6oz plain flour
¼ teaspoon salt
10 eggs
1·2 litres/2 pints milk
150ml/¼ pint olive oil
Extra olive oil, for cooking

Spread:
250g/8oz unsalted butter, softened
6–8 cloves garlic, crushed
175g/6oz flat-leaved parsley, chopped
8 tablespoons lemon juice
500g/1lb feta cheese

Filling:
20 thin slices cured ham (Parma ham or jambon de Bayonne)
500g/1lb whole black olives
16 black olives, halved lengthwise and pitted, to garnish
Flat-leaved parsley, to garnish

Heat a dry frying pan and toast the oats over high heat, tossing constantly, until aromatic and a rich brown. Cool and keep aside.

Make the pancake batter by putting the flour, salt and eggs into a food processor or bowl. Mix briefly. Add the milk and oil, mixed, in a steady stream, continuing to process, blend or whisk until a thin batter results. Add the toasted oats and mix in briefly. Refrigerate for at least 30 minutes.

Heat a non-stick 25cm/10in frying pan until very hot. Brush or wipe the pan (use a heatproof brush or wad of kitchen paper) with a generous film of olive oil. Stir the batter each time (to distribute the oats evenly) and pour enough into the pan to cover the base thinly. Cook over high heat for 55–60 seconds, then use a palette knife to turn it over. Alternatively, invert the pancake on to an oiled flat plate. Slide the pancake back into the pan, cook the second side for 20–30 seconds, then remove from the pan. Stack the pancakes between sheets of foil or baking parchment. Continue until all the mixture is used (it should make 20–24 pancakes). Allow all the pancakes to become cold (if wished wrap and refrigerate for up to 2 days, or wrap and freeze).

Meanwhile prepare the pancake spread: put the butter, garlic, parsley and lemon juice into a food processor or bowl and process or beat to a rough paste. Crumble in the cheese and process or beat briefly until smooth. Spread the mixture out on to a flat plate and mark into one portion per pancake.

To assemble the two pancake 'towers', spread 2 pancakes with a share of the filling spread. Pit the olives and roughly chop the flesh. Dot both pancake surfaces with a twelfth of the chopped olives. Repeat the process using two more pancakes and the next two portions of the spread but top both layers with slices of ham so that they come close to the edges. Continue this process until all the ingredients are used. Garnish, if wished, with extra herbs on top. For a more curious visual effect, leave off the top pancake to reveal the cheese-herb filling.

To serve *Serve each pancake 'tower' whole but marked into 16 neat wedges to be eaten in the fingers or with forks. Put a halved black olive on top of each serving wedge and decorate with small sprigs of parsley.*

EXTRAS

Sugared almonds, in pastel colours and white – bitter-sweet tokens of life's forthcoming events – are traditional treats given to guests at a name-day ceremony. Allow 6–8 per guest. Using pinking shears cut out circles of fabric 25cm/10in in diameter, one per guest, and 30cm/12in lengths of white satin ribbon. If wished add scented herbs such as lemon scented verbena, scented pelargonium leaves or dried lavender before tying up each group of bonbons into a parcel and securing it with a bow. Allow children to hand them out from pretty baskets.

This is a tea party so buy superb tea such as Earl Grey, really fresh. Allow one generous teaspoon of tea or one sachet or teabag per person, with an optional 'one for the pot'. Rinse out the chosen vessels with boiling water. Add the tea and fresh-boiled water immediately, stir once, cover and place on trays. Leave to infuse.

If guests prefer, let them pour their own or else encourage teenage guests to participate. Ensure, however, that the teas are poured when at the optimum fragrance. Do not allow the drink to become tannic, cloudy or bitter from long standing – brew a new pot. Have additional boiling water circulating at regular intervals.

Technically 250g/8oz of tea should make 48 cups, but it might be considerate to have 250g/8oz China tea, 250g/8oz Formosa Oolong or Darjeeling and 250g/8oz Indian or Ceylon tea. Allow also 1·5litres/3 pints of milk, 300ml/½ pint half cream, 4 sliced lemons and 500g/1lb white sugar lumps (now available in hearts, spades, clubs and diamond shapes).

Opposite **OAT PANCAKES LAYERED WITH HAM, HERBS AND OLIVES, LITTLE ANGEL CAKE WITH HONEY AND RUM SABAYON SAUCE, BLUE CHEESE AND CRAB FILO PASTRIES**

BLUE CHEESE AND CRAB FILO PASTRIES

Forget about crimped pasty edges and fiddly blind baking – here's a great new trick: lacy crisp leaves of filo pastry are used instead of short or puff pastry for these stylish open tarts. One contains pungent blue cheese and the other crab. Yogurt gives particular interest to the egg custard mixture. For speed and simplicity use two non-stick roasting tins with curved sides, though large Swiss roll tins could work satisfactorily. Ideally, prepare and refrigerate then bake an hour before guests are due to arrive, so they're hot and fragrant.

12 eggs
300ml/½ pint milk
450g/14½oz strained Greek yogurt
1½ teaspoons salt
1½ teaspoons hot paprika
250g/8oz blue cheese (ideally Gorgonzola)
12–16 spring onions
175g/6oz butter, melted
4 tablespoons sunflower oil
400g/13oz filo pastry, defrosted
15g/½oz chopped fresh dill
375g/12oz fresh crab meat, brown and white
Freshly ground black pepper
2 lemons, cut into twists or wedges, and spring onion fans, to garnish (optional)

Lightly beat the eggs with the milk, yogurt and salt. Divide the mixture into two (about 750ml/1¼ pints each). Add the freshly ground black pepper to one half and the paprika to the other.

Derind and thinly slice the cheese, then cut into small pieces. Slice the spring onions crosswise, separating white parts and green tops.

Mix the melted butter and oil together. Using a soft 10cm/4in wide paint brush, grease two non-stick 30 × 37cm/12 × 15in roasting tins with the butter and oil mixture.

Unwrap the filo pastry and unroll carefully on to a clean dry surface. Count the complete sheets (about 16–18), roll half of them back up and enclose in a plastic bag to stop them drying and becoming brittle.

Working with 2 sheets of pastry together at a time, line one of the roasting tins first lengthwise, then crosswise, twice (that is 8 layers). Brush the top surfaces with the butter and oil mixture between each layer. Repeat the entire procedure with the remaining filo, including fragments, to line the second tin. Do not be concerned about tidy edges: they'll cook to a crisp prettiness even if uneven.

Cover one pastry case with the chopped blue cheese and green spring onion tops. Pour over the half of the egg mixture that was seasoned with black pepper, then sprinkle with the dill. Spread the other pastry case with the crab and white spring onion stems, then pour over the pink paprika-seasoned egg mixture. (If necessary refrigerate at this stage.)

Bake the 2 flans in a preheated oven, 230°C, 450°F, Gas Mark 8, in the two top oven positions, for 40–50 minutes or until the filling is firm and risen and the pastry crisp and golden, changing the positions of the tins half way through cooking.

If serving immediately, leave to stand for 8–10 minutes then cut each flan in the tin into 30 even portions. Lift them out and arrange them in lines or circles, crisp edges outermost, on two or four heated serving dishes or trays.

If making the pastries in advance, leave to cool before cutting them in the tin and then reheat briefly for 10–12 minutes at 200°C, 400°F, Gas Mark 6, before serving.

To serve *If wished, add cut lemon and spring onion garnishes. To make spring onion fans, slash 5cm/2in pieces of green or white spring onion almost to the base in several places and leave in iced water overnight. They will fan out into 'petals'.*
SEE PAGE 176.

PLANNING AHEAD

Few christenings take place at home these days so you will need a trusted neighbour or helpers in the house until the guests and family return.

In advance: Make up the parcels of sugared almonds. Make the ice garland and keep in the freezer. Make up plenty of ice cubes for the peppermint tea fizz and the punch.

Two days before: Make the christening cakes, frosting and sabayon sauce – freeze them separately in lidded plastic containers. Make the club sandwiches, arrange on serving plates, cover and freeze. Make the pancakes and the spread. Assemble the filling. Pit the olives. Chill everything.

The day before: Extract the crab meat and refrigerate. Make the peppermint tea syrup and chill. Make fruit loaves, chill. Make the meringues and keep in airtight containers (unfilled).

The day of the party: Defrost the christening cakes, frosting the sabayon at room temperature.

Assemble and garnish the pancake towers and chill. Prepare both filo cases and part-fill; mix the custard to add later. Refrigerate. Defrost the club sandwiches at room temperature and leave wrapped. Make, fill and arrange the chicken pocket pittas; cover and keep cool.

Two hours before the party finish filling the filo cases, bake and garnish; keep covered. Slice the banana and nut loaves and decorate. Fill the meringues. Ice and decorate the angel cakes. Add the ice garland to the punch, discarding soggy fruits; do not add the Champagne yet. Put the ice cubes and Champagne into buckets. Add the Champagne to the punch just before serving.

CLUB SANDWICHES

These memorable little sandwiches contain freshly cooked green bean 'coins', a herb butter whipped especially light, smoked fish and a grainy mustard. Use same-sized square-shaped loaves.

CLUB SANDWICHES, SPICED CHICKEN POCKET PITTAS

300g/10oz cold butter, cubed
15g/½oz fresh dill, chopped
15g/½oz fresh parsley, chopped
200ml/7fl oz hand-hot water
250g/8oz dwarf green beans
5cm/2in piece fresh root ginger, peeled and grated
10 slices medium-sliced wholemeal bread from a large loaf
20 slices medium-sliced white bread from a large loaf
Red-wine-flavoured mustard
375g/12oz smoked salmon trout, sliced
Salt
Freshly ground black pepper
Herb sprigs, edible flowers, herb flowers or seed heads, to garnish (optional)

To make the herb butter, put the butter, dill and parsley into a food processor. Process briefly. Add the hand-hot water gradually with the machine running, to form a fluffy spread. If mixing by hand, whisk continuously, adding water gradually until light and smooth.

To prepare the beans, top and tail with a pair of scissors. Holding the beans in bundles of 6 or 8, cross-cut into tiny 'coins'. Add the 'coins' to a large pan of boiling salted water, bring back to the boil and cook for 2–3 minutes. Drain. Refresh briefly in cold water then put back into the still-hot pan. Add the grated ginger, salt and pepper and set aside.

To assemble the sandwiches, spread the herb butter over one side of all the 20 white and 10 wholemeal bread slices. Stack these in two piles. Spread ample mustard over 10 of the white slices. Cut and arrange the salmon trout slices on top of these 10. Next place the wholemeal bread slices, buttered side down, on top. Butter the top surfaces of these slices. Spoon a tenth share of the beans on to each. Put on the remaining top slices, buttered sides down, and press firmly together. Pile up the completed sandwiches and trim off the crusts (children enjoy these as nibbles) and cut each sandwich evenly into 6 rectangles – 60 in all. If wished press a herb sprig prettily on to each sandwich.

Keep in airtight containers or cover with clingfilm on serving dishes until serving time. If necessary, freeze in this ready-to-serve state. Thaw at room temperature 4–6 hours ahead. Do not unwrap until serving time.

To serve *Decorate the sandwiches with edible flowers – yellow nasturtiums, primroses or flowering herbs or seed heads (dill or fennel) – at serving time if wished.*

SPICED CHICKEN 'POCKET' PITTAS

Small round 'mini' pitta breads make charming sandwiches and can be held with ease. Turkey breast could be substituted or game such as guinea fowl, pheasant, wild duck or pigeon in season, but ensure that the shreds are small and well bound with thick mayonnaise.

750g/$1\frac{1}{2}$lb skinned chicken breast fillets
2 teaspoons five-spice powder
Juice of 1 fresh lime
$1\frac{1}{2}$ tablespoons toasted sesame oil
3 tablespoons light soy sauce
300ml/$\frac{1}{2}$ pint lemon mayonnaise
75g/3oz capers
16 mini pitta breads
2 cucumbers, thinly sliced
1 large Cos lettuce, washed and dried
Red chillies, deseeded and sliced

Rub the chicken with the five-spice powder then, on a clean dry surface, beat using a meat hammer or rolling pin until thin (this tenderizes and aromatizes and cuts down cooking time). Steam half the chicken, in one layer, on a covered rack over boiling water for 10 minutes, turning over half way through, then repeat with remaining chicken breasts.

For the marinade, mix together the lime juice, sesame oil and soy sauce. Shred the still-hot chicken using a sharp knife or pull apart using 2 forks. Add to the marinade, refrigerate and leave to stand for an hour or until the marinade is absorbed. Blend in mayonnaise and capers.

Cut the pittas crosswise and open carefully to make pockets (32 half-pittas). Thinly slice the cucumbers and cut the lettuce into narrow strips. Pack lettuce then chicken then a little more lettuce into each pitta, tucking in 3–4 overlapped slices of cucumber at the same time. Stack upright in napkin-lined baskets or trays. Cover and keep in a cool place until serving time. Garnish with chillies if wished.
SEE PAGE 179.

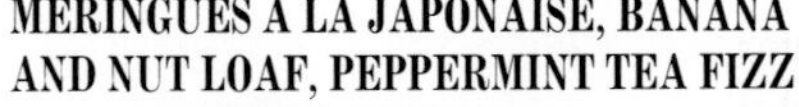

MERINGUES À LA JAPONAISE, BANANA AND NUT LOAF, PEPPERMINT TEA FIZZ

BANANA AND NUT LOAF

This fragrant banana bread is pleasant served plain or with butter or curd cheese, with thin slices of star fruit overlapped on each slice. The recipe makes 3 loaves, each giving 10–12 slices.

175g/6oz butter, cubed and softened
1lb 2oz/18oz caster sugar
175g/6oz vanilla sugar
1·5 kg/3lb very ripe bananas
4 eggs
4 tablespoons lemon juice
1lb 2oz/18oz plain flour
1½ teaspoons salt
1 tablespoon ground cinnamon
2 teaspoons grated nutmeg
2 tablespoons baking powder
250g/8oz shelled almonds, walnuts or pecan nuts, chopped
4 star fruit, sliced, to decorate

Prepare 3 loaf tins (20 × 7·5cm/8 × 3in, and 10cm/4in deep): butter them and line with a continuous strip of baking parchment to cover the ends and base of each tin. Cream the butter until fluffy. Add the caster and vanilla sugars gradually, whisking until the mixture is pale and airy. Mash the bananas and add. Mix the eggs and lemon juice with a fork, add and beat all together until smooth. Mixture may curdle. Sift together the flour, salt, spices and baking powder and add. Fold through until no pockets of flour remain. Do not overmix. Stir in the nuts and pour into the prepared tins. Bake at 180°C, 350°F, Gas Mark 4, for 80–90 minutes or until the cakes have shrunk slightly from the sides of the tins and a skewer, when inserted, comes out clean. Leave in the tins for 20 minutes. Loosen loaves, invert on to a rack.

Remove the paper and leave until cool enough to slice. Decorate with thin slices of star fruit.

MERINGUES À LA JAPONAISE

Toasted cashew nuts and walnuts give particular interest to these chewy-centred meringues. Don't forget baking parchment.

175g/6oz unsalted cashew nuts
50g/2oz shelled walnuts
10 egg whites
¼ teaspoon salt
¼ teaspoon cream of tartar
375g/12oz caster sugar
450ml/¾ pint double cream, chilled
200g/7oz skimmed milk soft cheese
2 teaspoons vanilla essence
150ml/¼ pint soured cream, chilled
Icing sugar, to decorate

Roast the nuts for 15 minutes in a preheated oven, 220°C, 425°F, Gas Mark 7. Chop coarsely by hand and allow to cool. Reduce the temperature to 110°C, 225°F, Gas Mark ¼. Put the egg whites, salt and cream of tartar into a large bowl standing in hot water. Whisk into fairly stiff peaks. Add the sugar gradually, whisking until glossy and very stiff. Fold the nuts carefully and evenly through the mixture. Wet 3 baking sheets, cover with baking parchment and wet again. Using a large piping bag with a 1·5cm/⅝ plain nozzle, pipe about 30 5cm/2in turban shapes on to each sheet. Bake for 6 hours in the lowest 3 oven positions, then turn off the oven and leave overnight until cold.

To make the filling, whip the double cream until fairly stiff then fold in the cheese and vanilla. Add soured cream and whisk again until stiff. Refrigerate.

No more than 2 hours before serving, sandwich meringues together with filling to give 45 doubles. Arrange on serving plates. Dust lightly with icing sugar.

PRESENTATION

A name-day is welcome! White, gauzy cloths, pretty pastels, wrapped gifts, delicate china, polished silver and gleaming glass create pleasurable lightness. Ribbons, bows, draped lace, family albums and portraits help remind children of family links.

The two rather unorthodox cakes with fruit, leaf and flower decorations look and taste sensational. Have them prominent on the table.

Beg, borrow or hire a pretty punch bowl for the archbishop's punch – a glorious old-fashioned concoction which, when served ice-decorated from polished silver, glints and dances in the bowl with a gilded splendour.

Instead of ice cubes, chill the punch with a beautiful ice garland prepared days before the party. Use boiled and cooled water: water straight from the tap will not set clear. Set the ice in two stages. Use a ring mould (as for the christening cakes) with the decorative elements set into the first half layer: sliced peach, nectarine or apricot segments, whole unhulled berries and leaf bunches or twigs containing green leaves, or use mint, lemon balm, lovage or salad burnet. Once this has set, top up with cooled freshly boiled water. Refreeze as before. Turn out, store in a plastic bag and refreeze. Use it to enhance and chill the punch.

Check and freshen the flowers early in the day; white, green, gold and budding flowers come to mind. Gypsophila is useful. Smallish, informal spring flowers are particularly pretty as posies in modest little vases, teapots or jugs. One large arrangement, however, placed between the cakes looks wonderful on the main table.

Although it's a finger food buffet (bliss for kids – all the food out at once) have some chairs and little tables on which guests can perch themselves and their plates.

Oz Clarke's *WINE NOTES*

I've always found at christenings that the adults are too quiet and respectful while the kids are straining at the leash and take the slightest opportunity to whoop it up and create mayhem. Well, it's not the kids I'm worried about. Sure, the actual christening itself should have an air of consecration and spirituality about it, but I do think once we're out of the church and back home we should remember that this is a celebration we're involved in, and we should act accordingly.

In which case a glass or two of Champagne right at the start will do no end of good in releasing the tension and soothing any frayed nerves. And there should be triumphal toasts to parents, to child, to vicar, whoever, right at the start. It breaks the ice and gets the business end of things out of the way.

The rules for Champagne at christenings are the same as those for weddings – buy as good and ripe a Champagne as you can afford – and make sure it is as cold as can be. But christening parties are usually much more intimate family affairs than weddings and, except for the rioting juveniles, they're generally a good deal less rowdy. You may have room in the fridge for Champagne – in which case make sure it's been in for several hours – but if not, buy a bag or two of ice and fill a sink or a large insulated picnic box or the bath – it depends on how many bottles you've got! – with a mixture of ice and water, because this is simply *the* most efficient way of chilling bottles; half an hour will give you an extremely cold bottle of fizz. If you don't want to splash out for the full vintage Champagne treatment, the safest, ripest, easiest-to-employ alternatives are from Australia, although some of the dry fizzes from northern Italy such as Prosecco are also increasingly good.

LITTLE ANGEL CAKE WITH HONEY AND RUM SABAYON SAUCE

Here is a truly unusual, handsome and delectable cake: ring-shaped, decorative, snow-white both in frosting and crumb and decidedly refreshing. It is inexpensive, far less cloying than many traditional cakes and contains no egg yolks or butter, though some cream cheese is used in its lime-sharp frosting. (The recipe makes two cakes.)

Cakes:

10 large egg whites
½ teaspoon salt
1 tablespoon hot water
Freshly squeezed juice and grated rind of 3 limes
425g/14oz icing sugar, sifted
150g/5oz plain flour
1 teaspoon cream of tartar
1 teaspoon vanilla essence
½ teaspoon almond flavouring
500g/1lb full-fat soft cheese
175g/6oz fromage frais
500g/1lb seedless grapes and some scented white roses, to decorate (optional)

Sauce:

10 large egg yolks
250g/8oz honey
4 tablespoons dark rum, warmed
300ml/½ pint double cream

Whisk the egg whites (reserving the yolks for the sauce), salt, hot water and a tablespoon of the lime juice in a large bowl until stiff peaks are formed. Gradually add 375g/12oz of the sugar, whisking until the meringue becomes glossy and thick. Sift the flour with the cream of tartar and carefully fold in, a quarter at a time.

Fold in two thirds of the lime rind with the vanilla and almond essences. Divide the mixture between two ungreased ring moulds of about 1·2 litre/2 pint volume and 20–23cm/8–9in diameter. Cut through the mixture with a palette knife to break up any air pockets.

Bake in a preheated oven, 180°C, 350°F, Gas Mark 4, side-by-side towards the top of the oven for 35–45 minutes or until the cakes are slightly risen, pale golden and springy to touch.

Leave to stand, in the tins, for 15–20 minutes to cool before unmoulding. Tilting each cake tin up at a 45° angle, give it a sharp rap with the flat of the hand on the upper edge. Continue this procedure, turning the tin round little by little to free the edges, then give the base of the tin a sharp knock to loosen the contents. Invert each cake quickly on to a large flat plate. Relax; any imperfections will be concealed by the frosting.

To make the frosting, put the broken-up cheese into a food processor or mixing bowl and combine with the fromage frais and the remaining icing sugar and lime rind. Add the remaining lime juice (about 5 tablespoons) until the mixture forms a firm but pliable icing texture. Spread the outer sides and tops of the cakes with frosting. Use a palette knife to swirl or feather it all over.

To make the sauce, put the egg yolks into a large heatproof bowl. Whisk over barely simmering water until frothy and light. Stand the honey over a second pan of boiling water and heat to near-boiling. Add the rum. Drizzle the honey-rum mix into the egg yolks, continuing to whisk until the mixture becomes thick, pale and high. Remove the bowl from the hot water and continue whisking till cool. Whip the double cream until thick. Fold it into the mixture gently.

Serve with the cake as a sauce or separately later.

To serve *Decorate the iced cakes with little bunches of green grapes at intervals round the bases. Fill the centres with halved grapes or edible flowers such as white scented roses. Cut the cakes into 16ths, using a sharp serrated knife and 'sawing' gently so as not to compact the tender crumb. Offer sabayon sauce if wished.*

Drink a cheerful toast to the celebrant: the little angel!

PEPPERMINT TEA FIZZ

Peppermint tea fizz is an interesting alcohol-free drink for children and non-drinkers alike. If peppermint is not your favourite or is unavailable then use an apple or fruit tisane.

LITTLE ANGEL CAKE WITH HONEY AND RUM SABAYON SAUCE, ARCHBISHOP'S PUNCH

8–12 sachets (or teaspoons) peppermint tea
900ml/1½ pints boiling water
Thinly pared rind of 1 lemon, in one piece (no pith)
4 tablespoons lemon juice
50g/2oz caster sugar
2·5ml/½ teaspoon citric acid granules
2 trays ice cubes
Sparkling mineral water, soda or lemonade
Thinly sliced lemon and fresh mint leaves, to decorate

Brew the super-strong infusion (2–3 times the normal strength) in the usual way but leave it to infuse for 25–30 minutes, stirring occasionally. Squeeze out all the liquid from the sachets and pour the tea into a jug, through a strainer if necessary. Stir in the rind, juice, sugar and citric acid granules. Chill for 12–24 hours or so. Strain carefully.

To serve *Put 3–4 ice cubes in a long glass, pour over half a glass or so of the light syrup, add sliced lemon and top up with half the volume (not equal volumes) of sparkling water or (for very young children) slightly sweeter lemonade. Decorate with fresh mint.* *SEE PAGE 180.*

ARCHBISHOP'S PUNCH

This old-fashioned brandied punch is utterly suitable for happy and relaxed toasts. If possible, serve it from a silver punch bowl.

1kg/2lb strawberries or peaches
6 tablespoons caster sugar
1 tablespoon Angostura (or orange) bitters (optional)
300ml/½ pint brandy
Rind of 2 oranges
3 bottles chilled Chardonnay
2 bottles non-vintage Champagne, chilled
Ice cubes

Slice most of the fruit into a bowl, reserving a few for decoration. Add sugar, bitters, brandy and rind. Leave for 1–2 hours.

At serving time, discard the now-soggy fruits. Add the wine and ice cubes or, if wished, an ice garland (see page 181). Slice the remaining fresh fruits into the punch. Pour in the Champagne.

Frugal Feast
for 20

This rather homely all-season menu is easy to prepare and organize, has relatively few difficult-to-locate ingredients and is pleasantly uncomplicated both to serve and to eat.

The informal 'comfort-foodish' style makes it ideal for a young person's birthday party treat, a teenage celebration or an all-ages family celebration. Toddlers, and not-so-young, all appreciate dips, rice and ice cream.

None of these recipes would defeat a young cook and the pudding, particularly, is impressive. Although it uses some ready-made components it is relatively economical.

One or two recipes contain some aromatic surprises: chilli, cardamom, coconut milk, saffron, harissa, cod's roe, lavender, home-made caramel.

Of the ethnic ingredients the most essential is tahini: sesame seed paste of Middle Eastern origin. Sambal oelek and harissa are spicy seasonings, one Far Eastern and the other North African, but they are optional.

Ideal as a buffet lunch on the terrace or in the garden, these dishes also group usefully into an indoors fork-supper formula or indeed a sit-down but serve-yourself meal for 20 as long as table-space and chairs permit.

MENU

*

PEA AND BEAN DIP WITH RAW VEGETABLES

SCENTED SALAD

SUNSHINE SEAFOOD RICE

*

CHEAT'S ICE CREAM CAKE WITH RUM FUDGE SAUCE

*

Vin de Pays des Côtes du Tarn
Muscat Vin Doux Naturel
Cafetière Coffee

PEA AND BEAN DIP WITH RAW VEGETABLES, LEAFY SALAD WITH PARMESAN SHAVINGS

PEA AND BEAN DIP WITH RAW VEGETABLES

In our enthusiasm for fresh food we sometimes forget that canned or bottled foods also have their charms. This purée capitalizes on the mellow sweetness of canned peas and beans. The hot sauce is optional but it gives a good final note. Use any seasonal, crisp, raw vegetables but try to vary colour and texture.

Dip:
425g/14oz can petits pois
475g/15oz can cannellini beans
4 tablespoons tahini (sesame seed paste)
2 large garlic cloves, peeled and crushed
3 tablespoons lemon juice
1 teaspoon ground cumin
1½ teaspoons salt
2 teaspoons sambal oelek (hot pepper condiment) or tabasco sauce (optional)

Vegetables:
5 celery sticks cut into 7cm/3in pieces
2 each yellow, green and red peppers
125g/4oz mangetout
250g/8oz fresh baby corn cobs
1 large mooli

Put the petits pois, beans, tahini and garlic into a food processor. Add the lemon juice, cumin and salt, and process to a rough sticky paste. Alternatively mash the ingredients well together. Spoon into serving dishes and sprinkle a teaspoon of hot pepper condiment over each dish. Chill while the vegetables are prepared.

Cut close, parallel slashes to the middle of each celery piece. Put into iced water and leave for 30–45 minutes or until they curl.

Slice the peppers into rings or strips. Wash and drain the mangetout and baby corn; leave whole. Top and tail the mooli and, using a swivel blade peeler, remove the skin. Use the peeler to make long ribbons and tie these into loose knots. Chill all the vegetables if time allows.

To serve *Put the chilled dips in the centre of 2 large platters and surround each with grouped vegetables. Serve with toasted or oven-dried bread, or bought-in Naan or puppodums.*

SCENTED SALAD

There's a Mediterranean feel to this all-season salad: hotness, sweetness, aromatics and the balm of good oil set off by lavender. Blood oranges are stunning, but any good juicy orange will suffice.

Dressing:
2 teaspoons harissa (spicy, hot seasoning)
2 tablespoons clear honey
300ml/½ pint light olive oil
4 tablespoons lemon juice
1–1½ teaspoons salt

Salad:
2·25kg/5lb tomatoes
5 red onions, skinned
750g/1½lb mixed red and black grapes, preferably seedless
12 blood or other oranges
4 lavender flowers (optional)

Combine the dressing ingredients.

To prepare the salad, halve the tomatoes, then cross-cut into semi-circles, or cut into rings. Slice the onions thinly and separate into rings. Halve the grapes lengthwise, flicking out any pips. Scrub, dry, then remove the rind from 3 of the oranges. Cut away the skin and pith from all oranges and slice thinly. Arrange on platters and scatter grapes and onion rings on top. Crumble lavender flowers over the salads. Dress them at serving time.

SEE PAGE 186.

EXTRAS

You'll need bread to serve with the dip. Use toasted or oven-dried bread or buy in some of the delicious ethnic breads available. Naan – large flat Indian bread – is perfect (buy about 6). Just before serving heat them in the oven for 4 minutes.

Serve a handsome DIY salad: guests dress their own leafy salads as they wish. Provide a variety of leaves, the wherewithal for dressings and shavings of Parmesan cheese to act as seasoning.

In the rice dish, use good-quality vegetable stock cubes for economy and ease and if time is short. If you have a good vegetable garden or readily available vegetables make your own: pour the required volume of boiling water over 2·5kg/5lb combined weight of the following: onions, leeks, carrots, celery, jerusalem artichokes, parsnips, black peppercorns, fresh thyme and parsley. Bring back to boiling and leave to infuse. Strain and season to taste.

With the coffee, serve chilled bitter chocolate squares or praline-filled chocolate 'sea-shells'.

As an alternative to wine, add crushed mint or lovage leaves to the juice and finely grated rind of 3 lemons and 3 oranges. Sweeten with honey and top up with ice cubes and sparkling water.

PLANNING AHEAD

Three days before: Make the ice cream cake and refreeze. Make the rum fudge sauce, cover and chill.

The day before: Make the pea and bean dip; cover and chill.

The day of the party: Prepare the vegetables for the dip; chill. Unmould the ice cream cake on to a serving plate, decorate and refreeze.

Make the scented salad (keeping the dressing separate), arrange the vegetables and dip. Make up drinks. Prepare and cook the seafood rice.

SUNSHINE SEAFOOD RICE

PRESENTATION

The general feeling is informal and carefree. Use simple china with wooden platters, bowls and serving boards. Sometimes a cheerful mix of colours can give a casual look to the occasion. The seafood rice, when served (probably in large 'paella' dishes) could be carried to the table on a large plank of wood.

If it's an outdoor party pretty rugs are important. Baskets of white daisies and bunches of scented, flowering herbs tied with braid, look fresh and pretty and can be picked up to accompany the action if the party should move from one place to another.

For this easy one-pan peasant-style party dish it's essential to use a large pasta pan, a preserving pan or other copious lidded vessel: the rice swells to four to five times its original volume. The perfumed rice should cook rich and creamy; select and add seafood which is available according to choice. Saffron adds special appeal.

4 tablespoons olive oil
5 large cloves garlic, sliced
3 large onions, sliced
5 tablespoons tomato purée (double concentrate)
1 large chilli, deseeded and chopped
1·2kg/2½lb long-grain rice
4·8 litres/8 pints boiling vegetable stock
Pinch of saffron threads (optional)
2 tablespoons sea salt
3 tablespoons cardamom pods, crushed
50g/2oz sun-dried tomatoes, cut into strips
2 tablespoons dill seeds
1 tablespoon sweet paprika
425ml/14fl oz coconut milk
1kg/2lb smoked mackerel fillets, skinned and flaked
250g/8oz shredded smoked chicken (optional)
500g/1lb peeled prawns
2 litres/4 pints fresh mussels, cooked, or ready-cooked mussels (optional)
250g/8oz smoked cod's roe, sliced
50g/2oz flat-leaved parsley, chopped, and 5 limes, to garnish

SCENTED SALAD, SUNSHINE SEAFOOD RICE

Heat the oil in a very large heavy-based pan. Add the garlic and onions and sauté for 5 minutes. Stir in the tomato purée and chilli. Add the rice. Stir to combine ingredients, cooking for 1–2 minutes. Stir in 600ml/1 pint of the boiling stock with saffron and salt dissolved in it. Bring back to the boil then add 2 litres/3½ pints more boiling stock. Stir and simmer for 15 minutes, covered. During that time add the cardamom pods and sun-dried tomatoes. At the end of that time add remaining stock. Stir briefly and cook for another 15 minutes.

Meanwhile dry-fry the dill seeds and paprika for 1–2 minutes until aromatic. Add to the pan along with the coconut milk, adding the mackerel, chicken and prawns on top. Cook for 10–15 minutes more, adding the finely sliced cod's roe (skin and all) and cooked mussels 5 minutes before the end of cooking time.

To serve *Spoon carefully into large pans or dishes. Garnish with chopped parsley. Cut the limes into wedges and add to the dish.*

CHEAT'S ICE CREAM CAKE WITH RUM FUDGE SAUCE

For those who rarely bake and have no ice cream maker, this fifties-style pudding is a godsend: purchased Madeira cake drenched with rum is layered with ice cream, crumb-covered in stripes and refrozen.

1kg/2lb Madeira cake or cakes
4 × 750ml/1¼ pint rectangular cartons dairy ice cream, butterscotch or fudge flavoured
Apricot jam
8–10 tablespoons dark rum
50g/2oz shelled hazelnuts, chopped
1 tablespoon ground cinnamon

Sauce:
2 × 400g/14oz cans condensed milk
600ml/1 pint double cream
3 tablespoons dark rum

Oil a 20 × 30cm/8 × 12in non-stick roasting tin. Line with waxed paper in both directions with enough to fold double edges above the rim.

With the curved top of the cake uppermost, cut into lengthwise slices 3·5cm/1½in thick. Trim to make even rectangles (keep the trimmings).

Freeze the ice cream hard. Quickly press the blocks of ice cream into the paper-lined tin, pushing them together into one neat rectangle. Place the cake slices firmly on top of the ice cream, sandwiching the cut edges together with jam. Trim to fit and keep the trimmings. Trickle rum all over the cake layer. Clingfilm-wrap the whole tin and refreeze.

Coarsely grind the cake trimmings, nuts and spice in food processor (or crumble in the fingers and add the nuts and spice). Wrap and freeze the crumbs along with the cake.

To make the sauce, put the unopened cans of condensed milk into a saucepan. Cover with boiling water, put on a lid and boil gently for 2 hours, to caramelize the contents. Make sure the cans remain covered with boiling water, topping up if necessary. (Do not allow them to boil dry as this may cause the cans to burst, and for this reason avoid leaning over the pan.) Open the cans carefully and spoon the hot caramel into a large bowl. Blend in the cream until smooth, then the rum. Pour into serving jugs.

To complete the cake, invert tin on to a board. Remove tin and covering paper. Coat cake sides with apricot jam and pat frozen crumbs all over the sides, and in diagonal stripes over the top masking with strips of greaseproof paper to make an even pattern. Refreeze. Serve with the rum fudge sauce.

Oz Clarke's *WINE NOTES*

I *love* this kind of food: serve me the dip, especially with Naan bread, or puppodums, and I'm likely never to make it to the main course. And that utterly wonderful seafood and rice is totally yummy. So if this is budget cooking – I'm all for saving money.

Even so, to find good enough wine without breaking out of the financial constraints is quite a challenge. But I think we can do it. One of the most encouraging events in the wine world during the last few years has been the emergence of the South of France as a low-cost, high-quality producer of white wine. In areas like Gascony and the Tarn, centuries-old wine-making traditions which had somehow got lost are now being rediscovered. This delicious, super-fresh, lemony Vin de Pays des Côtes du Tarn will go beautifully with the spicy flavours of our feast.

Some sweet Muscats are being made in France outside the *appellation contrôlée* system, but they're cheap and good and should just about cope with that rum fudge sauce.

CAFETIÈRE COFFEE

Really good coffee for crowds creates some practical problems. The best coffee is unblended, made from freshly ground arabica-type beans, freshly made, then served very hot, but for convenience you may have to buy the medium-ground, medium-roast equivalent. I allow 50g/2oz per 8-cup measure cafetière (volume 1 litre/1¾ pints), allowing one cafetière for each 5 guests.

Ideally fill 4 cafetières and take to the table simultaneously. If only one cafetière is available make 4 pots of coffee one after the other. Leave to brew for 3–4 minutes then pour into heatproof non-metal jugs. Cover loosely with plastic film and microwave to near-boiling on full power for 15–18 minutes from cold. Alternatively, stand the jugs in a saucepan of boiling water over moderate heat and bring back to near boiling though this will never taste as good as the microwave-reheated variety, let alone freshly made coffee.

Accompany with jugs of cream or hot milk, sugar cubes and crystals.

CHEAT'S ICE CREAM CAKE WITH RUM FUDGE SAUCE

Wedding Feast for 80

A wedding should always be the occasion for a gay and cheerful uproar: family members at all ages and stages of life along with well-loved friends come together to share the joy and expectations of the bride and groom. Since some guests may have travelled long distances, refreshments are not only a courtesy but a necessity.

A wedding reception needs meticulous organization: last-minute panics about flowers and food destroy the fun. Although shopping for some items can be done weeks in advance (dry goods, wine) others cannot be bought until three or so days ahead – the turkeys, fresh fruits, the avocados, smoked salmon and so on. Others such as the lamb joints, the vegetables, salad stuffs, herbs and dairy products will probably need to be purchased one day ahead, to be prepared on that or the final day.

If you have only one refrigerator and freezer you may need to recruit space in neighbours' fridges or larders. Keep aside a cool, dark, dry room to act as a larder if you, like most households these days, don't have one. Metal or plastic trays for storing prepared foods covered with foil or clingfilm, which will fit into a fridge and can stack up, will save much effort. Extra trays for storage and carriage to where the food is to be set out will save time and temper.

Since the croquembouches require some early-on-the-day preparation, do allow room and sufficient time. Cooking and eating are convivial activities: so detail willing family and friends to assist with the food preparation – it's more enjoyable as well as more efficient!

Some rather unorthodox dishes and preparation techniques allow for informality and a democratic approach: it pleases me to think of both bride and groom dispensing servings of their two cakes! Carving of the turkeys can be done during the reception by any moderately capable persons. Since all bones, apart from the drumstick bones, are removed it's merely a matter of crosswise slicing. The main dishes and first course dishes are each designed to serve about 50 people, but with a choice of two there should be more than enough to go round.

If it's to be a buffet meal provide seats for those who prefer to eat on their knees. Though all the food is planned for ease of eating even if standing up, some people will always prefer to use both knives and forks, rather than merely forks.

As for toasts, do allow for both formal and informal impromptu speeches (the bride may wish to make her own speech too); these are often the most delightful and will be recalled in later years with affection.

Non-alcoholic drinks (sparkling mineral water, ice and sliced lemon or lime seems to please almost everyone) definitely matter too.

Most of all, bear in mind that what most people recall of a good party are faces, talk and laughter: rarely is it a calamity if any one dish is not perfect. What is disastrous is a stressful, tense occasion.

So relax and bon appetit!

Menu

*

SMOKED SALMON ROULADES
or
AVOCADO, CUCUMBER AND WATERCRESS SOUP

GLAZED LAMB WITH SPICED FRUIT COMPOTE
or
BONED TURKEY STUFFED WITH COUSCOUS AND LIME

BROCCOLI WITH SAFFRON DRESSING

POTATO GRATIN SQUARES

STUFFED TOMATO CUPS

ROSY SALAD

*

GRAND TIERS OF FRUITS

CROQUEMBOUCHE PYRAMIDS WITH SPUN CARAMEL

*

Champagne

Bianco di Custoza

Côtes du Rhône-Villages

Coffee and Tea

SMOKED SALMON ROULADES

This is an elegant and practical recipe which uses smoked salmon in a fresh-tasting and pretty arrangement with carrot and orange. Allowing six slices per person this makes about 50 servings.

AVOCADO, CUCUMBER AND WATERCRESS SOUP, SMOKED SALMON ROULADES

750g/1½lb carrots, trimmed
175g/6oz onion, peeled and quartered
3 oranges
550g/18oz (about 6) smoked mackerel fillets with peppercorns, skinned and flaked
625g/1¼lb full-fat soft cheese, broken up
72 slices smoked salmon (about 2kg/4lb)
175g/6oz parsley stalks, finely chopped
150ml/¼ pint Pernod or Ricard
1·2 litres/2 pints mayonnaise
150–300ml/¼–½ pint boiling water
50 sprigs flat-leaved parsley, to garnish

To serve:
50 slices wholemeal bread, crusts trimmed
250g/8oz butter, softened, for spreading

Grate the carrots and onions finely in a food processor or by hand. Put these into a sieve, squeeze well to extract all juices and leave to drain while remaining filling ingredients are prepared.

Fit the chopping blade in the processor. Grate the orange rinds finely by hand, reserving the whole fruits. Put the smoked mackerel, soft cheese and orange rind in the processor bowl and process minimally to a paste. Add this fish-cheese paste to the carrot-onion mixture, stir well and chill.

Cover the work surface with a 25cm/10in length of clingfilm. Arrange 4 slices of salmon on this to cover an area about 20 × 15cm/8 x 6in. Using a palette knife spread a 75g/3oz portion of filling evenly over the fish. Sprinkle about 2 tablespoons of chopped parsley stalks over all. Roll up tightly from one short side using the clingfilm to achieve a smooth, even-sized sausage shape. Enclose in clingfilm, twisting the ends of the plastic very tightly to make a firm 'package'. Continue until all 18 rolls are completed. Leave to chill overnight or longer.

Meanwhile add the Pernod to the mayonnaise and whisk or blend with enough boiling water to make a thin smooth sauce. Chill. Remove the pith completely from the oranges and discard it. Cut the oranges crosswise into slices and then into tiny dice. Drain in a sieve and chill.

A little before serving time unwrap each roulade and cut neatly, using a serrated knife, into 18 or so slices.

For each person, arrange six slices of roulade on a plate, slightly overlapped in a half-moon shape. Pour a pool of sauce at one side of the slices, scatter over a few orange cubes and add a herb sprig to the other side.

To serve *Butter the bread and cut into triangles to serve with the roulade.*

AVOCADO, CUCUMBER AND WATERCRESS SOUP

EXTRAS

If you want to make Melba toast to accompany the soup you'll need about 50 slices of medium-sliced white bread. Toast the slices in batches, on both sides, under a preheated grill until golden. Immediately cut off and discard the crusts. Split each slice into two thinner slices by sliding a knife blade horizontally all the way through. Cut each slice into two triangles. Toast the fresh-cut surfaces until golden and curled. Cool on wire racks. Store in airtight containers. Heat through in a warm oven before serving with the chilled soup.

To accompany the rest of the meal, serve small easy-to-handle bread rolls, or huge round country-style loaves, such as *pain de campagne*, sliced or placed on bread boards with sharp cutting knives.

Butter should be room temperature and easy to manage. Serve smoothed into pretty lidded dishes or as butter balls, curls or cubes.

Ensure there is plenty of mineral water sparkling and still.

At the end of the meal serve good quality tea and coffee on trays with bowls of sliced lemon, sugar lumps and jugs of thin cream or milk.

Sugared almond bonbons (white only) are a traditional 'take-home' present. Allow 6–8 almonds per guest, tied up in white tulle with ribbon (see Champagne Christening Tea Party, page 176).

Serve this stylish, chilled first course in small pretty soup cups. Its refreshing taste is strengthened by really good turkey stock, homemade using the turkey carcasses. Organizing large quantities of liquids can, however, create real difficulties when soup-making for crowds. My instructions help make handling easy: the cucumber and watercress mixture and the avocado mixture are prepared separately and then combined. Hot Melba toast is a classic accompaniment.

6 tablespoons extra virgin olive oil
3·7 litres/6½ pints turkey stock (see page 000)
375g/12oz spring onions or leeks, trimmed and sliced
4 cucumbers, peeled
8 tablespoons cornmeal (polenta)
4 bunches watercress
12 ripe avocados
1·5 litres/2½ pints low-fat natural yogurt
Salt
Freshly ground green peppercorns (optional)

Heat the oil in a very large (preserving-sized) heavy-based pan. Add the spring onions or leeks and soften until aromatic. Cut the cucumbers in half lengthwise then crosswise into chunks. Add to the pan and cook, stirring occasionally, for 10 minutes. Meanwhile heat the turkey stock, covered, in another pan. Stir the cornmeal into the pan with the vegetables then pour in about half the hot stock. Bring to the boil and simmer for a further 10 minutes. Remove both the pan of soup base and the pan of stock from the heat.

Trim the roots and coarser stalks from the watercress (discarding these) and put a quarter of it in the bowl of a food processor with a ladleful of the soup base. Process to a green-speckled purée then transfer to a large bowl. Repeat three times with the remaining watercress and more ladlefuls of soup base then set the bowl aside. Process the rest of the soup base on its own and return it to the pan.

Remove the flesh from 4 of the avocados, chop and put in the food processor with one third of the natural yogurt. Process in bursts until fairly smooth. Add one third of the puréed soup base from the pan and process again until completely smooth. Whisk this mixture into the pan of stock. Repeat this process twice more with the remaining avocados, yogurt and soup base.

Stir the contents of the bowl of green-speckled purée and pan of soup mixture together until uniform in colour and texture. Cover the surface with clingfilm to prevent discoloration and chill for up to two days.

This recipe makes about 50 servings of 175ml/6fl oz. Do not pour the soup out too far in advance of serving since oxidation of the surface will spoil its pastel green colour.
SEE PAGE 189.

GLAZED LAMB WITH SPICED FRUIT COMPOTE

Lamb, glazed deep gold and surrounded by jewel-like fruits in a spiced brandy syrup, makes succulent wedding fare. Serve cool for fullest flavour. Carve in front of the guests into good generous chunks or wedges. Each of the four joints should provide 12 or so servings.

1·4 litres/2½ pints boiling water
5 tablespoons Earl Grey or Lapsang Souchong tea
1kg/2lb dried apricots
1kg/2lb dried prunes
8 cinnamon sticks, crushed
20 cloves
4 × 2·25kg/5lb legs of lamb, at room temperature
150ml/¼ pint non-vintage brandy

Glaze:
6 tablespoons apricot jam
2 tablespoons lemon juice
1½ tablespoons rich soy sauce
1 teaspoon five-spice powder
2 tablespoons soft light brown sugar

To prepare the compote, make the tea using the boiling water and Earl Grey or Lapsang Souchong. Put the dried fruits in a large heatproof bowl and strain the tea over them. Add the aromatics. Leave to stand for 1–1½ hours. Remove and discard the prune stones if wished. Divide the fruit mixture between two large, preferably non-stick, roasting tins.

Place 2 of the legs of lamb on racks in two roasting tins. Insert meat thermometers in the centres of the thickest muscles of each leg. Set one tin of fruit near the base of the oven.

To make the glaze, heat the ingredients together in a small, heavy-based saucepan until syrupy. Cool slightly. Generously brush a quarter of the total glaze over each of the first two roasts. Cook, one above the other, in a preheated oven, 200°C, 400°F, Gas Mark 6, for about 1¼ hours or until the meat thermometer registers 65–70°C/148–157°F for very pink or 70–75°C/157–167°F for barely pink lamb, changing position of joints halfway through cooking time. Remove the roasts and fruit and leave to cool.

Glaze and cook the next two joints of lamb and the second tin of fruit in the same way.

Pour off all meat juices. Put this liquid in a bowl in the freezer and allow to set. Remove and discard all the fat leaving the lamb 'essence'. Pour this into a pan and bring to the boil. Remove from heat, add the brandy then cool before pouring over the cooked fruits.

To serve *Carve the cool (not chilled) lamb and serve with spoonfuls of the fruit in its spiced brandy syrup.*

POTATO GRATIN SQUARES, GLAZED LAMB WITH SPICED FRUIT COMPOTE, ROSY SALAD

BONED TURKEY STUFFED WITH COUSCOUS AND LIME

PLANNING AHEAD

In advance: If you will not have time on the day before the wedding, make the choux buns for the croquembouches in advance and freeze them.

Two days ahead: Make the smoked salmon roulades and refrigerate. Cook the turkeys, cool quickly and refrigerate. Make the avocado, cucumber and watercress soup and refrigerate.

One day ahead: Make the sauce and orange garnish for the roulades and the dressing for the broccoli; refrigerate. Make the Melba toast and store in airtight containers. Cook the glazed lamb and spiced fruit compote and keep in a cool place or in the refrigerator (allow several hours for them to return to room temperature before serving). Cook the potato gratin squares and stuff the tomatoes; refrigerate. Defrost choux buns if necessary.

The day of the wedding: Re-crisp choux buns. Cook the broccoli, cover with foil and refrigerate until needed. Prepare the rosy salad but do not add the radicchio and lettuce. Assemble the grand tiers of fruit – spray them with water occasionally to keep them looking fresh until serving time. Glaze the choux buns; when the glaze has cooled and set fill the buns and assemble the croquembouches.

Just before serving time slice the roulades and arrange on individual plates; butter the bread to accompany them. To serve, reheat the Melba toast, potato gratin squares (unless serving cold) and stuffed tomatoes; add the radicchio and lettuce to the rosy salad and toss briefly.

As centrepieces for the feast one huge and two large turkeys are boned out then reassembled into compact shapes. The birds contain pork, spiced pork sausagemeat and lettuces stuffed with couscous, so that, when carved, a pattern of tasty layers is revealed. Most of the stock obtained from the bones is used in the first course to enrich the flavour of the soup; the rest is used in the stuffing. These birds can be cooked one or two days ahead if they are cooled quickly then refrigerated.

1 × 5kg/11lb turkey (with giblets)
2 × 3·4kg/7½lb turkeys (with giblets)
6 litres/10½ pints water
4 onions, quartered
8 garlic cloves, crushed
2 handfuls parsley stalks
2 tablespoons salt
3 large Cos lettuces
25g/1oz butter
Fresh flat-leaved parsely, to garnish

Stuffing 1:
1 teaspoon salt
1 teaspoon harissa paste
2 teaspoons mild paprika
3 tablespoons virgin olive oil
500g/1lb couscous
250g/8oz roasted salted cashew nuts
6 tablespoons mango chutney
1 whole lime, finely diced

Stuffing 2:
1kg/2lb minced lean pork
1 teaspoon salt and freshly ground black pepper
9 stems fresh lemon grass, finely sliced crosswise (optional)
6 large garlic cloves, skinned and chopped
6 teaspoons crushed, dried chillies
2·75kg/6lb pork sausagemeat
175g/6oz parsley, roughly chopped

To serve:
750g/1½ guava or redcurrant jelly
750g/1½lb mango chutney

Bone the turkeys as described on page 193. To make the stock, divide the carcasses and giblets (reserve and chill the livers and hearts) between two large pans, adding half the water, onions, garlic and parsley stalks to each one. Bring to the boil, cover and simmer for 45 minutes. Remove from heat and leave to stand for 30 minutes. Strain and season.

For the first stuffing pour off 900ml/1½ pints of the boiling stock into another pan. (Use the remaining stock for the soup.) Chop the reserved livers and hearts. Add them to the boiling stock and cook for 5 minutes, then add the salt, harissa, paprika and oil. Stir in the couscous all at once. Reduce the heat and cook gently until the liquid is absorbed and the couscous tender (8–10 minutes). Stir in the nuts and chutney and diced lime. Spread out the mixture on a tray and leave until completely cool; the stuffing and shaping cannot begin until all the ingredients are very cold.

To stuff and shape the birds, lay them breast down on a work surface. Using one third of the ingredients for the second stuffing per bird, pat out a layer of minced pork over the breast area. Season with the salt and black pepper. Mix the lemon grass, garlic and chillies well into sausagemeat. Using wetted hands, pat the mixture all over the minced pork and down into the leg cavities. (Do not stuff the wing flaps.) Cover with parsley.

Wash and trim the bases of the Cos lettuces but leave them whole. Lay a lettuce in the centre of the stuffing on one of the birds with its base over the vent area. Pack one third of the chilled couscous mixture among the leaves as evenly as possible. Close the tips of the lettuce, and holding it firmly in position, wrap the stuffed 'back flaps' over it into a 'normal' turkey shape, overlapping them enough to secure them easily. Thread a long metal skewer in and out down the entire length of the bird's back attaching the wing flaps to it. Fold the neck-skin flap back over the wing flaps so they stay beneath as the bird cooks. Secure with a metal skewer.

Turn the bird over on to its back and pat into an even shape. Cross and secure the legs over the lettuce base using string (about 1·75 metres/6 feet) to loop about the drumsticks, cross diagonally over the thigh areas (pat shapes smooth) then pass underneath the bird. Cross the ends beneath and bring them up at opposite sides near where the wings would normally be. Cross the strings over the breast (knot the strings in the centre here) then take the two ends beneath at a 45° angle, loop them beneath a skewer or under the string then bring back both strings together at mid-neck position to the top knot. Secure again. This helps make a neat 'parcel' shape, protects the skin from bursting while cooking and keeps the bird compact so it is easy to lift. Prick any air pockets using a needle. Stuff the other two birds in the same way.

Place the two smaller birds in two roasting tins and rub all over with butter. Roast one above the other in a preheated oven, 200°C, 400°F, Gas Mark 6, for 30 minutes then reduce the heat to 180°C, 350°F, Gas Mark 4 and roast for a further 2 hours 40 minutes to 3 hours. Cover with foil after $1\frac{1}{2}$ hours total cooking time and at the same time pour off and reserve all the pan juices. Change turkeys' position halfway through cooking time. A meat thermometer inserted into the lower thigh should register 88–98°C/180–190°F when cooked and the juices should run clear yellow, not pink. Leave birds to cool completely, then refrigerate. For the larger bird, rub with butter and cook for 30 minutes at 200°C, 400°F, Gas Mark 6 and a further $2\frac{1}{2}$ hours at 180°C, 350°F, Gas Mark 4, using a meat thermometer for accuracy. Cover with foil after 1 hour cooking time, pouring off juices as before.

To serve *Remove the strings and skewers. Garnish with parsley. Slice each bird crosswise at the table. Serve with guava or redcurrant jelly and mango chutney.*

BONED TURKEY STUFFED WITH COUSCOUS AND LIME, STUFFED TOMATO CUPS, BROCCOLI WITH SAFFRON DRESSING

BONING THE TURKEYS

Lay bird breast down on a work surface and, using poultry shears or kitchen scissors, cut the bird in half down one side of the backbone. Open it out flat, skin side down, and, with a small sharp knife, scrape free flesh from backbone and ribs, exposing the bones. Snap wing joints and turn the wings inside out, freeing the bone completely. Cut through sinews. Remove wing tips. Cut forward always to avoid damaging the skin. Snap the leg bones from their joints. Cut through connecting tissues. Turn legs inside out to remove the thigh bone but leave the drumstick bone intact. Pat flesh back into shape. Cut through tail bone. Remove the vent. Keep the bones for stock.

BROCCOLI WITH SAFFRON DRESSING

Using hotel chefs' tactics, rapidly cook the broccoli then quick-chill in iced water to retain the brightness and texture.

7·2kg/16lb broccoli florets
6 tablespoons sweet dessert wine
Pinch of saffron threads
150ml/¼ pint hazelnut oil
900ml/1½ pints light olive oil
175ml/6 fl oz raspberry vinegar
6 tablespoons Dijon mustard
Salt and cayenne pepper

Cook the broccoli in 7 or 8 batches in a large pan of boiling salted water for 3–4 minutes, part-covered, until tender, crisp and a brilliant green. Drain immediately. Plunge into iced water and leave until cold. Drain, cover and chill. To make dressing, heat the wine in a small pan with the saffron, stirring until brightly coloured. Cool and blend with remaining ingredients to a smooth yellow emulsion. Season to taste.
SEE PAGE 193.

STUFFED TOMATO CUPS

Apple, shallot and the curious savour of fennel seeds transform the ordinary tomato into something much more interesting.

4kg/8lb (or 50) ripe tomatoes
150ml/¼ pint extra virgin olive oil
375g/12oz shallots, skinned and finely sliced
1kg/2lb red-skinned dessert apples, quartered and cored
2 tablespoons fennel seeds
Parsley sprigs, to garnish

Halve the tomatoes crosswise. Scoop out the pulp, chop and reserve. Heat the oil in a heavy-based pan and add the shallots. Sauté for 3–4 minutes. Cut the apples into 5mm/¼in cubes and add to the pan with the tomato pulp and fennel seeds. Stir until the apple is tender but still firm and the fennel aromatic. Spoon filling into tomato cups. Arrange on heatproof trays. To serve, warm through under a preheated grill for 5–8 minutes.
SEE PAGE 193.

POTATO GRATIN SQUARES

This classic potato recipe tastes as good cold or warm as hot. Prepare a quarter at a time (otherwise the potatoes may discolour).

8kg/17lb even-sized waxy potatoes
4 tablespoons fine sea salt
4 teaspoons ground white pepper
300g/10oz butter
16 eggs
2·4 litres/4 pints single cream
8 garlic cloves, skinned and chopped
Freshly grated nutmeg

Dealing with a quarter of the ingredients at a time, wash and dry the potatoes then slice them thinly. Season well. Rub a large, preferably non-stick, roasting tin, 30 × 45 cm/12 × 15in, with a tablespoon of the butter. Whisk the eggs, cream and garlic together and pour evenly over the seasoned potatoes. Dot butter over the top and dust with nutmeg. Bake in a preheated oven, 200°C, 400°F, Gas Mark 6 for 1¼ hours or until golden. Cool and refrigerate.

To serve *Cut the contents of each pan into 20 and serve cold or warm in a preheated oven, 180°C, 350°F, Gas Mark 4, for 20–25 minutes.*
SEE PAGE 191.

PRESENTATION

If timing schemes and serving suggestions for all recipes are followed your presentation should be stunning! Open house means best feet forward, so have all flat surfaces sparkling and flower-filled: any dust on cornices will never be noticed! The same applies to village halls. All hiring and borrowing of utensils must be resolved long ahead.

Flowers will scent the air if arranged one day ahead. A yellow and white colour theme always succeeds. Ribbons, ruches, gathers, swags and pleats using yellow and white fabrics look great.

Exploit a garden if you have access to one: stretches of lawn and lavender borders are lovely. Ponds however mean one must watch out for toddlers!

Trees in pots, with ribbons and silk flowers among hired evergreens, and dried flower posies are a winter alternative.

Food choices become clear if menus are on display. Name cards help. The top table should be clearly visible to all.

If there is to be live music; a gentle jazz trio, a string quartet or pianist, then consider the acoustics. Over-loud music is intrusive.

Should any unexpected dramas occur, all will be well so long as smiling helpers keep the Champagne circulating.

Ensure that the salmon or soup course starts when the time is right: otherwise some guests will be ready for their second course before others have even tasted the first. Ensure that every glass is filled as toasts begin – then let the celebrations commence.

ROSY SALAD

This is a pretty pink salad to enliven the palate after the main course and before the dessert.

40 tamarillos
900ml/$1\frac{1}{2}$ pints vinaigrette (olive oil, wine vinegar, mustard)
10 ripe pawpaws
20 pink grapefruit
10 red onions, skinned and sliced
20 medium heads of radicchio
5 lollo rosso lettuces

Halve 10 of the ripest tamarillos crosswise. Scoop out the flesh. Discard the skins. Chop, then blend or process the flesh into the vinaigrette.

Slash the skins of the remaining tamarillos lengthwise. Pour over boiling water and leave to stand for 3–5 minutes. Drain, peel and discard skins, and slice flesh into rings. Peel the pawpaws. Halve the fruit then discard the seeds. Cut the flesh crosswise into slices.

Add pawpaw and tamarillo slices to the dressing. Remove the skin and pith from the grapefruit. Sever the segments from their membranes to give perfect pink 'moons'. Add the grapefruit and the onion slices to the dressing.

Tear the radicchio and lollo rosso into even-sized pieces. Add to the dressing mixture and toss all together briefly just before serving *SEE PAGE 191.*

GRAND TIERS OF FRUITS

Build two magnificent arrangements of fabulous fruits choosing from whatever fruits are available. Allow a maximum of about 7kg/16lb weight of fruit. Select fruits which are scented, ripe, colourful, beautiful and easy to eat in the fingers, such as cherries, grapes (red, green and black), physalis, lychees, strawberries, peaches, nectarines, apples, pears, kumquats and so on. Have evergreen, glossy leaves for decoration. The intention is to arrange the fruits in ascending size: large at the base, smallish at the top. Try to obtain two three-tier china, glass or silver stands on which to arrange the fruit. Otherwise, find two large baseplates and four stemmed glass stands or six stemmed stands, two large, two medium and two small: place one on top of another to give three levels for each arrangement. Secure the stands in position with lots of strong tape.

If necessary, cut the fruits into conveniently sized pieces. Leave the green husks on strawberries, and any leaves on the figs, cherries and so forth. Arrange the fruits on the tiers as prettily as possible. Spray them with water from time to time to keep them fresh and cool. Present them with the croquembouches.

GRAND TIER OF FRUITS

Oz Clarke's
WINE NOTES

I never *know* anyone at weddings. I wander round the place watching gaggles of groom's friends all queuing up to kiss the bride and the bride's family all cooing with pleasure, and there am I actually looking forward to the speeches so that I'll feel someone is talking to me!

Well, I may not know anyone to start with, but there's one person whose acquaintance I very quickly make – the chap who's doling out the Champagne, because somehow, if you're standing there with a glass of Champagne in your hand trying to work out how you'll get the morning dress back to the hirer before you go to work on Monday, there's nothing more reassuring than an ice-cold glass of Champagne. You can almost hear the tinkling of the stream of bubbles over the chatter in the room, you can feel the refreshing chill of the glass as you begin to broil in your finery, and as the icy liquid cascades down your throat, the bubbles bursting in your mouth like a thousand stars, ah yes, well, haven't I met that chap over by the door somewhere? I'll go and ask him – and that girl looks a bit lonely, I'll go and offer her a glass of Champagne. I *do* feel better.

I'm never sure whether the most important thing at a wedding is to make sure that the Champagne is *good* or that it is cold or that there's enough of it! So if you possibly can, try to splash out on the Champagne a bit. To be honest, the grand French names are becoming silly in price, but luckily we still have very good own-label Champagne.

Many people will drink fizzy right the way through given the chance – but you should have alternatives – it'll save you money for a start – and I'll go for a gentle low-acid white from north-east Italy like a Lugana or a Bianco di Custoza, and robust fruity Côtes du Rhône-Villages red from France.

CROQUEMBOUCHE PYRAMIDS WITH SPUN CARAMEL

No-one could pretend that this splendid wedding cake is quick to make, but it is neither difficult nor expensive. At the end when the towers of profiteroles clouded in spun sugar are flanked by two 'grand tiers' of fruits your efforts will seem well worth while.

Do follow the construction details carefully for absolute success. To make two sufficiently grand croquembouche 'towers' about 300–320 buns are needed. Make the paste in eight separate batches; the results are better with smallish quantities.

Ideally make these one day (no more) ahead. They must stay crisp. Freezing is not ideal, but if buns are frozen and defrosted then re-crisp them in the oven (see later notes).

Choux paste:
8 × 125g/4oz salted butter, cubed
8 × 300ml/½ pint water
8 × 150g/5oz plain flour, sifted
8 × 4 eggs

Glaze:
5 × 250g/8oz caster sugar
5 × 150ml/¼ pint water
5 × 1 tablespoon distilled malt vinegar

Filling:
2 × 900ml/1½ pints double cream, chilled
2 × 450ml/¾ pint whipping cream, chilled
2 × 600g/1¼lb fruit-flavoured fromage frais

Spun caramel:
250g/8oz caster sugar
150ml/¼ pint water
1 tablespoon distilled malt vinegar

To make the choux paste, heat one quantity of the butter and water in a saucepan. Bring to the boil, remove from the heat and beat in one quantity of the flour all at once using an electric whisk. Continue until the mixture leaves the sides of the pan clean and forms one mass. Cool slightly. Beat in 4 eggs one at a time, whisking well between each addition. Chill until cold and firm.

Spoon the paste into a large piping bag fitted with a 1·5cm/¾in plain nozzle. Pipe 30 × 5cm/2in rounds on to two, preferably non-stick, wetted baking trays. Push down any peaks with a wetted teaspoon. Spray with a mist of water.

Bake in a preheated oven, 200°C, 400°F, Gas Mark 6, for 1 hour, changing tray positions half way through. The buns should be well risen, golden and crisp. Make 1cm/½in diameter holes in the bases of the buns. Leave them to cool upside down on wire racks.

Repeat this process seven more times producing one more batch of 30 buns, four batches of 40 buns of a smaller size and two batches of 55 buns of a smaller size again. Do not crowd the trays: the 30 and 40 bun batches will fit on two trays but for the 55 bun batches use three trays.

Baking times for the buns will vary depending on sizes. Reduce cooking time to 50–55 minutes for the medium-sized buns and 45 minutes for the small ones.

When completely cold, store in airtight containers overnight in a cool, dry place.

If it has been absolutely essential to make the buns days or weeks ahead and freeze them, defrost them for 3 hours. Set the buns upside-down on baking sheets and 're-crisp' in a preheated oven, 200°C, 400°F, Gas Mark 6, for 10 minutes. Cool.

To prepare the glaze – ideally no more than 12 hours ahead of serving time – heat one quantity of the ingredients in a small heavy-based saucepan. Swirl or stir until the sugar dissolves, then bring to the boil and continue boiling for 8–10 minutes without stirring until the temperature reaches 138°C/280°F – 'small crack stage' on a sugar thermometer

CROQUEMBOUCHE PYRAMIDS WITH SPUN CARAMEL

(syrup at this stage is clear, not golden at all). Remove the pan from the heat and reduce the heat to low. Swirl the contents of the pan to ensure an even temperature. Return the pan to the hob and heat gently for an additional 5–8 minutes or until the thermometer registers 165°C/325°F and the caramel is bright golden. Remove from the heat.

Place two racks each holding 33 buns over non-stick baking trays. Using two spoons drizzle the caramel in a fine, steady stream over the buns until all are criss-cross glazed and all the caramel is used up.

To clean the pan, add a little vinegar, fill with boiling water and boil for 5 minutes. Dry the pan then repeat with successive caramel batches until all the buns are coated.

When ready to construct the croquembouche and dealing with one quantity of the filling ingredients at a time, whip the two creams together until very stiff. Add the fromage frais, then whip again until very stiff. Fill a piping bag fitted with a plain 1cm/½in nozzle with some of the cream mixture. Pipe into the base of the buns, reserving some for anchoring the towers of buns. Repeat the process with the remaining ingredients until all the buns are filled.

To assemble the two pyramids – ideally a two-person task – have ready two large platters at least 35cm/14in in diameter. Dot the platters with the reserved filling, then cover with an even circular layer of the largest buns then make a second circular layer on top. Continue to stack up the layers of the prepared buns, gradually using the medium and finally the small buns until there are two completed pyramids, approximately 30cm/12in high and about 10 layers deep.

Make up the spun caramel following the instructions for the glaze exactly. Then, with the help of a second person, use two pairs of forks to repeatedly dip into the caramel, lift out, then up, scraping the two forks across each other. Pull them wide apart until fine threads can be seen forming as the caramel cools. Now work quickly and repeat this process many times, spinning these fine threads all around the pyramids to encase them. Work until all the caramel is used up and before it sets. The pyramids will shimmer with a gauzy sheen.

To serve *Decorate the base of each pyramid with leaves and flowers. Set the pyramids together on a separate table flanked by 'grand tiers' of fruits.*

Late Autumn Feast for 24

As summer's light begins to fade and we lament the shortening days, autumn provides us with a paradise of good ingredients to bring us solace.

This ambitious party menu celebrates the profusion and diversity of products which are at their peak and easily available at this time of year: field mushrooms, celeriac, sweet potatoes, squash, beef, certain cheeses, apples and passionfruit.

Autumn provides many occasions to celebrate: in September thanksgiving for the harvest and Michaelmas, in October there's the trick-or-treat of Hallowe'en, in November Guy Fawkes Day and later the American Thanksgiving feast. Late autumn is often, too, the point when summer holidays are over and people are back at home again, so it can be a good time for far-flung families and groups of friends to get together to talk over the summer's foibles.

Ideally – if you can put together enough tables and chairs – this is a seated dinner party so some days of planning and organization are needed to ensure that the party runs without a hitch.

Some recipes can be made ahead: mushrooms with sage, and the passionfruit pudding, if closely wrapped and airtight, are perfectly satisfactory made one day prior to the party. Some cheeses can stay in the cool for days. Many of the other recipes can be weighed, measured and semi-prepared ready for last-minute combining and cooking.

Menu

*

MUSHROOMS WITH SAGE

SIRLOIN STUDDED WITH GARLIC AND BRESAOLA

SQUASH, SWEET POTATO AND CELERIAC PURÉE

SEEDED AROMATIC GREENS

ROSY ROASTED POTATOES

*

CHEESE AND SALAD PLATTER

PASSIONFRUIT MIST PUDDING WITH SAUCE MOSCATINA

*

Lambs' Wool Punch
Barolo *or* Rioja Reserva
Chartreuse
Cardamom Coffee

MUSHROOMS WITH SAGE, LAMBS' WOOL PUNCH

Mushrooms with Sage

Briefly cooked dark triangles of open-cup mushrooms make an unusually delicious cold starter when combined with sage and lemon.

1·5kg/3lb large mushrooms
225ml/7½fl oz olive oil
3 tablespoons lemon juice
2 tablespoons chopped fresh sage
1½ teaspoons salt
Freshly ground black pepper
Fresh sage sprigs, to garnish

Slice the mushroom stalks thinly. Cut the caps into wedges. Heat 3 tablespoons of oil in a large heavy-based, non-stick frying pan. Add about a third of the mushrooms and cook briefly, gill sides down, then toss over a brisk heat until all the oil is absorbed. Drizzle over another 2 tablespoons of oil, continue tossing the mushrooms and cook for a further minute. Pour in 1 tablespoon of the lemon juice, 2 teaspoons of the sage and ½ teaspoon of the salt. Cook for a further 1–2 minutes, until the juices run. Season with pepper to taste. Spoon into a deep bowl.

Repeat the process twice more with the remaining ingredients. Chill for several hours or overnight.

To serve *Divide the mixture among individual pots, ramekins or plates. Garnish with sage and serve with crusty bread to mop up the juices.*

SIRLOIN STUDDED WITH GARLIC AND BRESAOLA

Prime beef cooked till pink and perfumed with garlic and the sweetness of cured beef is an updated version of a well-loved classic. Standing the meat on a rack prevents 'steamy' cooking and promotes browning. Choose a good red wine, such as Barbera, for the sauce.

SQUASH, SWEET POTATO AND CELERIAC PURÉE, SEEDED AROMATIC GREENS, ROSY ROASTED POTATOES, SIRLOIN STUDDED WITH GARLIC AND BRESAOLA

2 × 2·5kg/5½lb boned, rolled sirloin joints
24 garlic cloves
24 slices bresaola
Freshly ground black pepper
Fresh bay leaves and rosemary twigs, to garnish (optional)

Sauce:
350ml/12fl oz red wine
600ml/1 pint hot stock
350g/12oz rowan or redcurrant jelly
2 tablespoons arrowroot
4 tablespoons water
450ml/¾ pint horseradish sauce, to serve (optional)

Prepare the first joint: using a pointed knife, make 24 cuts into the top and sides of the beef. Halve the garlic cloves lengthwise. Cut the bresaola slices in halves lengthwise and fold into thinner strips. Enclose each garlic piece in a 'pocket' of bresaola then push a bundle down into each cut. The ends should stick out beyond the meat. Prepare the second joint the same way.

Season the joints with pepper and stand them on a rack in a large roasting tin just above mid-oven level. Cook in a preheated oven, 200°C, 400°F, Gas Mark 6, for 1–1½ hours, or longer for those who prefer their beef less pink. To ensure accuracy insert 2 meat thermometers: 60°C/140°F is for very rare, 70°C/160°F for pinkish brown meat. Lift out the joints, foil-wrap and rest them in a warm place for 10–12 minutes.

Add ice cubes to the meat juices in the pan to solidify the fat. Remove the fat. Add the red wine to the degreased meat juices in the pan. Boil over a lively heat for 5–10 minutes or until syrupy. Add the stock and jelly and bring back to boiling. Mix the arrowroot with the water, stir into the sauce and heat, stirring, until smooth and slightly thickened.

EXTRAS

If wished, for a bonfire night special serve hot chestnuts while guests stand out of doors, as the hot punch is served and before going indoors for the first course. The handling is more sociable if you thread them – three at a time – on to wooden skewers or satay sticks (soak the sticks overnight). Cook them in the embers or roast the chestnut 'kebabs' under a fierce grill until the skins char to black. Provide salted butter and black pepper for those who like them. You will need about 1kg/2lb chestnuts. Such DIY fare breaks the ice!

Buy two French loaves to serve with the mushrooms and thinly slice them or break into chunks.

You will also need horseradish sauce to serve with the beef.

Provide a selection of oils and vinegars to accompany the salad. Nut oil (hazelnut or walnut, for example) mixed 1 : 4 with extra virgin olive oil combines superbly with a fruity vinegar. My favourites are raspberry, strawberry and blackcurrant vinegars. Other delectable vinegars for salads to serve with cheese are Champagne vinegar, balsamic and good red wine vinegar.

Scented aromatic coffee is doubly welcome if it is also decaffeinated, since many these days prefer it. Serve it with a hint of extra spiciness: cardamom (crushed whole pods, six per pot) is said to help the digestion. Serve, too, fragments of *turrón* – a famous Spanish confection – or nougat or *panforte*. Arrange prettily on serving dishes or stemmed glass dishes.

SQUASH, SWEET POTATO AND CELERIAC PURÉE

The sweetness of this autumn vegetable purée makes it superb with any roast. Avoid preparing and cooking this too far ahead. It tastes and looks best if freshly prepared and cooked. Reheating, should this be necessary, would be most efficient in a microwave.

1·1kg/2¼lb butternut squash
1·3kg/2¾lb onion squash or pumpkin
1kg/2lb celeriac
1·1kg/2¼lb slim orange-fleshed sweet potatoes
25g/1oz butter, cubed
1 teaspoon salt
½ teaspoon grated nutmeg
½ teaspoon ground cinnamon
Black pepper

Peel the squashes and celeriac and remove and discard the seeds from the squashes. Cut all the flesh into 2·5cm/1in cubes. Wash and peel the sweet potatoes.

Put the cubes of celeriac into a large pan. Cover with boiling, generously salted water and bring back to the boil, then simmer for 5 minutes. Meanwhile, cut the sweet potatoes in half lengthwise then cut crosswise into 2·5cm/1in thick semi-circles. Add both the squashes and the sweet potatoes to the part-cooked celeriac and barely cover with more boiling salted water. Bring back to the boil, reduce the heat and simmer for 12–15 minutes or until all the vegetables are tender. Drain well, return to pan and dry off over a low heat. Mash the vegetables in the pan, using a potato masher, still over a low heat. Stir in the butter and seasonings.

Serve the purée in creamy spoonfuls with the beef.

SEE PAGE 199.

SEEDED AROMATIC GREENS

Green vegetables, when cooked in volume, all too often lose their crunch, colour and charm. Not, however, in this recipe: timings are carefully observed with perfect results. Herbs and seeds, too, add a pleasing earthy touch. Don't begin to cook these tasty greens until the cooked beef is close to its carving time because this is one recipe that should definitely not be reheated.

2 tablespoons fennel seeds
500g/1lb leeks, trimmed
1kg/2lb sprouts
900ml/1½ pints boiling water
1 tablespoon sea salt
50g/2oz butter, softened
25g/1oz parsley, chopped

Using a heavy-based, non-stick frying pan, dry-fry the fennel seeds until they begin to brown, pop and become aromatic. Tip the seeds out of the pan immediately to avoid scorching and keep aside.

Cut the leeks (both white and green parts) crosswise into 5mm/¼in slices. Rinse well in a colander under running water. Drain.

Trim away and discard the bases of the sprouts and then halve the sprouts lengthwise, quartering any which are very large. Put the sprouts into a large pan (such as a preserving pan) and cover with salted boiling water. Bring back to the boil and add the leeks. Part-cover the pan and return to the boil then cook for a further 4–6 minutes. Drain well. Push the vegetables to one side of the pan. Add the butter and parsley, allowing the butter to melt, and stir gently through the vegetables until they are evenly coated.

Serve quickly, while the vegetables still look vivid, in 2 heated serving dishes and sprinkle with the reserved toasted seeds.

SEE PAGE 199.

ROSY ROASTED POTATOES

Red-skinned potatoes, such as Romano, are halved but not peeled before being parboiled, spice-coated and roasted.

3 tablespoons mild paprika
2 tablespoons salt
3 tablespoons mustard powder
150ml/¼ pint olive oil
2·75kg/6lb red-skinned potatoes

Mix paprika, salt and mustard together. Divide the oil between two large roasting tins and heat in the oven at 200°C, 400°F, Gas Mark 6.

Halve the unpeeled potatoes. Put them into a large pan, cover with boiling salted water. Bring back to boiling point, then boil for 1 minute. Drain and dry on kitchen paper. Score the potatoes then roll them in the seasoning mix. Divide between the tins, cut sides down. Cook in lower part of the oven for 1½–2 hours, basting with oil and turning them over twice.

SEE PAGE 199.

CHEESE AND SALAD PLATTER

Texture, colour and flavour contrasts are much of the charm of cheeses: so a blue, a creamy and a goats' cheese should please all.

750g/1½lb blue cheese (such as Stilton or Roquefort)
250g/8oz soft, creamy cheese (such as Brie, Camembert or Brillat-Savarin)
3 small goats' cheeses
16 little gem lettuces
375g/12oz watercress

Arrange the cheeses on a cheese board or platter. Wash and dry the lettuces and trim into quarters lengthwise. Wash and dry the watercress and tear into neat lengths. Arrange in a salad bowl. Serve accompanied by a variety of oils, vinegars and seasonings.

PRESENTATION

For flowers: reds and golds with bronze foliage and dried bleached bundles of wheat and herbs in carefree but bold arrangements will probably proliferate. Tassels and swags, too, somehow make sense as do candles and embroidered cloths. Richness should predominate. Bleached wood or dark oak tables help the theme.

Name cards can be tucked into starched and pleated linen napkins at the table which can be cloth-covered or bare if wooden.

Don't forget both a knife and fork are required for the cheese and salad course, and cheese knives for the cheese board itself.

Glass, embossed white china, old silver or pewter, and simple classic objects fit the bill well. Have the room warm and fragrant with burning wood and pine cones.

CHEESE AND SALAD PLATTER

PASSIONFRUIT MIST PUDDING WITH SAUCE MOSCATINA

PLANNING AHEAD

The day before: Prepare the salad stuffs: wash, trim and plastic wrap. Chill them. Make the passionfruit pudding and keep airtight. Make the sauce. Chill both. Prepare the mushrooms with sage and put in the refrigerator to chill overnight.

The morning of the party: Prepare the beef for roasting and chill until 4 hours before the party. Measure out the sauce ingredients. Measure out the butter, seasonings and spices for the purée, and the butter and parsley for the greens.

Two hours ahead, make the lambs' wool punch apart from adding the cider. Make the vegetable purée. Arrange the mushroom servings. Slice the bread. Preheat the oven. Put the potatoes on to cook.

Ninety minutes ahead, cook the beef. Make the sauce for the beef as the chestnuts and punch are served. Leave the cooked beef to 'rest' on ovenproof serving dishes. Arrange the cheese and salad platters.

Cook the green vegetables between the mushroom and main courses. Reheat the purée.

This layered froth of passionfruit and orange set upon freshly made sponge cake is a sensational finish to an autumn meal.

25g/1oz butter, softened
9 eggs, separated
¼ teaspoon salt
200g/7oz caster sugar
50g/2oz vanilla sugar
275g/9oz self raising flour, sifted
6 tablespoons Moscatel (sweet dessert wine)
750g/1½lb (about 20) ripe passionfruit
4 tablespoons (40g/1½oz) powdered gelatine
600ml/1 pint freshly squeezed orange juice
600ml/1 pint double cream
600ml/1 pint whipping cream
Physalis berries, to decorate (optional)

Sauce:
875g/1¾lb skimmed milk soft cheese, chilled
300ml/½ pint Moscatel
300ml/½ pint freshly squeezed orange juice

Grease a 30cm/12in square, deep cake tin well with the softened butter. Whisk the egg whites and salt in a large bowl until they form soft peaks. Add the caster and vanilla sugars in three stages, whisking continuously until the egg whites form stiff peaks. Continue whisking, adding the egg yolks one after another. The mixture should remain high, pale and fluffy. Add the sifted flour in several lots of 3 heaped tablespoons each, folding it in with a palette knife using figure-of-eight movements. Avoid overmixing. (The mixture should have a similar volume after adding the flour as before.)

Pour into the prepared cake tin and bake in a preheated oven, 190°C, 375°F, Gas Mark 5, just above mid-oven, for 30–45 minutes or until the sponge has slightly separated from the edges of the tin and centre feels firm and springs back when lightly pressed. Leave to cool in the tin for half an hour. Pierce the cake all over with a skewer, then drizzle the Moscatel evenly all over it.

Halve the passionfruit and scoop out all the pulp and seeds using a teaspoon.

Measure 300ml/½ pint of the orange juice into a heatproof bowl. Add the gelatine all at once, stirring well. Leave to swell for 10–15 minutes, then stand in a saucepan of boiling water over very low heat. Stir until dissolved.

Stir in a further 150ml/¼ pint of orange juice and the passionfruit pulp. Pour into a large bowl and stand in iced water.

Check the gelatine mixture every 2 minutes for setting; stir the bottom up to the top regularly to ensure no lumps are forming. Should the fruit-gelatine mixture set solid, gently reheat to melt it and repeat the chilling process as before.

Meanwhile, whip the two lots of cream in separate bowls: the double cream until thick and the whipping cream until soft peaks form.

When the gelatine mixture is on the point of setting (thick, jelly-like but not yet solid) whisk in the remaining orange juice and quickly fold in first the whipping cream, then the thicker double cream. Pour the mixture quickly over the sponge base, smooth the top level then refrigerate for 2–3 hours until set. Wrap well to keep airtight.

To make the sauce, put all the ingredients into a food processor or blender and process until the consistency of thin cream.

To serve *Mark the pudding into 25 squares with a sharp knife. Lift out using a fish slice and cut each square into 3 even slices. Fan these, overlapped, on a pretty dessert platter. Pour a thin ribbon of sauce across the slices, ending in a little pool on the plate. Add two opened physalis berries if wished.*

Oz Clarke's
WINE NOTES

Oh autumn, autumn. How far away summer seems as we dust down our overcoats, so joyously packed away six months before. How searing the sun that we remember from August or June. How exhilarating those spring showers, how refreshing the early morning dew as it glinted on green lawns in the first rays of the summer sun. Yet now the rain clouds hang like an eternal cold grey fug hardly above the level of the rooftops.

But this is no good! I can't let myself get all mournful like this. I've got to beat back those evenings closing in ever earlier, and march out into the gales and the whiplash flurries of rain and enjoy a bracing early winter storm. Think of harvest home, think of vintage – and think of all those steaming hot dishes and rich red wines which summer renders inappropriate. *That's* more like it. Summer will always come again, so let's make the best of autumn on its own terms.

The most autumnal of all reds are those of the Piedmont region in north-west Italy. Even the main grape's name – Nebbiolo – refers to the fogs which blanket the valley floors. And the greatest Piedmont red is Barolo. It's a tough wine, but not a massive one, and its sweetness of blackberries and cherries and violets, maybe even chocolate and prunes, only becomes evident after the bottle has been opened for several hours and is being enjoyed with a dish as richly indulgent as Clare's sirloin of beef. If you want a gentler autumnal extravagance, I'd go for the warm strawberry and vanilla softness of a Rioja Reserva from Spain.

You could match the pudding with a sweet Muscat wine, but I feel slightly mischievous in my new enthusiasm for autumn, and I'm going to serve the most aromatic and spice-laden of all the liqueurs – green Chartreuse.

LAMBS' WOOL PUNCH

Here's just the thing to sip on a cool night, out of doors standing up around a bonfire or indoors as guests roll up. This hot spiced punch foams and froths up in the glass at the moment of completion – just like lamb's wool.

5 Cox's Orange Pippin apples
50 whole cloves
15g/½oz cinnamon sticks
1 teaspoon ground allspice
2 litres/3½ pints lager
250g/8oz dark soft brown sugar
1 litre/1¾ pint clear apple juice
2 litres/3½ pints dry cider
Calvados (about 350ml/12fl oz), to serve

Stud the apples with 8 cloves each. Slash around the 'middle' with a sharp knife. Split and crush the cinnamon sticks. Add these, the remaining cloves, the allspice, lager, sugar and apple juice to a large pan. Simmer vigorously for 15 minutes to allow the flavours to blend. Add the cider and straight away remove from the heat.

Measure a generous tablespoon of Calvados into each cut and ladle in the hot punch. Serve immediately.

Top **PASSIONFRUIT MIST PUDDING WITH SAUCE MOSCATINA**

INDEX

F

G

H

I

J

K

L

T

V

W

Y

ACKNOWLEDGEMENTS

The publishers are grateful to the following individuals for the help which they contributed towards the preparation of this book:

Julia Adlard, Sarah Bird, Elspeth Collins-Taylor, Conran Shop, Vickie Downie, Jan Dunsford, Puff Fairclough, Fay Franklin, Elisabet Fredrikson, Nina and Henrik Hammerskjöld, Gemma Hancock, Anna Harrod, Fiona Holman, Meg Jansz, Kateryna Lysak, Monica Maxted Jones, David Mellor, Villeroy & Boch, Fiona Wild, Wycombe Abbey School

Editorial Director Sandy Carr
Art Director Douglas Wilson
Art Editor Vanessa Pryse
Sub-Editors Fiona Eves, Wendy Toole
Editorial Assistant Mary Pickles
Designers Alison Donovan, Penny Smith
Photography Martin Brigdale
Stylists Andrea Lambton, Vanessa Pryse
Photographer's Assistant Gus Filgate
Home Economist Bridget Sargeson
Illustrations Jenny Abbot, Carol Wilhide
Indexer Naomi Good